W9-CDN-211

KILIMANJARO
A COMPLETE TREKKER'S GUIDE

About the Author

Alexander Stewart is the senior buyer for Stanfords, the renowned map and travel specialist bookshop. He has a particular interest in Africa and a passion for mountains. Throughout his adult life he has walked in them, written about them and photographed them. However, he doesn't often find himself on top of them, except at home in the UK. Kilimanjaro made a significant impression on him during his first ascent in 1999, and he has subsequently been drawn back repeatedly to the 'Roof of Africa'.

WARNING

All mountain activities contain an element of danger, with a risk of personal injury or death. The treks described in this guidebook are no exception. Under normal conditions wandering the trails of Kilimanjaro will be neither more nor less hazardous than walking among big mountains anywhere in the world, but trekking involves physically demanding exercise in a challenging landscape, where caution is advised and a degree of stamina is often required, and it should be undertaken only by those with a full understanding of the risks, and with the training and experience to evaluate them. Trekkers should be properly equipped for the routes undertaken. Whilst every care and effort has been taken in the preparation of this guide, the user should be aware that conditions can be highly variable and change quickly. Rockfall, landslip and crumbling paths can alter the character of a route, and the presence of snow and the possibility of avalanche must be carefully considered, for these can materially affect the seriousness of a trek.

Therefore, except for any liability which cannot be excluded by law, neither Cicerone Press nor the author accepts liability for damage of any nature (including damage to property, personal injury or death) arising directly or indirectly from the information in this guide.

Readers are warned that sometimes a few unfortunate trekkers die of hypothermia or acute mountain sickness; while some simply lose their balance and fall from the trail due to a momentary loss of concentration. Since there is no organised mountain rescue service in Tanzania, such as exists in some mountain regions of Europe, if an accident occurs self-help may be your only option.

KILIMANJARO
A COMPLETE TREKKER'S GUIDE

Preparations, practicalities and
trekking routes to the 'Roof of Africa'

by
Alexander Stewart

2 POLICE SQUARE, MILNTHORPE, CUMBRIA LA7 7PY
www.cicerone.co.uk

BELLEVILLE PUBLIC LIBRARY

© Alexander Stewart 2004
Reprinted 2006, 2007 (with updates), 2010 and 2011 (with updates)
ISBN-10: 1 85284 413 2
ISBN-13: 978 1 85284 413 4

A catalogue record for this book is available from the British Library.
Photos by the author.
Printed by MCC Graphics, Spain.

Dedication

To my mum and dad, in whose footsteps I followed,
and for my brother, who was there the very first time.

Acknowledgements

First and foremost, a massive, heartfelt 'thank you' to Katie for her continued support, for always being there during the creation of this book, and in recognition of the fact that staying behind is often the hardest part. A particular mention too for Martin and for Darwin. I would also like to thank all of the people who gave their time and energy so readily to answer my questions and help me during the various ascents of the mountain. Special thanks go to Rick and Delulu, Dawn, Zoe and Ryan for their hospitality and generosity. I would also like to take the opportunity to recognise the help given to me by the various guides and porters who accompanied each trip. An enormous 'thank you' goes to Benjamin, Bonny, Dawson and Ambrose as well as all their team members; Sadie, Paul, Imani, Manuel, Joseph, Jesse, Desdere, Ali, Manase, Bruno and Robson.

Advice to Readers

Readers are advised that, while every effort is made by our authors to ensure the accuracy of guidebooks as they go to print, changes can occur during the lifetime of an edition. Please check Updates on this book's page on the Cicerone website (**www.cicerone.co.uk**) before planning your trip. We would also advise that you check information about such things as transport, accommodation and shops locally. Even rights of way can be altered over time. We are always grateful for information about any discrepancies between a guidebook and the facts on the ground, sent by email to info@cicerone.co.uk or by post to Cicerone, 2 Police Square, Milnthorpe LA7 7PY, United Kingdom.

Front cover: View across the Saddle to the Kibo massif (Rongai Route, Mawenzi Tarn to Kibo Hut)

CONTENTS

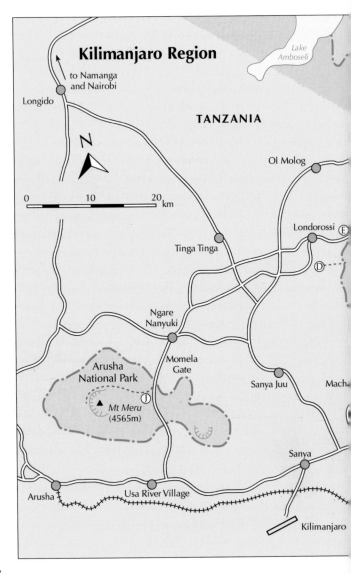

Kilimanjaro Region

Lake Amboseli

Longido

to Namanga and Nairobi

TANZANIA

Ol Molog

Londorossi (E)

(D)

Tinga Tinga

Ngare Nanyuki

Arusha National Park

Momela Gate

▲ Mt Meru (4565m)

Sanya Juu

Mach.

Sanya

Arusha

Usa River Village

Kilimanjaro

0   10   20 km

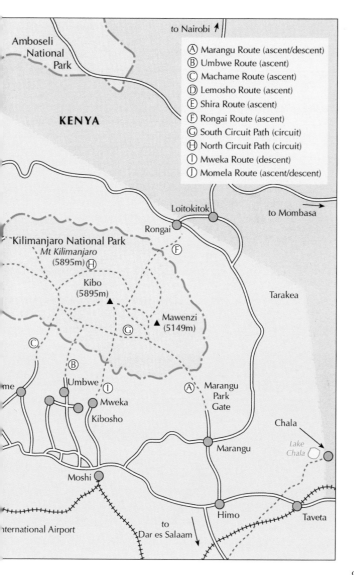

Map Key

→ Route

----------- Other paths in the area

Ⓧ Start point of North and South Circuit Paths

〜〜〜 Road (sealed roads and forest tracks)

▲ Peak (altitude in metres)

© Cave

++++++ Railway line

⬭ Glacier

■ Hut

🌳 Treeline

□ Park gate/trailhead

Contours		
		5600–6000m
		5200–5600m
		4800–5200m
		4400–4800m
		4000–4400m
		3600–4000m
		3200–3600m
		2800–3200m
		2400–2800m
		2000–2400m
		1600–2000m

PART 1
INTRODUCTION AND PRACTICALITIES

Every morning at about 8.30am, a battered combie van leaves from a small depot opposite the Norfolk Hotel on Harry Thuku Road in Nairobi. More than likely, some of the passengers aboard the shuttle will be trekkers. If all goes smoothly and the combie doesn't succumb to punctures or potholes, it will rattle into the town of Moshi, in Tanzania, some six hours later. Moshi is a pleasant if unremarkable town which is of little specific interest to the trekkers on the shuttle bus. It is, however, the first stop for many of them on their way to Kilimanjaro, Africa's highest peak. The massive bulk of the mountain dominates the town, looming over it like a colossus. To the uninitiated, it is quite a shock to be confronted by this new image of Africa.

East Africa is most often perceived as a flat, arid savannah. Famous for its wildlife safaris and coastal resorts, it is also an extraordinary destination for lovers of mountains, trekking and climbing. The history of walking in East Africa is relatively young and the area is rich in potential – the high mountains are the last secret places of the region. Walking on the high mountains of East Africa banishes the notion that Africa is only covered in tawny grasslands. As a result of its tremendous height and its location on the equator, Kilimanjaro's slopes are host to lush tropics, temperate climes, alpine moorland as well as barren high-alpine desert and permanently snow-capped summits.

The mountains of East Africa stand as solitary peaks above the surrounding plains. The single greatest attraction is, of course, Kilimanjaro. One of the world's highest volcanoes and the world's highest free-standing mountain, Kilimanjaro is a powerful visual symbol and a quintessential African image. Rolf Edberg was moved to write that 'Its might is strangely weightless. At a distance, the mountain can seem ethereal. When the sun is low and the clouds light, the mountain with its white- shimmering cap seems at times to be floating in space. At such moments, Kilimanjaro seems almost supernatural in its beauty.' The rounded, glacier-clad dome of Kibo is home to Uhuru Peak, the mountain's summit, whilst the shattered, jaggered spires of Mawenzi, Kilimanjaro's second summit, rear up across the blasted, desolate saddle. At 5895m, the square summit of Kilimanjaro is the highest point in Africa and, consequently, one of the coveted Seven Summits. Yet it is possible to reach the summit of Kilimanjaro without any technical climbing ability. Would-be mountaineers hoping to top one of the Seven Summits naturally gravitate towards Kilimanjaro. With its readily accessible, non-technical slopes, abundance of porters and relatively mild weather, the climb to the summit is considered a moderately easy ascent in mountaineering circles. Yet surprisingly few people make it to the top.

Among treks in East Africa, Kilimanjaro is a massive personal challenge in defiance of the extreme altitude. Walkers climbing the mountain move from the lush tropics, through temperate climes, alpine moorland and barren high-alpine desert to the permanently snow-capped summit, and back, in the course of only five or six days. This ascent is intensely gratifying and enlightening. Those who visit will be amply rewarded by what they encounter: diverse and colourful scenery, stunning natural beauty, endemic flora, warm and friendly locals and a unique sense of isolation. This last impression is reinforced by the knowledge that only a little more than 150 years ago this vast mountain was part of geographers' legend and remained unseen or unclimbed by Europeans, let alone accessible within six hours from Nairobi.

The ascent of Kilimanjaro is a gruelling, classic trek with magnificent views that are unmatched in Africa. The real magic of the mountain is its stunning beauty and fascinating natural history. To make the most of your trek, walk slowly with your eyes open and you'll come home with something far more important than a summit certificate.

CHOOSING A ROUTE

This book is a guide to all of the trekking routes on Kilimanjaro. It describes in depth the six approach routes through the forest and heath/moorland zones, the Circuit Path (which offers an alternative to ascending to the mountain's top and circumnavigates Kibo at 4000m) and the three summit routes leading to Uhuru Peak. It also details the available descent routes on the mountain. Each of these routes will reward the visitor with stunning panoramas and an incredible variety of scenic wonders.

Following the initial trickle of climbers to these slopes, the number of people attempting to reach the highest point in Africa has risen to

View from Kibo Hut across the Saddle towards Mawenzi on the Marangu Route

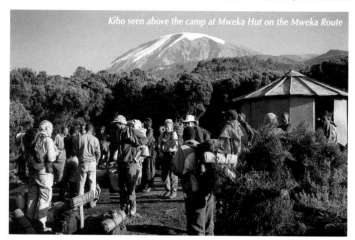
Kibo seen above the camp at Mweka Hut on the Mweka Route

around 40,000 per year, three quarters of whom tackle the Marangu and Machame Routes. Such a statistic may horrify you. The image of immense crowds of walkers and their porters traipsing across the slopes and the thought of squalid, cramped campsites and of broad, eroded trails strewn with litter are indeed horrific. Thankfully, the reality is very different and every visitor to these slopes ought to strive to ensure that this remains the case.

It is essential to select the route that is most appropriate for you. Be aware of the scenic variety, remoteness and popularity of each route, but most importantly, when choosing your ascent route, be aware of the degree of difficulty of that route. Don't let a false sense of bravado or an overestimation of your ability allow you to select a route that is beyond your capabilities. If you are inexperienced, less fit, have never been to altitude or have previously struggled

at altitude, you should tend towards one of the easier routes and consider the Marangu or Rongai Route.

If you are fitter, have some experience of walking and being at altitude you may wish to consider the Machame, Shira or Lemosho approach routes coupled with an ascent to the summit via the Barafu Route. If you are very fit and properly acclimatised you might like to consider one of the tougher ascent routes, such as the Umbwe Route, in conjunction with an assault on the Western Breach.

KILIMANJARO'S ROUTES

There are six official trekking routes on Kilimanjaro that provide a range of opportunities for experiencing the mountain. All walkers must follow one of these established paths. All of the ascents are quite difficult by virtue of the altitude, but some are harder than others.

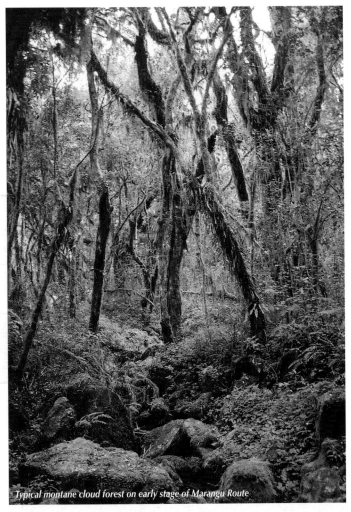

Typical montane cloud forest on early stage of Marangu Route

The most common ascent is via the **Marangu Route**. This relatively easy five-day trip ascends Kilimanjaro from the south-east. The lower sections provide fine forest and moorland walking. The lunar landscape of the Saddle then leads to the foot of Kibo, from where **the final summit bid is undertaken via the Normal/Marangu Route. You descend this route by retracing your steps.** This is the only route on which all overnight stops are made in purpose built huts. Since this is the shortest and cheapest route on the mountain, it is frequently very busy and there is the risk that the facilities along the trail can become stretched.

The second most popular ascent route is the **Machame Route**. This longer, six-day climb is harder and more spectacular. It climbs Kilimanjaro from the south-west and enjoys some of the finest forest and heath/moorland scenery on the mountain. **The final push to the summit is via either the tricky Western Breach or, more usually, the Barafu Route. The stipulated descent route for this path is the Mweka Route.** Increasingly popular and recently renovated, this path is no longer the

wilderness experience that it once was. Nonetheless it constitutes an exceptional, fully rounded expedition.

Of the more unusual ascent routes, the **Rongai Route** is the easiest. This six-day climb is an excellent alternative to the Marangu Route for those who don't feel capable of undertaking one of the more strenuous climbs. This is the only path that approaches the summit from the north-east. The path coils across the lower slopes and detours via Mawenzi, allowing you to explore this extraordinary second summit area more fully than on any other route. **It then makes the final summit bid via the Normal/Marangu Route. Descent from the mountain is along the Marangu Route.** Less heavily used and exceptionally scenic, the Rongai Route is a very fine outing on Kilimanjaro.

The **Umbwe Route** is the most direct, strenuous ascent route. Climbing stiffly through the thick forest on the

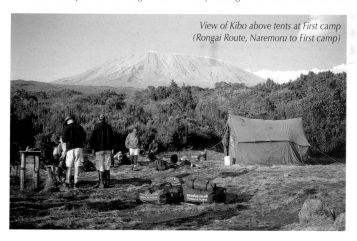

View of Kibo above tents at First camp (Rongai Route, Naremoru to First camp)

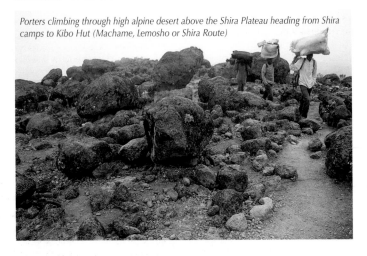

Porters climbing through high alpine desert above the Shira Plateau heading from Shira camps to Kibo Hut (Machame, Lemosho or Shira Route)

southern slopes of the mountain, it rapidly gains height and affords you little time to acclimatise properly. **The summit bid is often made via the Western Breach, but is sometimes conducted via the Barafu Route. Regardless, descent is via the Mweka Route.** For those who are fit and fully acclimatised, this is probably the most dramatic way to climb Kilimanjaro and experience many of its finest vistas. It must not be underestimated though, since it poses a very real challenge.

Both the **Shira** and **Lemosho Routes** approach the mountain from the west. They are variations on the same trail and merge above the forest on the Shira Plateau. The more enjoyable Lemosho Route is fractionally longer and allows you to ascend to the plateau on foot, where as the Shira Route begins much higher on the mountain and accesses the plateau by 4WD vehicle. **Both paths then either climb to the summit via the**

Western Breach or, more frequently, traverse the mountain beneath the Southern Icefields to ascend via the Barafu Route. Descent is once more along the Mweka Route. The Lemosho Route is longer than any other route on the mountain, and whilst being more expensive offers the best opportunity to acclimatise properly ahead of the summit bid. The isolation and space enjoyed as a result of the remoteness of both trailheads means that these are very good ways of escaping the crowds, at least on the early stages of the climb.

For those less concerned about claiming the summit's scalp, the **Circuit Path** that circumnavigates Kibo at around 4000m is an outstanding way to enjoy the mountain and explore some of its least visited features. The **South Circuit Path** is a superb traverse that provides you with fine panoramas of the Southern Icefields, whilst the **North Circuit Path** is very remote and rarely used, allowing you to enjoy the mountain in peace.

COSTS AND BUDGETING

Climbing Kilimanjaro is an expensive business. The Tanzanian government has understandably cashed in on the mountain's popularity and has intro-duced a series of mandatory fees that must be paid before you can even enter the Kilimanjaro National Park. The charges to climb Kilimanjaro have increased exponentially over the last few years and the combination of park gate fees, camping and hut fees levied by the authorities have now reached more than US$100 per day.

There is no cheap way to climb the mountain. The fees are compulsory. In addition to these, you must also hire and pay for a guide and a team of porters through a licensed outfitter. All food and transport need to be factored in as well. On top of all of the unavoidable costs, you must also include the amount of money that you will need to tip the guide and his porters once the climb is completed (see Guides and Porters).

The mandatory costs include the **national park daily gate fee**, which dou-bled in 2006 from US$30 to US$60. You must also pay either **camping fees** of US$50 per night or, on the Marangu Route, **hut fees** of US$50 per night. There is also a compulsory **rescue fee** of US$20 per trip. You must also pay US$1 per person per trip as **wages for each guide and porter** that accompanies you during your ascent. Thus, the basic cost of a five-day Marangu Route ascent using a guide, assistant guide and two porters rapidly

escalates to over US$500. By the time that your outfitter includes each member of your team's wages, approximately a further US$150 for a team of four, and the **costs for food and transport**, you will appreciate how the cost of the expedition very quickly increases. On top of this, you will inevitably be charged another **fee by, and for, your outfitter** in order to make the business profitable.

When all of these considera-tions are taken into account, expect to pay an outfitter somewhere in the region of US$1300 for a basic five-day Marangu trek. The Umbwe and Rongai Routes will cost somewhere between US$1300–1500, whilst the Machame Route costs around US$1500. The Shira and Lemosho Routes are both slightly more expensive and will set you back at least US$1800.

It pays to shop around and compare prices offered by each outfitter. Prices

Fresh provisions at the start of the trek

17

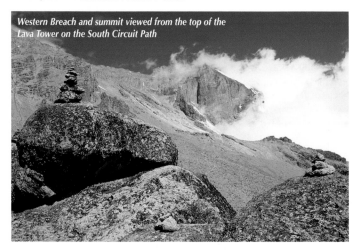

Western Breach and summit viewed from the top of the Lava Tower on the South Circuit Path

are often lower if you walk as part of a group rather than on your own. In most cases it is true that you get what you pay for, and the extra money spent on signing with a more expensive outfitter may pay dividends during your climb. Bear in mind that if you book your climb in the UK the costs will be much higher for each of the routes up the mountain.

Kilimanjaro is fairly unique in that you pay per day spent on the mountain. There is no option to make a one-off payment that would then enable you to make a slow ascent and several attempts on the summit. **Every additional day spent on the mountain is an extra cost.** This can prove particularly expensive on the longer routes, and consequently groups may be tempted to race up Kilimanjaro in a bid to save money. By charging a daily fee the Tanzanian authorities have created a system that encourages people to climb

too quickly, which increases the risks to these individuals' health. However, The additional cost is relatively inexpensive when compared to the frustration of having to descend without having made it to the highest point.

Don't let the cost discourage you though. The ascent of Kilimanjaro is an exceptional and priceless experience. Nevertheless, do consider spending extra on an additional acclimatisation day to ensure that you maximise your safety on the mountain.

WHEN TO GO

It is possible to climb Kilimanjaro all year round. That said, there are definitely more preferable times of year to attempt the climb, though even during the preferred months, the weather is erratic and difficult to predict. Ideally you will want to tackle the mountain during one of the two dry seasons that Tanzania enjoys. These last from mid-December to March and then from July to early October. During the dry spell at the start of the year, the weather is generally dry and warm, whilst during the middle of the year it tends to be dry but cooler. The hottest months are January, February and September.

The remaining months of the year fall within the two rainy seasons, when climbing Kilimanjaro is less easy or, indeed, pleasant. The long rains ('masika') last from April to June and the short rains ('mvuli') occur in November and early December, when thunderstorms are common. During this time, thick cloud shrouds the mountain and there are heavy downpours on the lower slopes, which can turn to snow higher on the mountain.

Temperatures on Kilimanjaro vary wildly. At the foot of the mountain the temperature can exceed 30°C, whilst on the summit it can plunge to below –20°C. Wind chill and the moisture in the clouds that swirl around the summits during the day can then make it feel even colder than this. Whilst climbing on Kilimanjaro, groups must always be prepared for cold weather and sudden storms. The high winds can mean that weather changes at very short notice and the exposed nature of the climb means that this can be very unpleasant.

At the equator, the sun rises and sets at a fairly consistent time throughout the year. Sunrise tends to occur around 6.30am and sunset takes place 12hrs later, at around 6.30pm.

As a consequence of these factors, the ideal months to climb Kilimanjaro are January and February, just after the major rains, as the weather improves and becomes relatively settled and the mountain is freshly covered by snow.

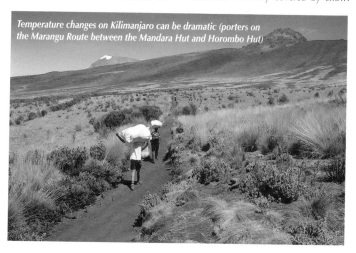

Temperature changes on Kilimanjaro can be dramatic (porters on the Marangu Route between the Mandara Hut and Horombo Hut)

AVERAGE MONTHLY TEMPERATURE/RAINFALL

Month	Max Temp (°C)	Min Temp (°C)	Rainfall (mm)
January	29	10	60
February	29	10	100
March	27	11	170
April	25	13	370
May	22	11	230
June	21	8	50
July	20	9	20
August	22	8	25
September	24	8	25
October	26	11	40
November	27	10	110
December	28	10	100

Alternatively, tackle the ascent from June to October after the short rains; though the forests are frequently encircled by cloud, the summits are often clear. This second set of dates tends to be the most popular time for people to make an ascent of the mountain as it coincides with European summer holidays.

Having plumped on a season in which to make the climb to the summit, it is also worth trying to coordinate your climb with the full moon since the final push to the summit is conducted in the small hours of the morning.

Almost all nights on Kilimanjaro are clear so climbing to the crater rim by

Silhouetted figures on Mawenzi ridge watching the sunrise (Rongai Route, Mawenzi Tarn hut to Kibo hut)

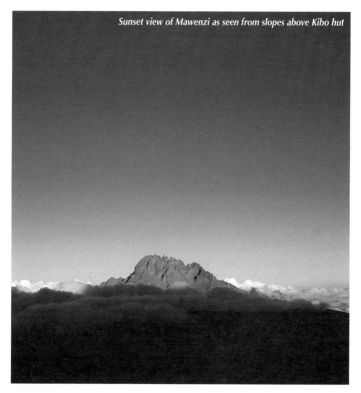

Sunset view of Mawenzi as seen from slopes above Kibo hut

moonlight makes the night time ascent more enjoyable and potentially even more beautiful. As a rough guide, a full moon rises at sunset and sets at sunrise, at about the time the sun actually becomes visible in the sky. The benefit of having strong moonlight illuminate the path during your ascent makes this the ideal time to tackle the last haul to the crater rim. However, the best conditions are probably a couple of days after the full moon as then the moon begins to set about an hour later each day. This means that at around 5.00am the sky is still lit by the moon and the critical section of the climb can be tackled relatively easily.

In order to coordinate your climb with the full moon and make the most of this period, those embarking on a five-day climb should aim to start the trek three days prior to the full moon and those completing the climb in six days should aim to commence their trip four days ahead of the full moon.

21

FULL MOON DATES 2010–2012

2010	2011	2012
Jan 30th	Jan 19th	Jan 9th
Feb 28th	Feb 18th	Feb 7th
Mar 29th	Mar 19th	Mar 8th
Apr 28th	Apr 18th	Apr 6th
May 27th	May 17th	May 5th
June 26th	June 15th	June 4th
July 25th	July 15th	July 3rd
Aug 24th	Aug 13th	Aug 1st and 31st
Sept 23rd	Sept 12th	Sept 29th
Oct 22nd	Oct 11th	Oct 29th
Nov 21st	Nov 10th	Nov 28th
Dec 21st	Dec 10th	Dec 28th

As you approach the crater rim, you may also become aware of the morning star, a planet (usually Venus), which becomes visible just before sun rise. The Chagga call this star 'Ngatunyi', which means 'the star that guides nocturnal travellers safely home'.

PRE-DEPARTURE PREPARATION

Kilimanjaro attracts a great number of trekkers who have never undertaken a multi-day walk, and certainly haven't contemplated doing so at altitude. The mountain's environment is regularly underestimated and the result can be

Mawenzi seen at dusk above band of cloud from Kibo hut (Rongai Route, Mawenzi Tarn hut to Kibo hut)

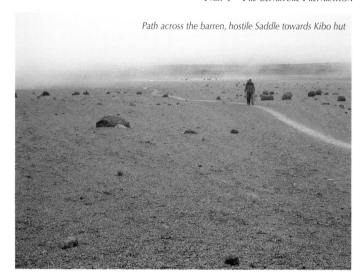

Path across the barren, hostile Saddle towards Kibo hut

fatal. Although many hundreds of people reach the summit without incident, many more don't make it because they fail to prepare and then ascend too quickly and suffer from altitude sickness. Uhuru Peak is several hundred metres higher than Everest Base Camp, yet climbers take at least two weeks to reach this height on Everest.

Getting to the top of Kilimanjaro demands mental preparation as well as physical fitness. Embarking on an ascent that will take several days and will culminate at almost 6000m is a very different proposition to a walking trip based in one place or predominantly at a single elevation. With a central base, you are able to choose whether or when to go walking. As a member of an organised group on a multi-day ascent, you will have a schedule to maintain and will be expected to

walk day after day, rain or shine, whether you fancy it or not. There are few opportunities to escape if you begin to falter, other than to stop and descend.

The most efficient way to get fit for climbing Kilimanjaro is to trek up and down hills. Jogging helps to build stamina and endurance, although there is little you can do to aid acclimatisation, short of spending time at altitude. By walking frequently, at the very least your body is becoming used to the rhythm and rigours of life on the path. When planning your trip, also carefully consider including an extra day for acclimatisation. The additional cost is relatively inexpensive when compared to the frustration of having to descend without having made it to the highest point. Once you arrive on the foothills of the mountain and the path winds away from you into the forest and ever upward, you will be grateful for the preparation and will be able to open your eyes and mind fully to the incredible experience ahead.

Mental preparation will be invaluable when high on the mountain, exhausted and facing potential extended periods of intense cold and discomfort. There will certainly also be times of confusion and times when your western sensibilities are overwhelmed by the sights and smells of life on Kilimanjaro. In order to successfully reach the summit, you must be able to adapt to a whole new range of conditions and circumstances.

If you have significant doubts, forget it. Three or four days into an ascent is no time to discover that you don't enjoy trekking. The financial outlay alone required to undertake an ascent of Kilimanjaro ought to be sufficient to ensure that you do think carefully about going, make suitable preparations and then savour every moment of the trip.

GETTING THERE

Information under this heading is particularly prone to change, especially those details relating to air travel; schedules and times can change and routes introduced or cancelled. Make sure to check all of the details with a travel agent or the airline in advance of making a booking.

By Air

It is possible to access Kilimanjaro by air from a number of directions, either flying to Nairobi in Kenya or to Dar es Salaam or, most conveniently, to Kilimanjaro International Airport in Tanzania. Many trekkers fly to Nairobi in Kenya, taking advantage of the more frequent flights and the cheaper deals. From here there are daily land and air connections to Dar es Salaam and Kilimanjaro airport. It is in fact far easier to access Arusha or Moshi by road from Nairobi than it is from Dar es Salaam (see 'By land' section).

The only realistic way of entering Tanzania from outside East or Southern

Porters on the trail above Machame hut (Machame Route, Machame hut to Shira Camp)

Africa is by air. There is a choice of two international airports; the international airport in Dar es Salaam and the smaller, more useful, Kilimanjaro International Airport. From either of these it is then possible to access the mountain.

It takes between 10–14hrs to fly to Tanzania, depending on the route taken and the number of stops made. However, because Tanzania is only three hours ahead of GMT (2hrs ahead of Brittish Summer Time), there is minimal jet lag to be overcome if you are flying from Europe.

Kilimanjaro airport is around 40km west of Moshi and 50km east of Arusha, to the south-west of the mountain. It has a small terminal that can be easily negotiated. The airport has been recently privatised and is likely to gain favour with more international airlines. It is a much more useful entry point to the country than Dar es Salaam. Currently **Kilimanjaro International Airport is serviced by** KLM (www.klm.com, three flights per week from Amsterdam on Mondays, Wednesdays and Fridays that continue on to Dar es Salaam), Air Tanzania (www.airtanzania.com, international flights suspended but still one flight per day from Dar es Salaam), Precision Air (www.precisionairtz.com, three daily flights from Nairobi and three to four from Dar es Salaam) and Ethiopian Airways (www.flyethiopia.com, who operate from Addis Ababa to Kilimanjaro six times per week). Precision Air is now partnered with Kenya Airways (www.kenya-airways.com), so you can fly Kenya Airways to Nairobi and then onwards to Kilimanjaro with Precision Air.

When flying into Kilimanjaro airport from the north, try to sit on the left-hand side of the plane so that when arriving by day (if it's clear) you will be able to have fantastic views of the mountain. If you are unlucky and end up on the right-hand side of the plane, content yourself with views of Lake Turkana in the north of Kenya. Lake Turkana is the world's largest permanent desert lake and is about 1hr flight north of Kilimanjaro.

There are several direct and one-stop **flights from Europe and other parts of Africa to Dar es Salaam**. Currently, the only direct flights from the UK to Tanzania are with British Airways (Tel. 08457 733 377, www.ba.com, three flights per week), who fly from Heathrow.

There are however a number of one-stop options that detour via various European, Middle Eastern and African cities. Emirates (Tel. 0870 243 2222, www.emiratesairline.com, daily flight to Dubai with connecting flight to Dar es Salaam four times a week), Ethiopian Airlines (Tel. 020 8987 7000, www.fly-ethiopia.com, daily flight to Addis Ababa with connecting flights to Dar es Salaam and Kilimanjaro three to five times per week), Kenya Airways (Tel. 01784 888 222, www.kenya-airways.com, daily flights to Nairobi, and two on weekends, with connecting flights to Dar es Salaam and Kilimanjaro), Egyptair (Tel. 020 7734 2343, www.egyptair.com.eg, weekly flights via Cairo), South African Airways (Tel. 020 7312 5000, www.flysaa.com, daily flight to Dar es Salaam via Johannesburg), Gulf Air (Tel. 0870 777 1717, www.gulfairco.com, flights to

Dar es Salaam via Muscat) and Swissair (Tel. 0845 601 0956, www.swissair.com, three weekly flights to Dar es Salaam via Zurich) are all worth comparing.

The cheapest direct **flights to Nairobi** are also currently with British Airways. Kenya Airways also run comparably priced direct flights. Alternatively, Emirates fly from Gatwick via Dubai; Ethiopian Airlines fly from Heathrow via Addis Ababa; Egyptair fly from Heathrow via Cairo; Gulf Air fly from Heathrow via Bahrain and Addis Ababa.

If you are flying from Ireland to Dar es Salaam or Nairobi, British Airways will sell you a through ticket from Belfast or Dublin. There are also convenient through-connections from Dublin to Nairobi with KLM.

There are currently no direct flights from North America to East Africa. To reach Tanzania from here you must change planes and possibly even airlines.

The quickest route is to fly from New York via London with British Airways. Otherwise, fly from New York via Amsterdam with North Western and KLM. Nonetheless, the total journey time is still going be over 20 hours. Fares for these routes are universally expensive. Whilst they may dip as low as US$1500 in the low season, it is not unusual for them to rise to more than US$5000 at peak times.

The alternative to these routes is to fly to a different African destination and then continue your journey from there. Popular options are to fly to Addis Ababa with Ethiopian Airlines or Cairo with Egyptair.

For those with a little time to spare and no fixed itinerary, the cheapest bet may be to fly to London, stay there for a couple of days and then try to pick up a last minute flight onwards.

If travelling from Australia or New Zealand to Tanzania you will have to stop over in Asia, Southern Africa or the Middle East.

The best deals are currently to be had either with Gulf Air, who fly via Singapore and Bahrain, Egyptair, who fly via Bangkok and Cairo, or Emirates, who fly via Dubai. All of these options cost A$2000 or more. It is quicker, but more expensive, to fly with Air Zimbabwe via Harare. Flights on this route start at A$2300.

Kilimanjaro towering above houses on outskirts of Moshi

Alternatively, fly to Johannesburg with Qantas (five times per week from Sydney and Perth) or South African Airways (four times a week from Perth) and pick up a connecting flight to Dar es Salaam from there.

The cheapest time of year to travel to East Africa is between January and May. Flights tend to be heavily booked and occasionally sold out between late June and late August. If you wish to travel during this time, make sure that you book your flights well in advance.

Once you have arrived at Kilimanjaro airport or Dar es Salaam, there are a number of bus connections that you can take that will shuttle you to Arusha or Moshi, from where you can commence your climb. Alternatively, your outfitter may arrange for you to be collected and transferred to the foot of the mountain. (For information on travelling on from Nairobi to Arusha or Moshi please see the 'By land' section.)

If you are flying out of Tanzania, you will be required to pay US$30 departure tax. The tax is only levied on flights, not overland departures from the country, and is usually incorporated into the price of your ticket.

The cheapest time of year to travel to East Africa is between January and May. Flights tend to be heavily booked and occasionally sold out between late June and late August. If you wish to travel during this time, make sure that you book your flights well in advance.

By land

An alternative and easy way of accessing Kilimanjaro is to fly to Nairobi and then travel overland to Arusha or Moshi

Jacaranda tree overlooking shacks on a street in Arusha

in Tanzania. The shuttle bus service is cheap and reliable. There are a couple of companies plying the same route, most of them operating 20-seat buses. Each company leaves at around 8.00am and again at 2.00pm from their offices in the centre of Nairobi. The companies will often offer to collect you from your hotel or from one of the main hotels in town, usually the New Stanley or the Norfolk. The buses cross the border at Namanga and then travel to Arusha, where they pause at the Novotel Hotel and where you may have to change bus, before continuing on to Moshi. The journey to Arusha takes 4–5hrs and the onward trip to Moshi takes a further 1½–2hrs – potholes, punctures and breakdowns allowing. A single ticket costs US$30–35.

The border crossing at Namanga is straightforward enough, although it is usually slow and time consuming. The crossing has been cleaned up considerably in recent years and is now much safer and less hostile to pass through. The hordes of beggars, sellers, charlatans and thieves that used to congregate here have been dispersed. There are still a number of Maasai that loiter here, but generally the crossing is hassle free.

At the border you will need to queue for a visa stamp and to have your baggage checked. You only ever need to pay for the visa. There are no other border fees or payments to be made, no matter what anyone tells you at the time.

In addition to the regular public buses that are run by Akamba and depart from the hectic River Rd area of central Nairobi at 7.00am, there are some companies that operate shuttle runs from Nairobi into Tanzania. By using these companies rather than the public buses, you are forced to pay a little extra, but are then able to board the buses in the comparative safety of downtown Nairobi. The best known and most established is Riverside (see Appendix C for contact details), although another operator, Impala (see Appendix C for contact details) is also a good bet. There is also a new option operated by Bobby (see Appendix C for contact details). Riverside depart from Nairobi at 8.00am and 2.00pm in order to drive to Arusha. The earlier departure then goes on to Moshi. The Moshi pick-up point is at the Tanzania Housing Board building near the New Livingstone Hotel (Tel. 027 275 0093). Single fares to Arusha cost from US$25

and those to Moshi from US$30. If you are prepared to haggle, there are residents rates available that cost Ks1000 and Ks1500 respectively.

Two other services are operated by Scandinavia Express and Pallsons (see Appendix C for contact details). Scandinavia Express run daily services between Nairobi and Dar es Salaam that depart at 6.30am and pass through Arusha. They also operate four buses a day between Dar es Salaam and Arusha. Pallsons only travel as far as Arusha.

PERMITS AND VISAS

Tanzanian visas

Most nationalities require a visa to enter Tanzania. The UK is no exception. Kenyans, Ugandans and the Irish are exempt though. The visa should be obtained in advance of your arrival. This can be done in person or by post from any Tanzanian embassy, consulate or High Commission. It is possible to download the application form in advance from the High Commission website, www.tanzania-online.gov.uk (see Appendix C for contact details). The visa application desks are generally open from 10.00am to 12.30pm on Mon–Fri. The visa request takes 24hrs to process and requires two passport photos and a passport that is valid for at least six months. A three month single-entry visa costs £38/US$50. A multiple entry visa costs roughly double that. The process can be completed in the same day if you are prepared to pay an additional £5.

It is possible to get a visa on arrival in Tanzania, but only at a couple of entry

View of Western Breach and summit amidst
cloud as seen on the South Circuit Path

points. You may also have to explain why you didn't get one in advance if there is a Tanzanian High Commission in your home country. The immigration points at Tanzania's three international airports (Dar es Salaam, Kilimanjaro and Zanzibar) and several of the major land border crossing points, including Namanga, are authorised to issue visas. If you are applying for a visa upon entry to Tanzania, US dollars are the most readily accepted currency, although sterling is usually accepted as well. Your passport will then be stamped to show how long you are allowed to remain in Tanzania.

As long as your Tanzanian visa remains valid, you can visit Kenya or Uganda and then return to Tanzania without having to reapply for another visa. You will still need to have your passport and visa stamp checked though.

Should you wish to extend your visa, you may apply at the immigration office in any major town. There is no extra charge, you do not require any extra photos and the extension is usually issued the same day. If you have already spent three months in Tanzania, you will need an acceptable reason to stay on. The alternative is to quit the country and reapply for a fresh visa. If you are intending to stay in Tanzania longer than three months, you may be as well to apply for a residency permit from the Tanzanian High Commission in your home country in advance of your trip.

YELLOW FEVER VACCINATION CERTIFICATES

Officially, Tanzania has stopped checking Yellow Fever Vaccination Certificates upon arrival in the country. Whilst this is probably fine for the airports, it may be advisable to get the jab anyway and have the certificate handy if you are travelling overland into the country. Try to ensure that you have the inoculation done in advance of departure, in your home country.

Kenyan visas

If you choose to fly into Nairobi and then transfer overland to Tanzania, you will also require a Kenyan visa. Most western and European nationalities, including the UK, need to obtain a visa in order to enter Kenya. This can be done in advance at any Kenyan embassy or high commission, where it generally takes 24–48hrs to process and requires two passport photos and an air ticket that confirms your departure from the country. A single entry visa costs £35/US$50 and is valid for three months. A multiple entry visa costs twice as much.

It is possible to secure a visa upon arrival at the airport in Kenya. This process is usually trouble free, but is very slow and time consuming.

Your visa allows you to re-enter Kenya after visits to Uganda or Tanzania, assuming that your Kenyan visa is still valid. This is particularly useful for those people who have a return ticket to Nairobi and are planning to use the shuttle services to access and return from Kilimanjaro.

If you wish to apply for a visa extension, you must present yourself at the immigration offices in either Nairobi, Mombasa, Lamu or Kisumu. It is only possible to extend the visa for a further three months.

ACCOMMODATION

There is no shortage of accommodation at the foot of Kilimanjaro. Most groups base themselves in Moshi before their climb. This is a small town that has benefited considerably from its proximity to the mountain. Set at just over 800m, it has grown to become a bustling, cosmopolitan place and is now the capital of the Kilimanjaro region. It is the home of the Chagga people and the centre of the region's successful coffee production industry.

The town itself is open and relatively spacious. The central streets are wide and the general pace of life is slow,

Kilimanjaro's summitt seen at sunset

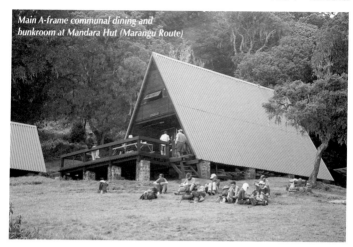
Main A-frame communal dining and bunkroom at Mandara Hut (Marangu Route)

making it an attractive and relaxing place to spend time. There are a number of hotel options in town to suit all budgets (see Appendix B), making this an ideal base for the climb up Kilimanjaro.

Once you begin your ascent of the mountain, your accommodation options are affected by the route that you have chosen to ascend. If you are going to climb the Marangu Route, then you will most likely take advantage of the huts constructed along the path. These are relatively basic structures that provide bunks and mattresses for their overnight guests. There are also communal dining areas, long-drop toilets, and, at the two lower huts, running water and solar powered lighting. More detailed descriptions of the huts and their facilities are provided in the description of the Marangu Route.

If you choose to climb Kilimajaro by any other route, you will need to camp throughout your trip. There are designated campsites on each of the paths. These are usually situated close to water sources, frequently streams or pools and adjacent to an old metal uniport. Outline details relating to these hut shells are given in the text wherever they can be found on the mountain. Each campsite has long-drop toilets in the vicinity.

It is worth bearing in mind that the final hut or campsite on the ascent are all dry, and water will have to be carried here from the last water points lower on the mountain

LANGUAGE

The official languages of Tanzania are Swahili and English. Swahili, or Kiswahili, has played a major role in uniting the people and solidifying the country's sense of self. Swahili was adopted as the country's national language after

31

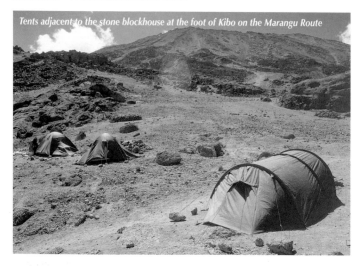
Tents adjacent to the stone blockhouse at the foot of Kibo on the Marangu Route

Tanzania secured independence. It has become the most widely spoken language used by Tanzania's ethnic groups and provides a degree of commonality. English is widely spoken in the main towns and tourist areas, but is much less common in rural or smaller towns. It is the official language of commerce, administration and higher education.

Swahili is technically a Bantu language, although it has assimilated a number of Arabic, Persian, Hindi, Portuguese and English words. Trade and immigration have influenced and moulded it, and it is now the lingua franca of central and eastern Africa. It is surprisingly easy to learn and is pronounced as it is written, with the stress nearly always on the penultimate syllable. Local people are often delighted if you make the effort to try and speak a little Swahili, even if it is just to say

'Hello'. Your guides will undoubtedly introduce you to a handful of phrases and essential words, most usefully the Kilimanjaro mantra, 'pole, pole', which means 'slowly, slowly'. A glossary of useful words is provided at the back of this book in Appendix E.

Besides Swahili, there are a host of local languages that can be categorised in four groups: Bantu, Nilotic, Coshitic and Khoisan. The vast majority of Tanzanians speak one of the Bantu languages as their first language. The Maasai are the main speakers of the Nilotic languages.

MAPS

There are a number of maps of Kilimanjaro itself available, both in Tanzania and abroad. Specialist map shops in the UK, such as Stanfords (branches in London and Bristol, www. stanfords.co.uk), carry a range of the best trekking maps available. Some of these are also available at the National Park headquarters at the Marangu Gate or in the towns of Moshi or Arusha. Most of the maps that are available are general overview maps of the entire mountain and are not really of sufficient detail to be used as trekking maps. Nonetheless, they help to put the mountain and the various routes into context as well as providing some useful and interesting details.

The Ordnance Survey produced an attractive map of Kilimanjaro at 1:100,000 scale in the early 1990s. Based on survey mapping, this shows contours at 100ft intervals. Varying grades of road and track are shown as are many of the main physical features, although the overlaid route maps are not entirely reliable. Unavailable in the UK since the end of the 1990s, this map can still be found in Moshi and at the park gates.

If you are simply in Tanzania to climb Kilimanjaro then you will have little need of a general road map of the country. Your outfitter will transport you to the trailhead and ensure that you are collected from the end of the track as well.

One of the most readily available maps is the attractive, hand-drawn *New Map of the Kilimanjaro National Park*, produced by Giovanni Tombazzi and published by Maco Editions in 1998. This colourful map is drawn at a scale of 1:125,000 and relies on shading to differentiate between elevations. Consequently, although it provides a good overview of the mountain and the routes, it is not as useful as a topographic map.

A revised edition of the ITMB (International Travel Maps) *Kilimanjaro*

View across the barren Saddle to the Kibo massif (Rongai Route, Mawenzi Tarn to Kibo hut)

map was published in 2006. Drawn at 1:62,500 scale, it shows all of the main trekking routes, campsites, huts and water points. Colour shading to show altitude is combined with 100m contours and spot heights. There is a comprehensive index that lists many of the caves, glaciers, mountain features and surrounding villages, as well as some short text providing additional information about the routes.

You will also come across the *Kilimanjaro Map and Guide* by Andrew Wielochowski and published by West Col Productions. This double-sided sheet features a 1:75,000 scale topographic trekking map of Kilimanjaro. There are contour intervals at 100m, and all of the routes are marked, as are the locations of campsites and water points. Whilst similar to the ITMB map, the physical features such as scree slopes, glaciers and cliffs are more clearly shown here. There is also a line drawing showing the approach roads to the foot of Kilimanjaro. On the reverse there are also more detailed maps of Kibo (1:30,000 scale) and Mawenzi (1:20,000 scale), in addition to text on the routes, climate, flora, fauna and suggestions for essential equipment.

Kilimanjaro-Kibo, by Sandra Greulich and Sacha Wettstein, was published by Climbing Map in 2008. It is an excellent 1:80,000 map that combines topographic coverage of the mountain with an enlargement for the Kibo crater, a list of GPS waypoints, profiles of the main routes and street plans of Arusha and Moshi. Contours are at 200m intervals and there are enhanced spot heights, graphics and colouring showing the type of terrain you are crossing.

EQUIPMENT

'We will trek over fifty miles, going from a few thousand feet to over nineteen thousand feet. During the course of our journey temperatures will range from 100 degrees plus at the jungle base to minus 20 degrees at Kilimanjaro's summit, and we must carry the gear and supplies essential for survival in both extremes. Every ounce must be counted, every square inch of space put to utmost use. To take too much will weigh us down and wear us out on the approach'.

Rob Taylor

Climbing Kilimanjaro is in no way technical and no mountaineering skills or equipment are required to make the ascent. In addition, a team of porters will carry the majority of your kit and supplies, leaving you to simply transport yourselves and a day pack to the next camp. Porters usually carry more than one person's gear, bound together with string or rope. Several outfitters now supply their charges with kitbags for the climb, so that the bags can be transported and identified more easily. Nonetheless, it is essential that you are properly equipped for all of the different stages on the mountain and that you recognise the need to restrict the size and weight of your rucksack to a manageable limit. There is a very real tendency for people to take far too much clothing and equipment on the climb. Just because you won't be carrying it is no reason to overload your pack. Besides which, the porters are restricted to carrying 15kg, and if

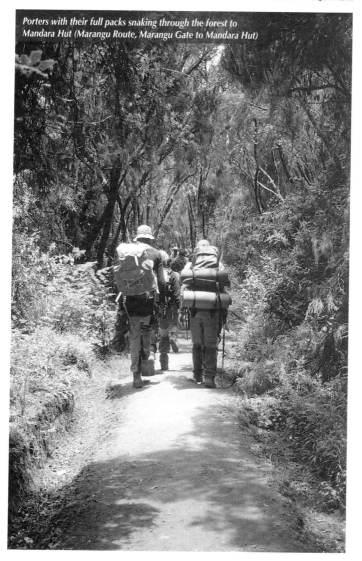

Porters with their full packs snaking through the forest to Mandara Hut (Marangu Route, Marangu Gate to Mandara Hut)

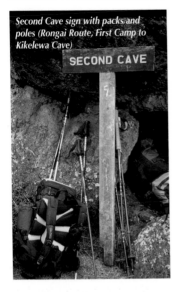

Second Cave sign with packs and poles (Rongai Route, First Camp to Kikelewa Cave)

SECOND CAVE

your gear comes to more than they can legitimately carry, you will be forced to hire additional men at additional cost.

Your choice of equipment is important and can influence your chances of succeeding on the mountain. You must be prepared for all eventualities and have sufficient resources to combat extremes of temperature, exposure and weather. Whilst shorts and t-shirts may be appropriate on the lower slopes, they are not adequate clothing at higher elevations and anything short of a full cold kit on the summit is potentially life threatening. It is worth remembering that whilst the daytime temperatures can be very high, at night the mountain gets very cold.

A warm **sleeping bag**, and if camping a good **ground mat**, can drastically improve your chances of getting a reasonable night's sleep when camping at altitude. You should also expect rainfall at some stage. Waterproof clothing is essential to prevent the disruption of, or even early termination of, your climb.

The type of boot that you wear can be critical to your enjoyment and success. Your **boots** should be comfortable, medium to heavyweight and of a good fit. It is essential that they are well broken in before your departure, in order to minimise the likelihood of you developing blisters during the trek. The boots must provide good ankle support and have thick cleated soles that give a degree of cushioning and excellent grip. Leather walking boots or indeed any other type of waterproof boot are ideal, since some of the ascent is through damp, wet forest or heath and the possibility of heavy rain can not be discounted. Make sure that there is enough room to prevent your toes hitting the front of the boot when descending a steep slope. You should also carry **sandals or other lightweight footwear** to change into at the hut or campsite.

Gaiters are a very sound investment prior to your ascent. The early stages in the forest can be exceptionally muddy and the use of gaiters helps to keep your feet dry and thus prevents potential blisters. On the heath/moorland, highland desert and summit ascent there are large quantities of scree and gravel to be negotiated. Use gaiters on these sections to stop the small shards of lava or rock from getting inside your footwear. The descent from the crater rim is on loose scree and the passage of feet tends to result in quantities of fine, penetrating dust being kicked up. Gaiters will once again prevent this material from getting into your boots.

A lot of walkers now use telescopic **trekking poles**. These are very useful when ascending or more particularly, descending steep or scree slopes. They provide extra balance and help to support your weight, taking the pressure off your knees. Use one or two poles, depending on your own personal preference.

Good **waterproofs** are an indispensable part of any Kilimanjaro climbers clothing. They are essential for protection against rain or snowfall, but also double up as a windproof outer layer. Jacket and trousers made from breathable fabric are ideal for this purpose.

All climbers should also take a fleece or warm jacket to wear in the evenings or on the upper slopes of the mountain. In order to combat the fluctuating temperatures on the mountain, adopt a layering policy when dressing. It is always easier to take something off than it is to put it on, especially if you don't have it with you. A woollen hat or balaclava, scarf and gloves are also a good idea

In addition to protective gear that combats the cold and wet, you should also have sufficient equipment to be able to endure extremes of sunshine and heat. The sun on the equator and at altitude is very strong. A **brimmed hat, sun cream (factor 15+), lip salve and sunglasses** are vital.

In addition to these items of clothing and kit, a **first aid kit** should be carried so that you can patch up minor injuries, such as blisters, cuts and grazes, or trail ailments (see Health and Safety Considerations). A **water bottle** with at least a 2 litre capacity is also essential. For the final ascent to the crater rim you will require a **headtorch**. A standard torch is also useful for when moving about inside your tent or around the campsite. Make sure to bring spare batteries and a spare bulb with you. Additionally, a **whistle** is useful for attracting attention if you are lost or separated from your group. A small amount of emergency, high energy **food**, such as chocolate or nuts, ought to

EQUIPMENT CHECKLIST

Clothing	boots and spare laces, light shoes or sandals, down jacket, fleece or jumper, shirts (t-shirts and long-sleeved, collared shirts), socks, trekking trousers, waterproof jacket and overtrousers, underwear (including thermals), gloves, woollen hat or balaclava, wide-brimmed hat.
Essential items	passport, rucksack, day pack, trekking poles, gaiters, sleeping bag (3 season+), floor mat, water bottle (2 litre+), water purifying tablets, headtorch, batteries, bulbs, first aid kit, penknife, lighter, sunglasses, sun cream (factor 15+), lip salve, towel and wash bag, money belt, map, whistle, toilet paper, plastic bags.
Optional items	camera, film, binoculars, altimeter, compass, notebook and pen, ear plugs, waterproof pack cover.

be carried as well. A **penknife** is also a handy tool to have. **Plastic bags** to store your rubbish in are also a good idea.

Whilst on the mountain, secure all of your valuable or important possessions in waterproof bags. This will ensure that they remain dry in the eventuality of rain or your pack leaking. At short notice a dustbin bag will double up as a pack liner.

Although you won't be carrying your full size pack, try to ensure that it is in good condition and is waterproof. The porters may or may not choose to carry it in the conventional manner. A sturdy day pack is essential. Make sure that it fits comfortably and is easily adjustable. It need not be especially large, 30 to 40 litre capacity is sufficient, but do make sure that it can contain all of your cameras, maps, water supplies, some food, additional clothing, waterproofs and sun cream.

INSURANCE

It is wise to take out a good insurance policy. When researching insurance policies, make sure that you mention that you are going to climb Kilimanjaro. Although this may result in an increase

in your premium, it will at least ensure that you are covered in case of an accident on the mountain. Make sure that you make a photocopy of the policy and leave it with a friend or family member.

HEALTH CONSIDERATIONS

'We were turning into geezers. Ratty beards sprouted. Fingers swelled. Faces grew puffy and wrinkled. Our rest steps slowed to funereal pace. We got gaseous … Why do people put themselves through this wringer?'

Tom Dunkel

First-time visitors to Africa can easily become obsessed with concerns regarding their health. Whilst the potential dangers of trekking in a developing country can seem overwhelming it is important to prevent these worries from becoming obsessive. In reality, Tanzania isn't a particularly dangerous country and very few travellers experience anything more than an upset stomach. In order to minimise the risks of becoming sick, have the requisite

FIRST AID KIT		
Plasters	Throat lozenges	Wet wipes
Blister kit	Imodium	Insect repellent
Bandages (both cotton gauze and elastic)	Iodine Tablets	Sterile needles
Knee supports	Sun cream	Any prescription medi-
Antiseptic cream	Lip salve	cines that you would
Aspirin or Paracetamol	Safety pins	usually take in your
	Scissors	home country

inoculations before leaving home, make sure that you carry a first aid kit and adopt a sensible attitude to food and hygiene whilst on the trek.

Pre-Trek Health

There are a number of steps that you can take before you even leave your home country to improve your chances

It would be sensible to safe guard against the following

• **Diptheria and Tetanus** – usually a combined vaccination that is initially administered in three injections and is then topped up every 10 years.

• **Polio** – usually administered during childhood, requires a booster every 10 years

• **Hepatitis A** – Havrix injection lasts for 10 years if you have a second booster shot after six months. Short term administration of gamma globulin provides immediate protection for up to six months.

• **Typhoid** – recommended for most parts of Africa. Available as an injection or as capsules to be taken orally.

• **Tuberculosis** – usually administered during childhood. The risk to travellers is low in Tanzania.

• **Rabies** – Low risk of contracting the disease, but should be considered if you plan to spend more than a month in Tanzania, particularly if you propose to work with animals. It is a three part injection that requires two booster injections upon being bitten.

• **Yellow Fever** – recommended for travel in areas where the disease is endemic, including Tanzania. Only becomes effective 10 days after it has been administered.

It is a good idea to carry proof of your vaccination, especially if you are entering the country overland.

• **Meningococcal Meningitis** – recommended for travel to parts of Africa, including Tanzania, particularly if you intend to stay for several months or work amongst the local population. Not necessary for short stays in the country.

• **Malaria** – the risk on Kilimanjaro itself is low since much of the mountain is too high and cold to support mosquitoes. However, there is a risk of contracting Malaria elsewhere in Tanzania and you should consult a GP or medical professional to gauge the risk posed to you. Your medical history, age and destination will all influence the advice given to you. Some anti-malarial medication is reported to have unpleasant side effects. Regardless, when on the mountain, especially in the forest and on the lower slopes, take precautions to avoid being bitten by mosquitoes. Cover exposed skin and use a repellent spray in the evenings to decrease the chances of being bitten.

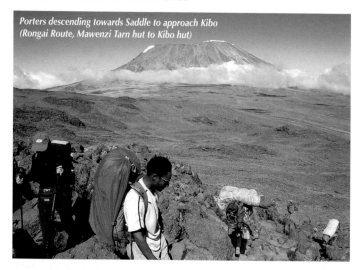

Porters descending towards Saddle to approach Kibo (Rongai Route, Mawenzi Tarn hut to Kibo hut)

of remaining healthy. For fully up-to-date health advice and for information as to which inoculations are necessary, contact the Department of Health Helpline (0800 555 777). Alternatively contact the Medical Advisory Service for Travellers Abroad (MASTA), Tel. 01276 685 040, www.masta.org, or the World Health Organisation (WHO) at www.who.ch. If you would prefer to talk to someone face to face, approach your GP or try visiting the Nomad Travellers store and medical centre in STA Travel in London or the British Airways Travel Clinic, also in London (see Appendix C for contact details).

Remember to plan ahead when getting vaccinations. Some vaccinations need more than one injection and others can not be administered together. Currently, Tanzania makes no requirements for visitors to show proof of immunisation, though in the past travellers have had to show a certificate of vaccination against yellow fever (this practice has officially been stopped – though you may still wish to have the vaccination).

On-Trek Health and Safety

The majority of individuals who set off to climb Kilimanjaro, complete their trip without any undue mishap. With the application of a bit of common sense and care, the mountain shouldn't pose an undue threat and the worst that will happen to you is that you have to deal with a blister. However, Kilimanjaro must not be underestimated and its very real dangers should be taken seriously. In 1884 Harry Johnston prematurely wrote that on Kilimanjaro, '… the most serious obstacles arise from mist and cold which would scarcely deter a cockney from ascending Snowdon.' He later noted on his climb to around 4850m that at one point he felt, 'as if I would never more regain the force to move, and must remain and die amid this horrid solitude of stones and snow.'

Although the path is generally well trodden and you are accompanied by a guide, the route to the summit passes through some wild and forbidding terrain. An accident here can have serious consequences. The National Park authorities are understandably cagey about the exact death toll on Kilimanjaro, but it is likely that between 10–15 people die on the mountain every year.

At the start of each day, **talk through your itinerary with your guide**. Pay particular attention to the amount of height to be gained and how quickly. Don't over-estimate your own physical ability or that of your group, it is far better to be realistic than optimistic in these circumstances. Make an allowance for delays, bad weather and innumerable photo stops to ensure that you have sufficient time to enjoy the day.

When trekking it is essential to **remain hydrated**. This is even more true at altitude, where the regular consumption of water helps to combat the effects of AMS (Acute Mountain Sickness). Drink water regularly and continually throughout the day. Although mountain water and runoff is generally okay to drink, it is well worth treating all drinking water before you consume it. Boil the water for three minutes, treat it with iodine or filter it using a portable filter to ensure that it is free from contamination by bacteria. Bottled water should come with an unbroken seal (equally true for water drunk in the towns). A host of organisms are active in the waterways of Tanzania that could lay you low with a variety of ailments. The

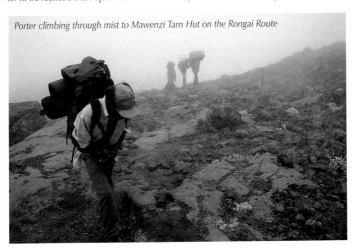

Porter climbing through mist to Mawenzi Tarn Hut on the Rongai Route

Various pieces of rescue equipment at Kibo Hut

same precautions should be borne in mind with regards to ice or water used for cleaning your teeth.

A **good standard of personal hygiene** throughout the trek will also minimise the risk of you becoming ill or suffering from gastro-intestinal problems. Try to clean your hands and fingers before you eat. Carry a pack of baby wipes for this purpose.

Carry a few emergency, high energy foodstuffs and a first aid kit with you on the trek. Keep an eye on the weather and be aware of the sudden build up of cloud or a rapid drop in temperature that may herald the onset of bad weather.

Whilst following the routes up the mountain, **stick to the approved paths**. Try not to leave the clearly marked track and resist the urge to take a shortcut. At higher elevations don't try to venture onto the glaciers unless you are properly

equipped and experienced enough to do so safely. Make sure that you keep an eye on all of the members of your group and watch out for anyone flagging or showing signs of distress.

In the unlikely event that you become separated from your group or have an accident, stay calm and try to draw attention to yourself. The **international distress signal** is six blasts on a whistle or flashes of a torch after dark, spaced evenly for one minute. Wait for a minute and then repeat the sequence. Continue to do so until you are spotted. The appropriate response to the signal from someone who recognises what it means, is three whistles or flashes evenly spaced throughout a minute, followed by a minutes pause and a second set of three.

Whilst climbing Kilimanjaro you will be subjected to extremes of temperature. Consequently **you must be conscious of the dangers of sunburn and**

hypothermia. Sunburn occurs quickly, particularly in the rarefied air and deceptive coolness of the mountain. Make sure that you wear the appropriate clothing and use sufficiently strong sun cream to protect yourself. Sunglasses can also protect your eyes from damage when walking on or near snow or ice. If you do get burnt, aloe vera or calomine lotion will soothe the burn. Continued exposure to high temperatures coupled with a low water intake can sometimes result in heatstroke. At the other end of the temperature gauge, hypothermia occurs when the body loses heat faster than it can produce it and the person's core temperature drops. A combination of wind, wet clothing, fatigue and hunger usually bring on the condition. To combat mild hypothermia, retreat out of the wind, put on dry, warm clothing and drink warm fluids. Do not rub the casualty, allow them to warm up slowly instead.

Mountain Sickness (AMS)

'Haraka haraka haina baraka'
'Hurry hurry has no blessings'
Swahili proverb

One of the main fears that people have when climbing Kilimanjaro is that they will succumb to Acute Mountain Sickness (AMS). This is a very serious condition that can affect anyone. However, it is alright to get AMS in its mild form and by being aware of the symptoms and by adhering to the rules of acclimatisation, you can significantly reduce the likelihood of suffering adversely from this condition. Other forms of varying severity of this condition, which are described later, include High Altitude Cerebral Edema (HACE) and High Altitude Pulminary Edema (HAPE).

As you gain altitude, the air gets thinner, the pressure drops and less

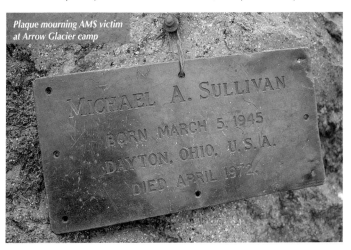

Plaque mourning AMS victim at Arrow Glacier camp

oxygen is available in the atmosphere. The drop in oxygen is noticeable above 2500m. 'High altitude' extends to 3700m and 'very high altitude' extends to 5500m. 'Extreme altitude' is defined as being above 5500m. Consequently, as you gain altitude your heart and lungs have to work harder to oxygenate the body. As the amount of oxygen in the lungs decreases, the blood becomes less and less efficient at acquiring and transporting oxygen. If you ascend slowly and carefully, your body adapts to the rarefied atmosphere and continues to deliver the necessary amounts of oxygen to the blood cells. Most people have the ability to adapt to altitude, if they expose themselves to it sufficiently slowly. However, acclimatisation takes different lengths of time for each individual and there is no hard or fast rule as to how long it ought to take to ascend a mountain. It is impossible to predict who will suffer from AMS. Neither youthfulness or physical fitness are guarantees that you won't be affected. In fact those young trekkers who forge ahead are the most likely to succumb to the debilitating effects of altitude.

Another vital consideration is water intake. When climbing at altitude, you must consume three to four litres of water per day in order to avoid dehydration. A lot of moisture is lost as you breathe or sweat during the climb. If your urine is yellow-coloured then you must increase your liquid intake.

A failure to allow sufficient time to acclimatise is almost certain to bring on AMS. The best way to avoid it is to ascend slowly. In this respect, the Kilimanjaro mantra, 'pole pole', meaning 'slowly, slowly', is wholly appropriate and accurate. However, there is no optimum period for acclimatisation. A conservative estimate for climbing high is that above 3200m (10,000ft) you should ideally only increase the sleeping altitude by around 350m (1200ft) per day. It is also recommended that whilst ascending you take a break every two or three days by sleeping at the same altitude as the previous day. To maximise the benefit of this, you should climb higher during the day, exposing your body to greater altitude, before returning to sleep at the lower elevation. In this way, an ideal ascent of Kilimanjaro should take seven to 10 days to acclimatise properly.

Most ascent routes on Kilimanjaro give you a fraction of that time to reach the top. The ascent is generally far too rapid and side effects of this are inevitable. The summit bid on the standard Marangu Route begins after three days. This is almost three times as fast as the recommended maximum rate of ascent.

At altitude, it is best to assume that any illness is AMS, until proven otherwise. Early indicators that something is amiss include extreme fatigue, persistent headache, dizziness, a loss of appetite and disturbed sleep caused by irregular breathing. In its mildest form it feels akin to a hangover. A tendency to run out of breath after minimal exertion is also an indication that you may be suffering from the condition. If any of these symptoms become apparent, you should pause until they have passed. As long as the symptoms remain mild, ascent at a modest rate can continue. If they persist after a day or two, consider descending

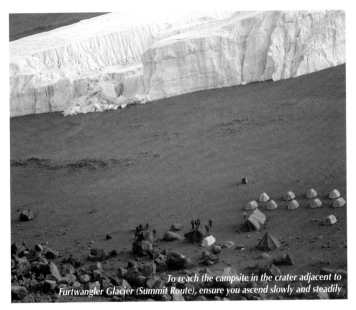

To reach the campsite in the crater adjacent to Furtwangler Glacier (Summit Route), ensure you ascend slowly and steadily

to a lower elevation. Try to avoid taking strong painkillers as they will mask these early symptoms and you will not be alerted to a potentially serious problem.

If the casualty's condition continues to deteriorate, they will become even more lethargic, confused, disorientated and out of breath. They will have wet, bubbly breath. The headache will become severe and they may start to cough harshly, sometimes producing pinkish or rust coloured sputum. They may vomit as well. They will also suffer a loss of co-ordination, known as ataxia, and will be unable to walk in a straight line or complete simple tasks. At this stage, the victim is enduring the onset of either pulmonary or cerebral oedema, both of which can result in

unconsciousness and death within 12hrs. AMS has been fatal as low as 3000m, but most commonly occurs above 3500m.

High Altitude Cerebral Edema (HACE)
HACE is a very severe condition. The brain swells and ceases to function properly. This can result in death very quickly.

The hallmark of HACE is a change in the ability of the victim to think. They may become confused, disorientated or very lethargic. There is a characteristic loss of co-ordination, called ataxia, that most often manifests itself as a staggering walk. If the victim can't walk in a straight line, even when not carrying a pack and on level ground, they should be presumed to have HACE.

45

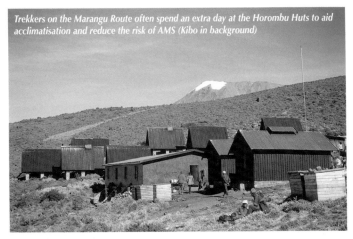

Trekkers on the Marangu Route often spend an extra day at the Horombu Huts to aid acclimatisation and reduce the risk of AMS (Kibo in background)

The treatment is to descend immediately, even if that means doing so in the dark. Delay, even until the following morning could be fatal. The casualty should be accompanied down at least as far as the last elevation at which they felt no symptoms of the condition. If uncertain, dropping 1000m is a good start. People with HACE usually survive if they descend sufficiently quickly and often recover completely.

High Altitude Pulmonary Edema (HAPE)

HAPE, another form of severe altitude sickness, is caused by a build up of fluid in the lungs. In addition to the usual symptoms of AMS, the victim may make a gurgling or rattling breathing sound. They may also feel a tightness around their chest. HAPE frequently occurs at night and may worsen with exertion. It is also common for HAPE to develop into HACE due to the extremely low levels of oxygen in the victims blood.

The treatment for HAPE is the same as for other forms of AMS. Immediate descent to a lower altitude is the optimal solution – even a descent of 500m and the associated increase in oxygen content of the air is often sufficient to reduce the symptoms to a manageable level. People suffering from serious AMS should be accompanied off the mountain – at no time should they be allowed to set off on their own. HAPE resolves itself rapidly upon descent and a couple of days' rest at a lower elevation should ensure a complete recovery.

If, when on your trek, you or your companions begin to suffer HAPE symptoms, descend at once with your group. If the casualty improves sufficiently, you may be able to continue. However, more than likely, once you have begun to descend, you will not be allowed to continue up the mountain. Do not let this fact cloud your judgement though. Be willing to admit that you have

PORTERS AND AMS

Whilst on the mountain it is important to remember that the porters can be affected by AMS just as readily as you. Although most of them have been to altitude before and are likely to be better acclimatised than their charges, they may still suffer from the condition. The fact that they are unlikely to know much about AMS, have a communication barrier that prevents them from explaining in detail how they feel and may actively conceal their symptoms so as not to lose their jobs, makes them susceptible to the more extreme versions of the condition.

altitude sickness. As soon as you begin to feel ill you must recognise the symptoms and act upon them.

Remember, the golden rules for avoiding AMS are: Ascend slowly. If you start to feel the onset of symptoms of AMS go no higher. If the symptoms persist, descend at once.

Diamox (acetazolamide)

Diamox can aid acclimatisation. However, it is not a substitute for a slow and appropriate ascent and should not be taken as a matter of course. Most people with a reasonable rate of ascent will not need it. You must seek guidance from a GP before taking Diamox. The dosage required is based on your body weight, though 125mg (half a tablet) two or three times a day is usually enough to have an effect. Diamox re-acidifies the blood, balancing the effects of the hyperventilation that occurs at altitude in an attempt to get sufficient oxygen. This in turn acts

as a respiratory stimulant, whose end effect is to accelerate acclimatisation.

It is not a magic cure though. Diamox doesn't cover up the symptoms of AMS. Neither does it protect you from worsening AMS if you continue to ascend after symptoms have been diagnosed. Although it may reduce the time it takes for you to acclimatise, it will not totally prevent you from suffering from AMS. If you still feel sick after taking Diamox, you must descend.

If you take Diamox remember to increase your level of fluid intake as the drug is a diuretic and you may become more prone to dehydration. There are also several other side effects of using the drug. You may feel a numbness or tingling sensation in your hands, feet and lips. These may be accompanied by a ringing sound in your ears. These side effects cease once you stop taking the drug.

ACCLIMATISATION TREK – MT MERU

In order to aid acclimatisation and their chances of success on Kilimanjaro, many people undertake an earlier acclimatisation trek that sees them climb to a reasonable altitude before descending once more. The climb closest to and most accessible from Kilimanjaro is the ascent of Mt Meru. Mt Meru is located in the Arusha National Park, which was once described by the British biologist, Sir Julian Huxley, as 'a gem amongst parks'.

At 4566m high, Mt Meru is the second highest mountain in Tanzania and the fifth highest on the African continent. Overshadowed by the larger mountain to the east, Mt Meru is nonetheless a very impressive freestanding volcano in its own right. It makes a superb four-day trek that is very rewarding and picturesque. The trek involves walking through forest and grassland on the lower slopes, before completing a dramatic and exhilarating ridge-walk to the summit that provides stunning views of the Ash Cone lying several hundred metres below in the crater.

The local Waarusha people maintain that the volcano is sacred. Although they conducted animal sacrifices on its slopes, it is unlikely that they ever climbed to the top. First sighted by Europeans in 1862, the mountain was probably first climbed in either 1901, by Carl Uhlig, or 1904, by Fritz Jaeger. It has since received far less foot traffic than Kilimanjaro.

Mt Meru is a perfectly conical shape. It was formed by volcanic activity associated with the creation of the Rift Valley a quarter of a million years ago. It has an internal crater surrounded by precipitous cliffs, some of which are more than 1500m high. More recent eruptions, some within the last 100 years, have resulted in the formation of a resurgent ash cone.

Mt Meru at sunset seen from Shira Plateau on Kilimanjaro

Over 400 species of birds and animals make their home on these slopes. The forests are also home to larger game than is seen on Kilimanjaro. As the mountain receives less visitors than Kilimanjaro, the animals are yet to be scared away by the frequent and heavy presence of people. Rhino, elephant, buffalo, baboon, warthog, duiker and black and white colobus monkeys have all been seen in the forest and on the moorland.

In order to climb Mt Meru you must pay the Arusha National Park entrance fee. This is US$35 per day. There are also hut fees (US$20 per day), a rescue fee (US$20 per trek) and, as all groups are obliged to take a guide, guide fees (US$15 per day) to pay. All fees are payable in cash at the Momela Gate. Although you don't need to take porters on the trip, you may wish to and this cost will also have to be taken into consideration.

The guide who has to accompany you is a national park ranger who is there to make sure that you remain safe on the mountain, rather than show you the way. The guides carry guns in case of unexpected contact with wild animals, but they will try not to have to use them.

There are opportunities to camp on the Momela Route – there are pitches adjacent to each of the huts along the trail. The huts can not be booked and instead operate on a first come, first served basis, so it may be as well to carry a tent in case you arrive late and find that the huts are already full. Whether you choose to camp or find yourself doing so out of necessity, you will have to pay the hut fees.

Most outfitters that organise climbs on Kilimanjaro will also be able to set up an ascent of Mt Meru. A four-day trek tends to cost between US$500–600. Tips for the guide and any porters that you hire are not included in this price and your budget ought to incorporate this.

MOMELA ROUTE

Time:	4 days
Length:	38km
Altitude gain:	3066m
Grade:	Moderate/hard
Start:	Momela Gate
End:	Momela Gate

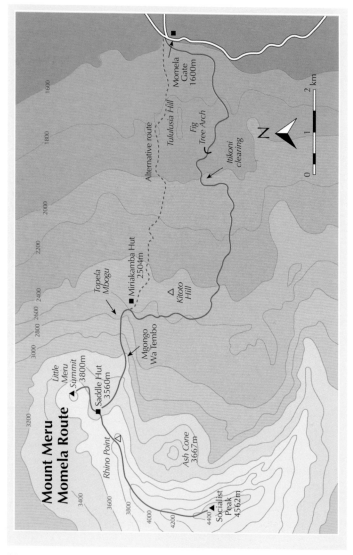

Mount Meru
Momela Route

This is the only available route to the summit of Mt Meru. The Momela Route begins on the eastern side of the mountain and climbs to the summit via the northern shoulder of a horseshoe-shaped crater. The climb takes four days. Since this is most often done as an acclimatisation trek, there is no point in rushing and wasting the opportunity on hand.

Day 1 The first day is a 4–5hr trek over 10km that ascends 1014m. The trek begins at Momela Gate (1600m), from where it crosses the Ngare Nanyuki River and climbs through the forest, past a sacred fig tree arch and the Itikoni clearing, towards the crater. The path crosses a number of streams and passes several excellent view points that show the wide open plains and Momela Lakes. It ascends steeply to the Miriakamba Hut (2504m). There are two bunkhouses here (with bunks and mattresses) that can accommodate 48 people. Long-drop toilets and a good water source are nearby.

Day 2 The second day takes you to the Saddle hut. The route covers 4km over 3–4hrs, climbing steeply to gain 1056m. The path winds through the pleasant forest, passing Buffalo Swamp (Topela Mbogo) and Elephant Ridge (Mgongo wa Tembo). From the ridge there are exceptional views into the crater. The path leaves the forest and continues up though the heath. It clambers onto a wide col between the slopes of Mt Meru and the secondary peak, Little Meru. Saddle Hut (3560m) is set here. There are two bunkhouses, one newer than the other, and long-drop toilets. Water is retrieved from a stream about 10 minutes away.

Due to the short nature of the day, it is possible to take a detour to the top of Little Meru (3800m). The ascent takes a further hour and affords you superb views of the summit and of Kilimanjaro.

Day 3 This is a 5km climb up just over 1000m to the peak followed by a descent to Miriakamba Hut for the evening. This will take 9–11hrs. By leaving Saddle Hut at 2.00am or just after, you ought to be on the summit of Mt Meru in time to see the sunrise behind the great bulk of Kilimanjaro.

The ascent to the top is along a narrow ridge. The drops on one side are sheer and the exposed nature of the path can prove too much for more timid trekkers. Aim first for Rhino Point, by heading across a plateau behind the hut before climbing steeply. The point is marked by a cairn and takes around 1hr to reach. From here you can see the inner walls of the crater being set aglow by the sun. The path then drops slightly before rising more steeply to edge around the rim of the crater. Walk around the rocky crater rim for a further 4–5hrs to reach the summit, Socialist Peak (4562m), from where the views are outstanding. The descent (2058m) is along the same path. It takes 3–4hrs to return to Saddle Hut, and a further 1–2hrs to descend to Miriakamba Hut.

Day 4 It takes 2–3hrs to descend the 10km from Miriakamba Hut to the Momela Gate the following day, along the same route that you used to climb the mountain.

Alternatively, some groups combine the third (summit) day and the fourth (descent) day. This is entirely possible, but does mean that the summit day is very lengthy, since you must descend right off the mountain in the same day.

SELECTING AN OUTFITTER

All walkers on Kilimanjaro must make the ascent with a licensed outfitter as independent trekking on the mountain was banned by the park authorities in 1991. There is now no independent trekking on the mountain at all. At the very least you must take a guide supplied by the outfitter, and the guide will require a porter to help carry all of the equipment and food supplies. Bigger groups will require much larger teams of porters, cooks and assistant guides.

Trekking on Kilimanjaro with a group is the norm for most people. It is always easier to undertake this sort of trip in the company of friends and is a very sociable way to climb the mountain. The companionship and camaraderie are highly desirable and can act as a positive incentive to succeed.

It is possible to organise a trip on your own, and use the services of an outfitter to obtain a guide. That way you can plan the trek that you want, without having to incorporate the wishes of others. Most outfitters will try to introduce you to a larger group and will encourage you to trek in the company of other

individuals, though. Even if you do opt to attempt the mountain on your own, you will never feel completely alone. Campsites are communal and lively places and there is a great deal of interaction between groups.

There are a great number of outfitters that organise treks on the mountain, based both in the UK and in Tanzania. They are responsible for ensuring the success and safety of your trip. It is important that you choose one that you think is best suited to your needs. Climbing Kilimanjaro is an expensive expedition, so it is worth spending some time comparing and contrasting the various organisations out there before parting with your money.

The vast majority of people book their climb on Kilimanjaro before they leave their home country. This is the easiest, least hassled way of organising the trip, since nearly all agencies will sell you a complete package, including airport pick up and transfers, accommodation and the ingredients for the climb itself. They may also be able to sell you flights as well. This is the least time consuming option and means that you can make all of the arrangements

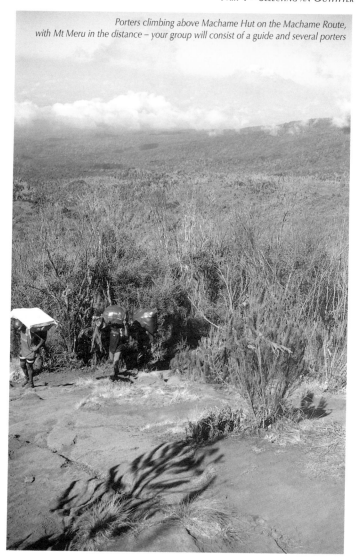

Porters climbing above Machame Hut on the Machame Route, with Mt Meru in the distance – your group will consist of a guide and several porters

Porters at Naremoru trailhead before heading on to the Rongai Route – ensure food and drink for the entire trip are included in the price

well in advance. Inevitably this costs a little more than booking direct with an outfitter in Tanzania, but the additional money buys you peace of mind.

There are a huge number of outfitters and agencies in Tanzania. Most are found at the foot of the mountain, in either Arusha or Moshi. Most of the larger and more established agencies now have online booking facilities, which mean that you can arrange your trek from outside Tanzania. Arusha tends to be a little more expensive than its neighbour, Moshi, not least because many of the agents here are working on behalf of outfitters in Moshi and need to take their cut. There are also higher transport costs to the trailhead from Arusha as it is further away from the mountain. Moshi has the largest number of outfitters (see Appendix C for a selection of the better outfitters in Moshi). Many of these are affiliated to agencies

in the UK. Booking directly with an outfitter in Moshi represents the best value in terms of how much you will pay and what your money will buy. As a result of the sheer mass of competition in the town and the fact that you have removed all of the middlemen, you are also likely to pay less than if you book your trip elsewhere.

The most important thing to bear in mind when booking your trip is that the agency must be licensed. Ask to see the licence and make sure that it is in date. A good way of comparing the different agencies is to ask other people about their experiences on the mountain. Check the visitors books and read the various comments. Shop around and consult several outfitters in order to get a feel for the types of service and price ranges on offer. Check the day-to-day itineraries proposed by the outfitters and, if possible, ask to see the standard of equipment that they propose to use. Make sure that you establish exactly what is and isn't included in the price. All national park fees, rescue fees, hut or camping fees for both you, the guide and all of the porters that will accompany you should be included. Food and drinks for the entire trip should also be part of the proposed deal, as should all equipment hire costs and the price of being transported to and from the trailhead by the outfitter. Most of the established, reputable outfitters will have standard contracts that stipulate all of this information, so that you know what you are signing yourself up for.

GUIDES AND PORTERS

With the outlawing of independent trekking on Kilimanjaro in 1991, groups were no longer allowed to pitch up at the foot of the mountain and just start climbing. Nowadays, all ascents of the mountain must be conducted with a guide and usually with a team of porters. Kilimanjaro National Park recommends that each individual making an ascent of the mountain do so with at least one or two porters. The guide will stay with you throughout the climb, accompanying you right to the summit should you be fortunate enough to make it that far. The porters will climb as far as the top camp, then wait for you to return from the summit bid before descending with you.

They are often interesting and entertaining companions, whose easy humour, ready laugh and knowledge of the mountain and the area can enhance your trip. Hopefully you'll be slightly more considerate towards your team than HW Tilman, who noted on his return to Gilman's Point from higher on the crater rim that, 'We picked up the

Porters gathered at the foot of the mountain

patient Solomon, now the colour of a mottled and overripe Victoria plum, and at twelve o'clock started down.'

Climbing the mountain with guide and porters is nothing new, though. In 1889, Hans Meyer was accompanied by a team of porters and guides. The group was led by 18-year-old Yohana Kinyala Lauwo, supported by an assistant, Jonathan Mtui, and several porters, Elia Minja, Tom Mosha, Makalio Lyimo, and Mamba Kowera. Their names are commemorated on a plaque at the Marangu Gate. Lauwo went on to guide people up the mountain for most of his life. He was present at the centennial celebrations when he was honoured in recognition of his role in the first ever ascent of the mountain. He died, aged 125, in 1996. The first Chagga to actually stand on the summit were the guides Oforo and Jonathan, who did so in 1925 and have been credited with the 11th and 12th ascents.

Most of the guides and porters are affiliated to one or other of the outfitters at the foot of the mountain. All guides must be registered with the national park authorities and will have a permit that confirms that. They are drawn from all walks of life and represent a broad spectrum of ages, tribes and backgrounds. That said, most of the porters are members of the Chagga tribe. Many are youngsters in their late teens and early twenties. Others have worked on the mountain for a decade or more.

Many porters volunteer to climb Kilimanjaro to supplement the income they generate from farming. Others are freelancers who have no other job. The role of porter is by no means a demeaning one and has long been a major source of employment in the Kilimanjaro

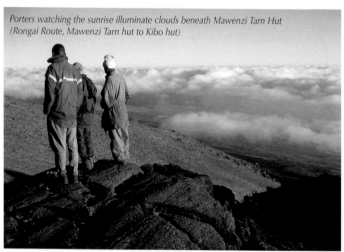

Porters watching the sunrise illuminate clouds beneath Mawenzi Tarn Hut (Rongai Route, Mawenzi Tarn hut to Kibo hut)

region. In an area where the unemployment rate is around 80%, it is a respectable and comparatively well paid job and money earned in tips supplements pay. Porters usually receive US$4–5.50 per day, although the official rate of pay is US$10. Cooks and assistant guides earn US$5.50–6.75 (official rate: US$15) and guides can expect to be paid US$6.75–8 per day (official rate: US$20). There was due to be a further attempt to enforce the official wages in 2010–2011 but the likelihood of the official salaries being enforced is very slim. Moses Kazimoto, himself a porter on the mountain, estimated in Audrey Salkeld's book, *Kilimanjaro*, that, '... if a porter manages only one trip a month on the Machame Route, he could expect to take home TS60,000 per year, which is equivalent to what a schoolteacher earns for the same period for far less arduous work.' Tsh60,000 is actually highly unlikely, and porters are more likely to make only Tsh25,000–40,000 per trip.

Porters are often open to exploitation, though. There is never enough work to go round and competition to become a porter is fierce. Only by serving an apprenticeship as a porter will they become an assistant guide and have a chance to progress to the level of guide. Although there are regulations in place to try to preserve porters' rights, these are sometimes flouted by unscrupulous outfitters or guides.

Tourism Concern (www.tourism concern.org.uk), a UK-based organisation that lobbies on behalf of porters' rights, noted that, 'There have been reports of guides bribing the rangers who weigh the porters' loads, for example, so that the porters end up carrying huge weights, and of guides choosing porters on the basis of payments and bribes. Porters who complain fear that they will be threatened by the guide and told that they will not climb again.' Porter conditions and standards vary considerably from one group to another. There are no standardised rates of pay and it is often the outfitters that get rich whilst the porters put in the hard graft.

Other organisations working for improved conditions for porters include the International Porter Protection Group (www.ippg.net) and the Kilimanjaro Porters Assitance Project (www.kiliporters.org). The latter lends out equipment and clothing, donated by trekkers, to porters for free, teach the porters English and first aid, and generally try to raise the issue of porter exploitation in the public mind by arranging for people to spend a day with a porter and see what his life is really like. They have also set up a 'Partner' scheme for trekking agencies, and there are lists online of those which have signed up to it.

The level of equipment given to porters has improved considerably over recent years. That said, the porters are still woefully kitted out for mountain climbing and often make do with whatever they can scrounge or cobble together. Outfitters are now obliged to provide tents for their teams since the porters have been banned from sleeping in caves along the routes.

Nonetheless, the porters are still at very high risk on the mountain. Although they appear superhuman, carrying massive loads, seemingly unaffected by altitude and surviving in the harsh conditions without the benefit of modern equipment or clothing, many of them are inexperienced, unsure of what to expect on the mountain and lack the proper equipment and clothing. They are still susceptible to appalling accidents, frostbite, altitude sickness and death. In bad weather it is not uncommon for a porter to die of exposure or hypothermia. In September 2002, the deaths of three porters in separate groups during one night, as a result of hypothermia developed during a violent storm, raised the concern about the plight of these individuals. The Kilimanjaro Porters' Association declared that the three men who died in September did so because of a lack of appropriate mountain clothing.

Though extreme, this example is symptomatic of a major problem of exploitation by unprincipled outfitters. There are a number of things that you can do as an individual to try and address this problem. Before booking your trek ask the tour operator or outfitter what policies they have in regard to porters' working conditions, and make sure that they know that it is important to you that your trip does not exploit its team of porters. If booking in the UK, only travel with an operator that has policies on porters' rights. Tourism Concern has a list of over 35 registered tour operators in the UK who have written policies on working conditions for porters. Before you set off, try to make sure that adequate clothing is available for the porters. Whilst on the climb check to see how the porters are being treated, noting the standard of kit they have, the amount that they have to carry and where they sleep at night. Once you have descended from the mountain,

tell the outfitter if you thought they were mistreated and report this to Tourism Concern. Equally, make sure that you tell the outfitter if you thought that the porters were treated fairly and make it clear that this was very important to you and your enjoyment of the climb. This sort of interest and concern will compel the trekking industry to improve itself and sharpen its practices.

TIPPING

In addition to the fee agreed with the outfitter for your climb on Kilimanjaro, you must include in your budget an amount to be allocated as tips for the guide and porters. Whilst it is not mandatory to tip those who accompany you on your climb, a situation has developed whereby the local people depend upon the tips to supplement their meagre income. To this end, tipping is no longer strictly discretionary and has become more-or-less obligatory. Nonetheless, do not let yourself be bullied into tipping excessively and make the team aware of the fact that the tip is for work well done. In fairness, once you see how much effort goes into making your climb a safe and successful one you will not begrudge the guide and porters the extra money.

When it comes to distributing the tips, you can either hand the money to the guide and allow him to share it amongst his team, or you may choose to give it to the individuals yourself. The second option is more personal and allows you to say thank you. It also ensures that each member of the group actually receives what is meant for them. If you do hand the money to the

WHAT TO TIP?

There are several ways of determining how much to tip the team. In the case of large groups, it has become common practice for each member of the group to contribute 10% of the cost of the climb to a tip kitty. The total amount is then shared between all of the porters and guides associated with that group. If there are only a few members in the group you should consider increasing the percentage donated to the kitty.

Alternatively, you might like to consider allocating a set amount to each individual in the team. Although there are no hard or fast rules, a general guideline for the Marangu Route would be to tip the porters US$20–25, the cook US$30–35, and the assistant guides US$35–45. The guide ought to have made the most effort on your behalf and accompanied you to the summit, and so should be tipped US$55–65. On each of the other routes, which are all slightly longer and more arduous, you should consider being slightly more generous. Thus for the Machame route, the porters might earn US$20–30, the cook US$30–40, the assistant guide US$40–50 and the guide US$60–70.

If the team accompanying you worked especially hard or did additional work, you may wish to recognize this by increasing their tip. Almost all of the local people will be very grateful for any shoes or clothes that you may wish to give them after the climb, but these should be gifts and not offered as an alternative to a cash tip.

guide, make sure that you write down what each member is to receive so that they can see that they have been treated fairly and haven't been swindled by an unscrupulous leader.

Bear in mind that tips can be sought quite aggressively and that there are a host of tricks designed to help you part with additional cash. The play-acting and aggrieved faces are designed to prick your conscience and open your wallet.

- Make sure that you are only tipping members of your own team.
- Ascertain how many people are associated with your group and make sure that you actually see them working on your behalf during the course of your climb.

- Don't let the guide persuade you that there was an additional porter accompanying the group that you simply didn't see. Be especially sceptical if this mysterious individual fails to appear to collect his tip and the others volunteer to take it on his behalf.

That said, try to bear in mind that what is a fairly small amount by western standards means an awful lot to the guides and porters on the mountain.

ENVIRONMENTAL AND CULTURAL CONSIDERATIONS

Kilimanjaro is a very important area of biodiversity and it has a very high

59

value to local people. The slopes of the mountain support high density populations, whose numbers have increased five times over the last century. These people rely on the mountain to provide them with water for drinking and irrigation and a pleasant and relatively disease-free environment. Consequently, in order to preserve this situation, the Tanzanian national parks' authorities have declared that Kilimanjaro should be at the centre of a substantial area of wilderness, where the evidence of man and man's activities are minimal. Thus all land above 2700m constitutes Kilimanjaro National Park.

The Tanzanian policy for park management is to conserve the natural environment with as little interference as possible. This involves the national parks' authorities taking responsibility for providing and maintaining facilities and routes on the mountain. Funds and man power are scarce, and they rely on trekkers adhering to the various regulations and making a conscious effort to not damage the mountain in the course of their visit.

Every trekker on Kilimanjaro will have an impact on the mountain and the region simply by virtue of being there. On its own, this may be minimal; but with up to 40,000 people visiting Kilimanjaro every year the effect on the environment and the people that live in the area is greatly magnified. Each visitor has the potential to make their impact a positive one. By being aware of your impact and responsible in regard to your trip, following the requests below, you will secure the future of the mountain.

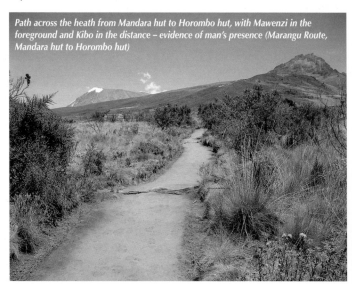

Path across the heath from Mandara hut to Horombo hut, with Mawenzi in the foreground and Kibo in the distance – evidence of man's presence (Marangu Route, Mandara hut to Horombo hut)

Remove all litter

Sadly, although steps have been taken to improve the state of the mountain and instill in trekkers the need to collect and remove from the mountain all of the rubbish that they generate in the course of their climb, the slopes are increasingly littered. This can pose a health risk and is dangerous to animals. Steps have been taken to improve the state of the mountain and instil in trekkers the need to collect and remove from the mountain all of the rubbish that they generate in the course of their climb.

You must pack-out everything that you carry in, including empty food packaging and detritus. Neither burning the rubbish nor burying it is acceptable – metal cans and many modern plastics do not burn completely, and buried rubbish will take years to break down and will, in the meantime, disturb the soil and promote erosion. The rubbish that you collect must be weighed by the park rangers at the end of your trek. If there is a suspicion that any has been dumped, the guide runs the risk of losing his license or being fined.

Toilet paper should be carefully burnt after use, in order to prevent it later becoming strewn across the mountain slopes. Carry a lighter for this purpose. If you are in the forest or heath/moorland zones and think that this will constitute a fire hazard then pack the paper out with you.

Don't pollute water sources

Water is a valuable resource on the mountain and should be treated as such. At the campsite use the long-drop toilets provided. If there are no toilet facilities to hand, select a spot that is at least 30m from any water source and the path, dig a shallow hole and bury the faeces. At the very least, make sure that you cover everything with stones.

Be careful when gathering water from streams and make sure that you leave the source uncontaminated. Also take care when washing not to pollute the water. Soaps, detergents and toothpaste can have a very negative impact on the flora and fauna. Even biodegradable soaps can harm wildlife. Your guide will make sure that, when in the campsite, you are brought warmed water several times a day for you to use to clean up. Dispose of the used water carefully, pouring it onto the ground away from other water sources.

Don't use bottled water

Abandoned water bottles are unsightly and can quickly build up. They aren't biodegradable and do not break down. Now that the huts along the Marangu Route have started to sell bottled water, there is a very real potential of littering. Instead, use water collected from the mountain and boil, filter or treat it before consumption. (See On-Trek Health in Health Considerations.)

Fires

Fires are capable of destroying enormous areas of forest and heath/ moorland vegetation, particularly in the dry seasons. The inaccessible nature of many of the slopes mean that if a fire does break out it is very hard to control or extinguish. The farmers below the national park boundaries use fires to remove dry grass from cropland. These are meant to be controlled but there is evidence to suggest that they have previously contributed to forest fires. Inside the National Park, fires can start as a result of carelessness – dropped cigarettes and roaring campfires are the worst culprits.

All of your meals should be prepared on kerosene stoves rather than on wood fires. Fires should not be lit at the hut or campsite areas either. The reason for this is twofold: it prevents the removal and destruction of timber along the routes and ensures that the risks of accidental forest fires are minimal. Huge forest fires have ravaged the heath/moorland slopes of the mountain above Horombo Hut in the past; the charred remains of these events are still evident beneath the regenerating vegetation. If you are cold in the evenings, resist the urge to light a fire and simply put on another layer of clothing.

Stay on the trail

In order to minimise the destruction of the flora and reduce the erosion of the mountain, you should stick to the clearly visible paths. Do not take short cuts across the slopes. Be especially careful in areas where the ground is boggy. These ecosystems are very fragile and can suffer irreparable damage if you trample over them. When descending from the crater rim, try to follow the switchbacks. It is very tempting to simply run down the scree in a straight line, but this dislodges enormous amounts of soil and gravel, shunting it off the slopes and hastening their deterioration.

Flora and fauna

It is illegal to remove any plants or animals from the mountain. Many of the flora species found on Kilimanjaro are unique or vulnerable. Do not pick any

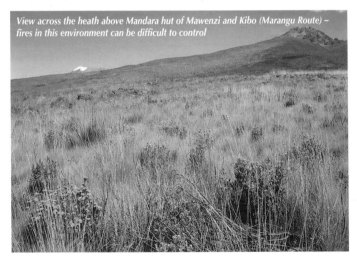

View across the heath above Mandara hut of Mawenzi and Kibo (Marangu Route) – fires in this environment can be difficult to control

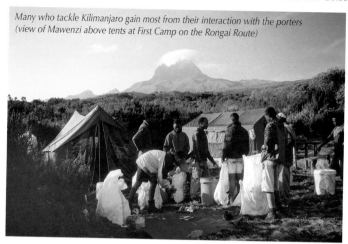
Many who tackle Kilimanjaro gain most from their interaction with the porters (view of Mawenzi above tents at First Camp on the Rongai Route)

of the flowers that you find on the mountain and do not disturb any wildlife that you come across. Everything should be left on the mountain for others to enjoy. Illegal hunting does occur in the forest zone. Poachers set snares and traps for duikers, hyraxes and monkeys. If you see any suspicious activity or find any evidence of poaching, report it to the park warden.

Cultural interaction

A lot of people who climb Kilimanjaro discover that the interaction that they enjoy with their guide and porters is one of the highlights of their trip. By rising above cultural prejudices and engaging with your hosts and companions on the mountain, you will become more sensitive to their ways of living and beliefs. To not do so will reduce the value of your trip and contribute to the cultural erosion of the country. Be patient, friendly and open when meeting people and the courtesy will usually be returned. Try to learn a few words of Swahili; the endeavour will be appreciated by the porters and guides, if only because your attempts to pronounce their language are so risible. If you hang on to your sense of humour and maintain a sense of perspective then your time on the mountain will be enriched. With a bit of effort you will cease to be the 'Mzungu Kichaa', or 'crazy European', and become a friend instead.

USING THIS GUIDE

The purpose of this guide is to add something to the experience of climbing this remarkable mountain by helping you to prepare for and then undertake the trek. By forewarning you of the nature of the climb and the potential seriousness of some of the routes, it is hoped

63

that you will be properly prepared for the challenge.

The first three parts contextualise Kilimanjaro and the experience of climbing this mountain. By now you will have been through **Part 1**. The aim of this section is to help you to prepare for your ascent by outlining the routes and the dangers; it suggests ways of making the most of your visit to the region, and highlights the need to appreciate both the porters and guides you will be walking with and the environment you will be walking through. **Part 2** tells the story of Kilimanjaro, providing an insight to the people of the region, the name of the mountain and its place in the exploration of the 'dark continent'. The mountain's natural environment is then discussed in **Part 3**. The history of the volcanoes and the glaciers, and information on the mountain's weather and animal and plant life aim to give you an idea of what you might see and experience on your trek.

Part 4 includes descriptions of all the ascent routes, circuit paths, summit ascent routes and then the descent routes. Though a detailed route guide to climbing Kilimanjaro is hardly necessary – the majority of the routes up the mountain are so well travelled that it's almost impossible to become lost – it is useful to know the nature of the paths, the distance you will be walking and the time it will take you to complete the different stages; and these details are included here in the route descriptions. In the following pages, all of the main routes up and down the mountain are described on a day-by-day basis, and are accompanied by a series of sketch maps showing the route and key features of the landscape.

The introduction to each route includes a box summarising the route. The ascent route summaries show the minimum total number of days you will spend on the mountain (ie. cumulative time spent on the ascent, summit ascent and the descent routes) if you choose to take that particular ascent route; the time spent on the summit ascent and the descent routes is included here. The time shown in the summit ascent and descent route summaries reflects only the time spent on that route.

An indication of how long each daily section takes is found in the summary of the daily schedule. The times quoted are average walking times only and will not correspond to everyone's experiences, but are intended as a rough guide. These approximations refer to the actual time spent walking and do not take into account breaks, photographic opportunities or any other delays.

The altitudes noted are taken from as reliable a set of sources as possible. There are wildly differing estimates of the height of each feature, and even of the summit, and the altitudes quoted here may not be in accordance with each map or every guide. The distances mentioned are also at best estimates that will provide as accurate an impression of the ascent of the mountain as possible.

Path through the forest zone on the
Machame Route – route finding is not a problem!

65

PART 2
THE STORY OF KILIMANJARO
People of the Region

Modern day man and his ancestors have probably been living in the shadow of Kilimanjaro for many thousands of years. Although little of actual antiquity has been found on the mountain itself, there is substantial evidence of ancient human occupation at nearby sites and throughout the Rift Valley.

Once Kilimanjaro's slopes had become safe to inhabit, they would have supported early hunter-gatherer tribes. The extensive network of springs and streams in conjunction with the temperate climate and bountiful supplies of food and wood, would have made this a highly desirable location for early man.

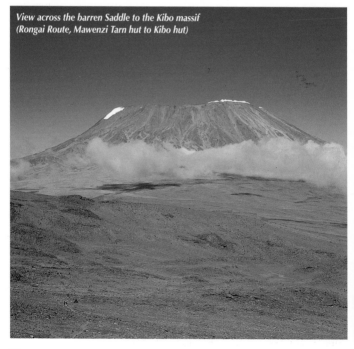

*View across the barren Saddle to the Kibo massif
(Rongai Route, Mawenzi Tarn hut to Kibo hut)*

As waves of people migrated through Africa, Cushites from the southern highlands of Ethiopia spread across north-east Africa. Some of this wave of humanity turned south and settled the plains and highlands of Tanzania. These agriculturalists may have been responsible for some of the early irrigation channels found on Kilimanjaro.

Within the last few thousand years, Bantu people from West Africa and Nilotic people from the Nile Basin have migrated to this region. They are represented around Kilimanjaro today by the Chagga and Maasai respectively.

The Chagga

The Chagga live around the southern slopes of Kilimanjaro, right up to the national park boundary and currently constitute the third largest tribal group in Tanzania. The last census, in 1988, estimated that they numbered over 800,000 people. They are also known as the Chaga or Shaka, and sometimes the tribe is referred to as the Wachagga (the prefix 'wa' meaning 'the people of '). They are descended from a variety of groups who migrated to the foothills of Kilimanjaro and took possession of the fertile mountain slopes **several hundred years ago**. The tribe was composed of around 400 main clans, most of which were descended from the Kamba, a Bantu-speaking people. They have since intermingled with the Taita, Maasai and other peoples.

The new homeland, Chaggaland, was divided into a number of politically independent chiefdoms, defined by natural barriers. Each chiefdom vied for supremacy over each other and gradually over the whole tribe. The tribe was almost united by the great chief Horombo in **the mid-18th century**. Nicknamed 'Kilimia', meaning 'the Conqueror', Horombo inspired respect and command throughout the Kilimanjaro region and was close to becoming the paramount chief of the Chagga. He would probably have succeeded had he not been slain by Maasai warriors. The policy of unification died with him and the tribe returned to fighting amongst itself.

The internal rivalry between chiefs vying to be the most powerful reached its peak in **the late 19th century**. The dominant chiefs of Moshi and of Marangu, called Rindi (or more usually, Mandara) and Sina respectively, were at this stage at the height of their powers. Kathleen Stahl, an authority on the Chagga, has credited both leaders, describing Mandara as 'The most illustrious ruler of Moshi, and the ablest diplomatist on Kilimanjaro', and Sina as, 'the greatest warrior chief that Kilimanjaro has ever known.'

Realising the potential benefits to be gleaned from the influx of colonials, the chiefs played each other off against these new arrivals. The German colonials took advantage of this and exploited the Chagga. They encouraged the spats and directed the tribe to attack those the Germans deemed unfriendly. Whilst Sina ruled by virtue of his powerful and ferocious army, Mandara proved to be the more astute and made a number of treaties with the wealthy foreigners. The result was that Moshi became an important staging post for the slave and ivory trade and consequently prospered. In 1885, Mandara held negotiations with the German colonists and agreed to allow them to use Moshi as their central base in this part of East Africa.

A number of years later, an overall chief of the Chagga did emerge, although it had little to do with the internal unification of the tribe and was in fact the work of the then colonial administration. Marealle, from Marangu, was nominated the paramount chief in 1893. Marealle's grandson, Thomas Marealle, is still the foremost chief of the Chagga, although the position has lost much of its official power.

Today, the Chagga have a reputation as being amongst the most organised and successful tribes in East Africa. The fertile nature of their land and the high-altitude climate of the region has contributed to their continued success. The creation of ingenious water irrigation channels with little more than wooden hoes is a marvel of primitive engineering. In addition to the advantageous location of their lands, they were also one of the first groups to have sustained contact with the European missionaries, in particular those from the Roman Catholic and Lutheran Churches. The initial provision of education in the region led to them being more advanced than many of the other tribes at that time.

As the population of the tribe has increased, so the Chagga have developed new intensive farming methods to sustain their numbers. This has resulted in the use of agricultural irrigation, fertilisers and crop rotation in the Kilimanjaro region, ensuring that the lower slopes can be cultivated all year round. The Chagga, who have proved to be **diligent, industrious farmers**, have realised the benefits of producing cash crops such as coffee and bananas, and now grow these alongside more traditional staple foods. They also brew beer from bananas and a small seed known as eleusine. The Kilimanjaro region is so clement and fertile that with sufficient water almost anything can be produced there. However the rains are erratic and the threat of drought is very real.

The Chagga are also fairly open-minded towards new ideas and developments. Consequently they consistently **participate in community activities** and are involved in the **cooperative production and marketing of coffee**. They are now responsible for producing the largest amount of arabica coffee in the Kilimanjaro region, selling the product worldwide. Their relatively high level of education and the ability to take advantage of cash crops has meant that the Chagga enjoy a comparatively high level of income.

Located at the foot of Kilimanjaro, they are also **ideally placed to take advantage of the boom in tourism** that the region has enjoyed. They have had sustained contact with visitors to the region over the centuries, beginning with the European missionaries, colonisers, mountaineers, geographers, botanists and, now, with the streams of trekkers from around the world. The majority of **guides and porters that accompany trekkers are Chagga**.

Despite having lived at the foot of Kilimanjaro for centuries, the Chagga formerly had no cause to climb the mountain, believing that it was full of evil spirits and djinns. Although there is evidence to suggest that the Chagga may have ventured as far as the snowline, it is thought that they considered the mountain too high to climb to the top. Charles Dundas wrote in his book, *Kilimanjaro and its People*, that, 'It is inconceivable that natives can ever have ascended to the crater rim, for apart from cold, altitude and superstitious fears, it is sheer impossibility that they could have negotiated the ice. Nor is there any tradition amongst the natives that anyone went up as high.'

Kilimanjaro Lager label – the most is being made of the tourist trade

Nonetheless, the tribe have always venerated Kilimanjaro. It gives them a very visible focal point and inspires a sense of identity and unity. It is also a provider of water and rainfall. Such is their reverence for the mountain that traditionally their dead are buried facing Kibo.

The Chagga traditionally worship a god known as Ruwa, who lives in the sky. He is the most important and powerful of all their deities and, although not responsible for earth's creation, did set man free and provided him with plants and fruit. The Chagga consider that all men are descended from him and that he is a great protector of men. Animal sacrifices used to be made to Ruwa in times of drought, famine or if the tribe was affected by an epidemic.

Sacrifices would also be made to the spirits of the dead, whom the Chagga hold in high regard. They maintain that when a person dies they move across to live in a different world in a different form. They also consider that the spirits of the dead are able to return to earth in order to demand from their relatives what is rightly theirs. These spirits only appear in dreams or visions but can communicate using animal noises.

However, there are also a number of modern Chagga who have **converted to Christianity** and are receptive to the various teachings of the different denominations of missionaries in the region.

Today, land shortages have altered their economic structure slightly and many Chagga are now wage earners in large cities. They are also prominent in politics and hold a number of important positions. As such, **they are important contributors to the country's economy and direction**. However, the success of the Chagga is not universally applauded and in some cases it is actively resented. Some Chagga businessmen and entrepreneurs find themselves affected by adverse discrimination and are the victims of anti-Chagga sentiments born of jealousy. It is worth noting that as a result of their increased involvement with the modern world, most of the Chagga's traditional practices have died out.

The Maasai

The Maasai are one of the best-known tribes in Africa. They have long been portrayed as the original 'noble savages', and initial reports from the missionaries and early explorers in the region confirmed this reputation. Ludwig Krapf recorded that throughout the mid-19th century the Maasai were engaged in a, 'useless and savage civil war', whilst Charles New described them as, 'congenital killers of the Dark Interior.' In reality, they are proud semi-nomadic pastoralists, whose wealth and well-being is largely dependent on their herds of cattle.

The myth of the origin of the Maasai is described in Joseph Thomson's account of his travels, *Through Masai Land*. He recorded that, 'The primal ancestor of the Masai was one Kidenoi, who lived at Donyo Egere [Mount Kenya], was hairy, and had a tail. Filled with the spirit of exploration, he left his home and wandered south. The people of the country, seeing him shaking something in a calabash, were so struck with admiration at the wonderful performance that they brought him women as a present. By these he had children who, strangely enough, were not hairy, and had no tails, and these were the progenitors of the Masai.' The more mundane reality is that the Maasai are descended from Nilotic pastoralists who migrated in to Tanzania from further north, following the course of the Nile from southern Sudan. The modern Maasai retain their original language, Maa.

Groups of Maasai migrated to East Africa in the 14th century and had drifted into Tanzania by the 17th century. The Maasai quickly earnt themselves a fearsome reputation as courageous and bold warriors. Ludwig Krapf noted that, 'When cattle fail them they make raids on the tribes which they know to be in possession of herds. They say that Engai [god] gave them all that exists in the way of cattle and that no other nation ought to possess any … They are dreaded as warriors, laying all waste with fire and sword, so that the weaker tribes do not venture to resist them in the open field, but leave them in possession of their herds, and seek only to save themselves by the quickest possible flight.'

During the 19th century, the Maasai overran huge tracts of savannah, including the area around Kilimanjaro, which they knew as Ol Doinyo Ebor, 'the white mountain'. Today, there are 12 distinct groups of Maasai, the largest of which lives in Tanzania. This biggest group is known as Otunlanyana loo Ngishu, which literally translates as 'people of the cattle'. Members of this group believe that all of the cows in the world have been given to them, as a right, by god.

The Maasai adhere to a **strict social structure**. Their society is heavily regulated and maintained by the highest ranking member of the tribe, the Olaibou – unlike many tribes, the Maasai do not have a paramount chief. The Olaibou is an important tribal figure and these men, since Maasai society is very much male orientated, are accorded a great deal of respect. He has the greatest wisdom and the most knowledge regarding the use of plant remedies (used as medicines). He also mediates between the people of his tribe and their ancestral spirits.

There are strict **rites of passage** to be endured by members of the tribe. They have to pass through several age divisions, each lasting seven years (apart from the Sokolyo which lasts three months): the Engayok are young children who are too young to leave their home; the Layooni are uncircumcised boys, who are taught to herd the cattle; newly circumcised boys awaiting the ceremony that formally makes them a Maasai Moran warrior are the Sokoliyo. These youths spend up to three months as Sokoliyo, during which time they must dress in black and paint their faces with white chalk and soot. They are also required to hunt and kill birds on the savannah in order to make their own headdress. Once they become Moran, they must spend seven more years protecting the community. After this they can marry (frequently more than one woman) and become Orpaiyan, after which they may have children. Finally, they become an Ilmoruak, an elder responsible for making the important decisions that affect the group's future.

A set of **traditional beliefs** based on the teachings of the god, Engai, and his messiah, Kindong'oi (from whom Maasai priests are believed to descend), govern the daily lives of the Maasai. All forms of worship are conducted either beneath fig trees, which are considered holy, or at Ol Doinyo Lengai, the 'mountain of god'. The Maasai do not believe in any form of afterlife.

The strict tribal regulations and the emphasis on a traditional way of life have made the transition to modern living particularly tough for the Maasai. Although they still attempt to maintain a pastoral, nomadic existence, they are faced by an increase in population numbers and the enforcement of tight boundaries. As a consequence, some Maasai have switched to cultivation rather than animal husbandry. Regardless, the rural Maasai continue to exist on a traditional diet of milk, meat and occasionally cow's blood. They are easily recognised by their proud, upright stance, large hooped earlobes and their red, frequently checked cloth robes, known as a shuka.

Many of the Maasai are highly educated and have very strong leadership abilities. They are respected and frequently secure important positions in the country's government.

Origin of the Mountain's Name

Kilimanjaro. Few names have such a powerful resonance. It echoes like a spell, evoking awesome images on a par with Xanadu, Timbuktu or Machu Picchu. It signifies

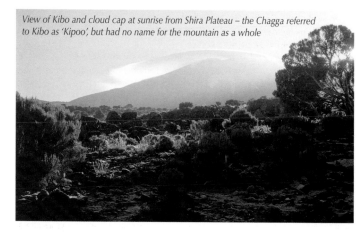

View of Kibo and cloud cap at sunrise from Shira Plateau – the Chagga referred to Kibo as 'Kipoo', but had no name for the mountain as a whole

somewhere special. Yet there is no consensus as to what it means or even as to how the mountain came to be known as this.

The origin of the name remains uncertain, but it probably evolved during the explorations of the 19th century. The missionary Johannes Rebmann reported that in the 1840s the Chagga referred to the two summits separately, calling them Kibo (or Kipoo) and Kimawenzi. Interestingly, they didn't have a name for the massif as a whole.

The coastal traders and local tribes had several versions of the name for Kilimanjaro, calling it **Kilima Njaro** or **Kilimanscharo**. In 1848 Rebmann surmised that the most probable definition of this name was, 'mountain of greatness'. He then undermined his theory by considering an alternative interpretation of the name, suggesting that if 'njaro' was a corruption of the Chagga word 'jaro', the name would translate as 'mountain of caravans', which he took to be a veiled reference to the traders and trade routes that used Kilimanjaro as a landmark. However, there is no philological explanation for either of these theories. It is also highly unlikely that the name is a composite of two languages. Consequently these theories have largely been disregarded. WD Cooley went so far as to rubbish the notions, describing them as, 'mere nonsense'.

However, **Swahili, the majority language in Tanzania, offers the the most likely derivation of the name**. The name 'Kilimanjaro' comprises two root words, '**kilima**', which is a corruption of the Swahili word '**mlima**' (meaning 'mountain'), and '**njaro**', which is the Swahili name for a type of devil that was reputed to be responsible for creating coldness. This particular rendition of the name seems most likely and appropriate, and also ties in with Chagga folklore, which is full of accounts of such devils.

The prefix '**ki**' in Swahili is often applied to make the noun diminutive or to reduce it in size. Thus the great mountain becomes a hill. The suggestion is that this is a term of affection for Kilimanjaro, or an ironic reference to its vast size.

In Swahili there is also a word, '**njara**', that means shining. This potential interpretation of the name seems an equally valid and apt reference to the mountain.

Other versions of the name have also been suggested. The Maasai word, 'njare', meaning 'font of water' has been proposed in association with the Swahili word 'kilima'. This version is unlikely though, since it involves the hybridization of two languages. Furthermore, the Maasai have their own name for Kilimanjaro, calling it Ol Donyo Ebor, which translates as 'the white mountain'.

There are also a handful of local variations of the name, which have most likely come about as a consequence of it being called Kilimanjaro, rather than as forerunners of the current name. Thus, you may hear the mountain referred to as Kilimoroyoo, or Kilemakyaro, which when translated literally means 'something that is impossible to climb'.

Exploration

Mount Kilimanjaro erupted from the savannah approximately **1 million years ago** as the result of a series of cataclysmic earth movements associated with the formation of the Rift Valley. This is recent, geologically speaking, and means that the volcano is one of the youngest in Africa. Formed within the time span that hominids have been on the earth, Kilimanjaro is likely to have been seen by at least four different Homo species, including Homo erectus and Homo ergaster, the forerunners of the Neandertals. However, little of great anthropological or archaeological antiquity has been found on the mountain itself. Primitive stone bowls fashioned from lava have been discovered on the lower western slopes of the mountain, leading archaeologists to conclude that hunter-gatherer tribes based themselves here from **1000BC** onwards, in order to take advantage of the good water, wood and food supplies found on the slopes. There is little evidence available though to conclusively prove what sort of life these tribes may have enjoyed.

It is unclear exactly when people outside of the Kilimanjaro region became aware of the giant peak. There are several allusions to such a mountain, but no specific references to Kilimanjaro. In the **5th century** BC scholars believed that the Nile sprang from snow clad mountains in equatorial Africa. This misfounded belief can be traced back to the writings of Aeschylus, who believed that Egypt was 'nourished by melting snows'. The Greek historian Herodotus propagated this myth by wrongly depicting the sources of the Nile as three great fountains astride the equator amidst what he called the 'Mountains of the Moon'. In the **4th century** BC, the Greek philosopher Aristotle referred to 'the so-called silver mountain' southwest of the Nile. The legend of a summit strewn with silver persisted amongst Swahili coastal people until the middle of the 19th century.

By the onset of the **1st century** AD, merchants from the Mediterranean were trading actively along the East African coastline. A Greek merchant, Diogenes, is alleged to have ventured inland from 'Rhapta' for 25 days and reached two great lakes and a snowy range of mountains, 'whence the Nile draws its twin sources'. (Rhapta's exact location is unknown, but it is probably modern day Pangani.) In AD 45 a book entitled *The Periplus of the Erythraeu Sea* was published, which described the town of Rhapta as 'the very last market town of the continent of Azania'. However, though there is no mention of Kilimanjaro in this particular text, in view of the distance travelled by Diogenes, it is possible that the 'snowy range of mountains' he described may be Kilimanjaro.

The Alexandrian astronomer and geographer Ptolemy incorporated the 'Montes Lunae' into his great *Geography*, which became the standard geographical textbook until the discoveries of the 15th century. Though the information Ptolemy recorded was most likely gleaned from hearsay, it is possible that this is the first written description of the mountain.

Potential references to Kilimanjaro continue to appear in Chinese and Arab texts during the **12th and 13th centuries**. Traders passing through the region probably used the mountain as a landmark since it is such a dominant feature in an otherwise unremarkable landscape. In addition to being an invaluable navigational tool, the mountain would also have been an excellent source of water and firewood for caravan troops.

During the **16th century**, the world's interest in the region shifted focus, as colonial interests replaced commercial ones. In 1507 the Spanish scholar and astronomer Fernandez de Encisco visited Mombasa and gained information from traders relating to the interior of the country. He reported that west of Mombasa lay 'the Ethiopian Olympus, which is very high, and further off are the mountains of the moon, in which are the sources of the Nile', echoing the theory circulated by Ptolemy almost 1400 years earlier. The 'Ethiopian Olympus' is thought to be Kilimanjaro and the 'mountains of the moon' the Ruwenzoris. In 1519 *Suma de Geographia*, a book based on Fernandez de Encisco's trip reports, was published in Seville and subsequently the 'Ethiopian Olympus' began to appear on maps of the region. By the 19th century, Arab slave traders regularly referred to a high snow mountain in Chagga country that had heavily populated, fertile slopes.

The 19th-century European fascination with the mountain

The British Royal Geographical Society, founded in 1830 with the intention of promoting geographical research, centred its interest in Africa on trying to pinpoint the source of the Nile; it seemed unthinkable to the Victorians that the Nile could rise from snow-capped peaks astride the equator. Remarkably, the society was uninterested in confirming the actual existence of Kilimanjaro or indeed the existence of snow on the equator, which it resolutely refused to acknowledge.

Interest in the region did increase, however, when in **1834** the then ruler of East Africa sent his envoy, Khamis bin Uthman, to Europe. He met a number of dignitaries and academics, including the English armchair geographer **William Desborough Cooley**, who later wrote that, 'The most famous mountain of East Africa is Kirimanjara, which we suppose, from a number of circumstances to be the highest ridge crossed on the road to Monomoezi'. Although the world was aware of other snow-capped mountains near the equator, Cooley was convinced that 'Kirimanjara' was only a fifth of the height required to sustain perennial snow in Africa. Bin Uthman's visit led to a flurry of academic interest in East Africa and inspired further exploration.

At this time missionaries were also focussing their attention on East Africa. In **1846** the Swiss-German missionary **Johannes Rebmann** joined the Protestant mission in Mombasa, originally founded by Ludwig Krapf. Krapf had arrived in Africa nurturing an ambition to create a chain of mission stations across the continent, which would spread the gospel and combat the perfidious slave trade. Rebmann enthusiastically embarked on a series of reconnaissance trips, journeying first to Kasigau to establish the first link in the chain, before relocating to the Jagga (now Chagga) region.

From the outset, Rebmann was captivated by the myth of Kilimanjaro. He had heard rumours that Jagga suffered from extreme cold; Rebmann's caravan leader, Bwana Kheri, confirmed this and described a giant mountain, which he called 'Kilimanshario', which was allegedly crowned with a strange white substance that glittered like silver. The locals simply called this substance 'cold'. Bwana Kheri reported that the local people believed the mountain was protected by djinns and evil spirits, who were capable of killing a man.

On the **11th May 1848** Rebmann had his first tantalising glimpse of Kilimanjaro from a distance of about 40km. Two days later he saw the mountain again. Captivated by the apparition, he made a second expedition to the region in **November 1848**. On this trip he reached Machame village and was able to obtain fine views of the mountain that enabled him to describe the two main peaks and the saddle-shaped depression that separated them. 'There are two principal summits placed upon a basis some ten leagues long and as many broad, so that the space between them forms as it were a saddle ... The eastern summit is lower, and pointed, whilst the western and higher one presents a fine crown, which, even in the hot season, when its eastern and lowlier neighbour can no longer support its snowy roof, remains covered by a mass of snow', he wrote in a report for the **April 1849** edition of the *Church Missionary Intelligencer* (a monthly periodical that was set up to raise funds for overseas endeavours). Rebmann became the first European in modern times to report a snow-capped mountain close to the equator when he wrote, 'At about ten o'clock I observed something remarkably white on the top of a high mountain, and first supposed that it was a very white cloud, in which supposition my guide also confirmed me, but having gone a few paces more I could no more rest satisfied with that explanation and while I was asking my guide a second time whether that white thing was indeed a cloud, and scarcely listening to his answer that yonder was a cloud but what that white was he did not know but supposed it was coldness – the most delightful recognition took place in my mind, of an old well-known European guest called snow.' Elated by this enlightenment, Rebmann was able to explain a number of the legends and stories that he had heard. 'All the strange stories we had so often heard about the gold and

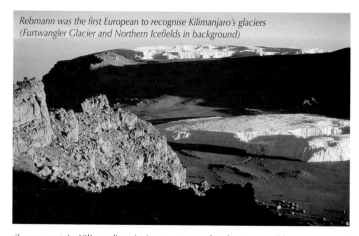

*Rebmann was the first European to recognise Kilimanjaro's glaciers
(Furtwangler Glacier and Northern Icefields in background)*

silver mountain Kilimandjaro in Jagga, supposed to be inaccessible on account of evil spirits, which had killed a great many of those who had attempted to ascend it, were now at once rendered intelligible to me, as of course the extreme cold to which poor natives are perfect strangers, would soon chill and kill the half-naked visitors', he wrote. Initially he believed that the members of his party had no word for snow, but subsequently learnt that the locals called the mountain Kibo, which also meant 'snow'. It transpired that it was only the coastal people who couldn't comprehend the concept of snow. Rebmann recorded a story told to him by Bwana Kheri concerning Kilimanjaro and the 'Madjame' tribe. The powerful king of Madjame, Rungua, was so intrigued by the substance that capped Kilimanjaro, that he sent a selection of his retinue to determine the exact nature of this unusual matter. Only one of this group, a man named Sabaya whom Bwana Kheri claimed to have spoken to, was to return from the mountain, his hands and feet hideously crippled. Rebmann reported the story in his piece for the *Church Missionary Intelligencer* in **1849** and surmised that the man had suffered severe frostbite and that his group had either frozen to death or fled and died on the mountain.

Scepticism over snow-clad peaks

The article in the *Church Missionary Intelligencer* caused a great deal of consternation in the western world. Geographers universally scoffed at the reports of a snow-capped peak. William Desborough Cooley was especially outspoken in his denial of the existence of such a mountain. Cooley was devising a map of Africa from the comfort of his study in England, based on his interpretations of classical and Arab reports. Although he had never been to East Africa, Cooley had written major essays on the region's geography in 1835 and 1845. His reputation as an Africa expert lent extra weight to his denunciation of the existence of snow on the equator. 'I deny altogether the existence of snow on Mount Kilimanjaro. It rests entirely on the testimony of Mr Rebmann ... and he ascertained it not with his eyes but by inference and in the visions of his imagination', Cooley wrote in the May 1849 edition of *Athanaeum*.

Cooley wasn't alone in ridiculing Rebmann's findings. Rebmann was no scientist and had no real geographical aptitude. His reports were vague and the references to latitude, longitude, altitude, direction and distances in them were incomplete. His extravagant writing style and lack of reliable observations caused people to doubt the validity of his writings.

In order to press inland and establish the third link of the proposed chain of mission stations, Rebmann returned to the region in **April 1849**, ahead of the publication of his article. Consequently he was unaware of the widespread scepticism that greeted his announcements. Though this expedition was much more organised than his previous efforts, Rebmann did away with Bwana Kheris' services and guidance. As he approached Machame village once more he declared that he seemed 'so close to the snow line that, supposing no impassable abyss to intervene, I could have reached it in three to four hours', this was a wildly optimistic and inaccurate assessment (being at least three or four days away from the snowline). Rebmann's expedition fell foul of the powerful local king in Machame, Mamkinga. Mamkinga extorted all of his possessions and eventually Rebmann fled from the greedy tyrant, a dispirited, humiliated, sick man. Thoroughly broken, he abandoned the project and refrained from further exploration.

Rebmann's missionary co-worker, **Ludwig Krapf**, continued to practise in the region, though. Krapf visited the Wakamba district to the north of Kilimanjaro in **November 1849**, and sighted the mountain twice, first on the 10th of November and again on the 16th. Krapf reported these sightings, only to be faced with the same scepticism that Rebmann's earlier descriptions had met. Cooley insisted that he had been hallucinating. However, it was harder for people to dismiss two independent European sightings of the snow-capped mountain. Doubts began to surface as to the accuracy of Cooley's rebuttals. In **1852** Cooley published his thoughts in the book *Inner Africa Laid Open*, reiterating his belief that Rebmann's sightings were, 'a most delightful mental recognition only, not supported by the evidence of his senses'. Cooley gained support from a number of powerful public figures including the president of the Royal Geographical Society, Sir Roderick Murchison, and esteemed explorer, Richard Burton, who declared that Rebmann's stories reminded him of 'a de Lunatico'. Burton, who was to cross Tanzania with John Hanning Speke in 1857, was cruelly dismissive of Rebmann, noting that although he was, 'an honest and conscientious man, he had yet all the qualities which secure unsuccess.' David Livingstone further undermined the reports by describing mountains topped by 'glittering whiteness' in the Zambezi valley as actually being topped by 'masses of white rock, somewhat like quartz', insinuating that this was the case in Jagga.

The first serious attempt to climb the mountain was made in **August 1861** by the Hanoverian naturalist and traveller **Baron Carl Claus von der Decken**. Supported by a team of fifty porters, von der Decken claimed to have reached 13,900ft only to be forced back by atrocious weather. He described the mountain rising from the savannah and the shapes of the two summits, portraying Kibo as a 'mighty dome, rising to a height of about 20,000ft of which the last 3000ft are covered in snow'. Both of these figures were exaggerated and it is likely that the group actually only reached 8200ft. However, his companion, the English surveyor and explorer Richard Thornton, correctly deduced that the mountain was in fact a volcano. His scientific background lent credence to his reports and carried extra weight in Britain. In **December 1862**, von der Decken returned to the mountain with Dr Otto Kersten and climbed as high as 14,000ft before becoming caught in a snowstorm. Von der Decken reported that, 'During the night it snowed heavily and next morning the ground lay white all around us'. He finished his report by boldly declaring, 'Surely the obstinate Cooley will be satisfied now.' Cooley responded by calling this latest report a 'traveller's tale' and poured scorn on its contents and 'so opportune a fall of snow', announcing that the whole thing had been cooked up to support Rebmann and Krapf.

Nonetheless, Cooley began to lose support. The Royal Geographical Society withdrew its backing for him and formally announced that it now recognised that Rebmann, who first declared that there was snow on the equator 14 years earlier, may have been correct. In 1863 the society awarded its Gold Medal to von der Decken for his contributions to the sum of the world's geographical knowledge of Africa. There were however no retrospective awards for Rebmann or Krapf. Despite all of the evidence to the contrary, Cooley maintained his disbelief to the day he died.

Reduced interest in the mountain

Once geographers had solved the mystery of where the source of the Nile lay, they lost interest in the topography of East Africa and exploration abated. Von der Decken was the only European to travel to Kilimanjaro in the 1860s, and during the 1870s only the English missionary Charles New explored the region. In **1871** New climbed Kilimanjaro from the south-east, at a point where the snowline dipped almost to the foot of Kibo. He recorded seeing 'mountains upon mountains of dark forest; loftier still, height upon heights of grassy hills' and ultimately 'barren, rocky steeps' beneath permanent snowfields, and became the first European to actually cross the snowline in equatorial Africa. New published his book, *Life, Wanderings and Labours in Eastern Africa*, in 1873, writing that, 'Of Kilimanjaro we have little more to say: its leading characteristics have been pointed out, and its 'eternal snows' must be regarded now as 'eternal verities''. In **1874** New returned to the village of Moshi with the intention of continuing his exploration. Unfortunately, he fell foul of the fearsome Chagga chieftain, Mandara, who claimed to have met every European explorer on Kilimanjaro and appropriated gifts from them in return for safe passage through his land; New was robbed of all of his possessions, including a gold watch that had been given to him by the Royal Geographical Society. Finding his path to the mountain blocked, New was forced to retreat from the region. Broken in health and spirit, he died on the return journey to Mombasa.

Arrival of the European colonialists

For several years explorers steered clear of the mountain and its hostile, greedy inhabitants. But in **1883** Dr Gustave Fischer passed to the south of Kilimanjaro on his way to Lake Naivasha and observed that the region seemed, 'well adapted to European settlement'. This statement heightened interest in the area as a possible colonial possession. Later the same year, the Scottish geologist Joseph Thomson journeyed to the north of Kilimanjaro, through Masai Land. He was awestruck by the mountain and rhapsodised, 'There is the grand dome or crater of Kibo, with its snow cap glancing and scintillating like burnished silver ... on its eastern flank, rise the jagged outlines of the craggy peak of Kimawenzi. What words can adequately describe this glimpse of majestic grandeur and godlike repose?' Thomson crossed the lower slopes of the mountain and was in turn robbed by Mandara. Undeterred, he went on to climb 9000ft in order to collect flora specimens. Having allowed only a day for the summit attempt, it is not surprising that he barely made it above the tree line. He was, however, the first European to see the northern slopes up close, and virtually completed a circuit of the mountain as part of his travels.

A year later, in **1884**, **Harry Johnston** fronted an expedition funded by a number of eminent British scientific societies, including the Royal Geographic Society. His mission was to collect flora and fauna specimens on Kilimanjaro for the herbarium at Kew Gardens. Johnston spent five months on the mountain, working out of a number of self-supporting base camps and gathered 600 species of new and rare plants, as well as six new species of bird, a new species of colobus monkey and various new butterfly and beetle specimens. He was responsible for collecting and naming the first specimen of the endemic *Impatiens kilimanjari* and described the unusual heath and moorlands,

*Porters today ascending through cloud to the Saddle,
the point at which Johnston had to descend*

detailing the strange *senecios* and *lobelia* found there. Johnston made an attempt to climb Kibo, but abandoned the ascent on the Saddle, as the summit was blanketed by cloud, which he likened to, 'a kind of London fog, very depressing in character'.

Johnston was able to reassure other travellers that the region was safe and exhorted the British government to colonise the country. 'I am on the spot, the first in the field, and able to make Kilima-njaro as completely English as Ceylon', Johnston wrote in his report 'The Kilima-njaro Expedition'. In his memoirs, Johnston claimed to be a secret agent, tasked with assessing colonial prospects in East Africa on behalf of the British government. There is however, no evidence to support this flight of fancy. Previously the British government had dragged its feet when considering its future role in East Africa. The Prime Minister William Gladstone was unable to imagine why anyone should be interested in that 'mountain country behind Zanzibar with the unrememberable name', and was astounded when his advisors suggested making Kilimanjaro a British protectorate.

Germany was also being urged to take control of the region by the fervent empire builder **Dr Karl Peters**, the founder of the GDK (Gessellschaft fur Deutsche Kolonisation). The Society for German Colonisation was a political party whose ultimate aim was to colonise East Africa on behalf of the German nation. Peters hoped that by acting independently of the German government, he would be able to establish German influence in the region and provoke the government into backing his policy of expansion. To this end, Peters travelled to East Africa to secure treaties with 12 local chiefs that granted Germany exclusive rights, at least on paper, to vast tracts of land in the Kilimanjaro region. He persuaded the local chiefs to reject the rule of the Sultan of Zanzibar, who was guided by the British, and throw in their lot with Germany. This direct action sparked a contest for land rights between the two great East African colonisers, Germany and Britain.

Britain's immediate response was to force twice as many chiefs, including some of the rogue leaders who had sided with Germany, to restate their allegiance to the Sultan of Zanzibar. By swearing this allegiance they indirectly aligned themselves with Britain. The situation in East Africa became increasingly unstable and war between the two countries appeared inevitable.

In order to prevent hostilities, the two countries agreed the **Berlin Treaty in November 1886**, which delineated their spheres of influence in the region. The result was the creation of German East Africa and a British administered East Africa Protectorate, with Kilimanjaro falling inside German East Africa. Stories abound as to why the border drawn up between the two new regions kinks to pass Kilimanjaro. The account of Queen Victoria gifting Kilimanjaro to her grandson Wilhelm II because he lacked a snow-capped mountain in his territory and Britain already boasted Mount Kenya in hers is appealing but fanciful. The border was kinked in order to ensure that Mombasa remained in Britain's East African territory, providing her with a port on the Indian Ocean; German East Africa had Dar es Salaam as its access port.

Karl Peters was given the task of administering German East Africa. The first period of German rule was considered to be very harsh: Peters has been described as 'short on ethics and long on cruelty', and even some of his contemporaries felt uneasy about the excesses of their leader. This draconian approach to governing the new territory led to the locals' burgeoning hatred of the colonists.

With the cessation of hostilities between Germany and Britain, English and American 'tourists' began to flock to the region to take advantage of the hunting opportunities. As a result of this explosion in interest, there was widespread and appalling slaughter of wildlife in the name of sport. The exploration of Kilimanjaro also resumed. The son of the king of Hungary, Crown Prince Rudolph, persuaded the Hungarian geographer, **Count Teleki**, and **Lt Von Hohnel** to lead an expedition to explore the Meru area in 1887. Teleki made a serious attempt on Kilimanjaro, following Johnston's route to the Saddle. He reached 15,800ft before exhaustion, bleeding lips and a 'rushing noise' in his head brought on by the altitude checked his progress. During the ascent, Von Hohnel made a series of astute observations and consequently, a new map of the mountain was drawn-up, which included the northern flank of Kilimanjaro.

The Race for the summit: Hans Meyer's expeditions

Motivated by Count Teleki's colourful tales, **Hans Meyer**, a geology professor from Leipzig, made the first of three visits to Kilimanjaro in **1887**. He made good progress on the mountain, following Teleki's advice and ascending from the village of Marangu. Abandoning the majority of his entourage, Meyer led a small group swiftly through the forest zone and onto the heath/moorland. It took the group five days to gain the Saddle, where they rested for a day before pushing on. As the weather worsened and snow began to fall, the group's morale deteriorated and their resolve weakened; Meyer pushed on alone until he came up against a solid wall of ice that marked the lower edge of the Kibo ice cap. Recognising that this obstacle could only be tackled with the proper equipment, and lacking crampons or an ice axe, Meyer retreated to rejoin the rest of his group. *The Alpine Journal* of November 1887 mistakenly wrote this trip up as a first ascent and Meyer was forced to correct them, pointing out that he was probably 1500ft shy of the summit, having only reached 17,800ft. He did manage to collect a large number of flora specimens, take a number of photographs and make a series of useful measurements. The failure to reach the peak merely fired his determination to conquer Kilimanjaro and he resolved to return.

Before Meyer could return to the mountain, **Dr Abbott**, an American naturalist who had spent a year and a half in the region making natural history notes, and the German **Otto Ehlers**, made an attempt to reach the summit in the autumn of **1888**. Dr Abbott abandoned the ascent at 17,000ft as a result of altitude sickness, but Ehlers persevered. He later claimed to have reached the 'north western side of the summit' at a height that 'could not have been less than 19,680ft'. Ehlers' claims are widely doubted, not least because he alleges he stood on a point considerably higher than Kilimanjaro's actual summit. Meyer and others disputed the claims at the time and Ehlers conceded that he might have been mistaken.

Later the same year, Meyer tried to return to Kilimanjaro with **Dr Oscar Bauman**. Unfortunately, their expedition became caught up in an organised insurrection against the German rulers of the region. Meyer and Bauman were taken prisoner by Chief Bushiri and ransomed. The chief was paid off and the pair released, although they forfeited all of their equipment and supplies. As a result they, unsurprisingly, called off the expedition. Bushiri was later executed by the Germans.

By early **1889**, Meyer calculated that 49 Europeans had battled their way to Kilimanjaro. He realised that if he wanted to be the first to summit the mountain, he couldn't afford to wait much longer before making a concerted effort on the peak. In the second half of the year he returned to the mountain with the celebrated Austrian climber **Ludwig Purtscheller**, for a third attempt. His climbing team included two local headmen, nine porters, a cook and a guide. Meyer stayed with Dr Abbott in Moshi. Having questioned him at length about the mountain, he recognised that the biggest problem in conquering the summit was the lack of food supplies at the top of the mountain, so established a series of camps along the route he proposed to follow. By stocking camps at 4260m (13,970ft) and 4580m (15,020ft), Meyer ensured that he didn't have to quit the mountain after every attempt on the summit.

Beginning from the Marangu Village on the **28th September 1889**, Meyer trekked through the forest zone for two days, climbing to the west of where modern day Mandara Hut is situated. He then contoured across the mountainside and camped in the vicinity of today's Rau Campsite. From here he climbed north onto the Saddle and stopped at a campsite previously established by Dr Abbott at 3894m (12,770ft). Meyer then launched himself directly at Kibo. From a base camp at the foot of the slope, Meyer and Purtscheller began to climb towards the Ratzel Glacier. Once they encountered the permanent ice, they began to carve out a series of steps, taking up to 20 strokes with an ice axe to chip out a small foothold in the ice cap. Reaching the crater rim on the 3rd October, Meyer realised that the pair were too exhausted and the weather too inclement to push on to the summit. The climbers retreated to the foot of Kibo and spent a day recuperating and taking essential readings and measurements before advancing to a higher bivouac site and making a final assault on the summit.

Beginning at 3am on the 6th October, Purtscheller's 40th birthday, the pair approached the summit. By dawn they had reached the foot of the glacier and located the steps in the ice that they had cut the previous day. They climbed the glacier and traversed a deep crevasse to crest the crater rim, becoming the first people to see into the crater, which Meyer declared, 'burst upon us with such unexpected suddenness that, for a moment, it quite took away our breath'. He went on to note that, '… the earth opened up there before us, revealing the secret of Kibo: Taking in the whole upper part of Kibo there opened up a great crater with precipitous sides …' The two climbers then trekked around the southern rim of the crater, climbing three hillocks that they encountered to **arrive at the highest point at 10.30am on the morning of the 6th October**. Meyer soberly recorded in his account *Across East African Glaciers* that, 'In virtue of my right as its first discoverer (I) christened this hitherto unknown and

HANS MEYER·1928
IM 70·LEBENSJAHR

ZUR ERINNERUNG AN HANS MEYER
DEN ER FORCHER UND ERSTERSTEIGER
DES KILIMANDSCHARO (ZUSAMMEN MIT
LUDWIG PURTSCHELLER 6·10·1889)
UND AN MAREALLE I VON MARANGU
SEINEN FREUND UND FÖRDERER
SEINER UNTERNCHMUNGEN.

KWA UKUMBUSHO WA BWANA HANS MEYER
NZUNGU WA KWANZA KUPANDA MLIMA
KILIMANJARO TAREHE 6·10·1889.

IN MEMORY OF HANS MEYER THE FIRST
WHITEMAN TO CLIMB MT KILIMANJARO
ON THE 6th OCTOBER, 1889.

Plaque at the Marangu Gate commemorating Hans Meyer's first successful ascent

unnamed mountain peak – the loftiest spot in Africa and in the German Empire – Kaiser Wilhelm Spitze. Then we gave three cheers more for the Emperor, and shook hands in mutual congratulation.' He then commented that 'Njaro, the guardian spirit of the

83

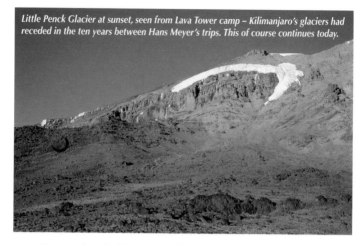

Little Penck Glacier at sunset, seen from Lava Tower camp – Kilimanjaro's glaciers had receded in the ten years between Hans Meyer's trips. This of course continues today.

mountain, seemed to take his conquest with a good grace, for neither snow nor tempest marred our triumphal invasion of his sanctuary.'

Meyer and Purtscheller then descended to the Saddle and attempted to climb Mawenzi. They reached the lower summit of Klute Peak but illness prevented them from attempting the highest point on Kilimanjaro's second peak. For good measure they returned to Kibo's crater rim on the 18th October via a similar route to that now ascended from Kibo Hut, and crested the rim at Hans Meyer Notch. Although they failed to reach the inner cone, they were able to confirm that it was made of mud and ash. In total, Meyer and Purtscheller spent an incredible 16 days above 15,000ft on Kilimanjaro and made four forays to the crater rim, reaching the summit on one of these occasions, in addition to making a number of sorties on Mawenzi.

Once the peak had been claimed, interest in Kilimanjaro waned and fewer expeditions were undertaken to explore the mountain. In fact, the summit was not revisited for 20 years. In **1898**, Hans Meyer returned to Kilimanjaro once more, to study the glaciers on the mountain. He was amazed and appalled to observe that the glaciers had retreated about 100m since 1889. The ice in the crater had all but disappeared and there were visible flows of meltwater at the snout of many of the glaciers. This process continues unabated today.

Advances of the early 20th century

At the onset of the 20th century, Kilimanjaro was declared a wildlife reservation by the German colonial government. The early years of the century were then dominated by private scientific explorations which, although undertaken in the name of science, frequently turned out to be nothing more than glorified hunting sprees. The specimen

These trips in the early 20th century were not without a human cost. The region's natives were still held in low regard and were considered expendable; on several expeditions inadequately equipped porters died as a result of exposure and hypothermia. In 1908 the Americans Peter MacQueen and Peter Dutkewich mounted an ascent that was beset with problems. Abandoned by their guides at the snowline, the pair began to retreat only for Dutkewich to fall and fracture several ribs. As the temperatures plummeted and the weather deteriorated, the porters attempted to assist the evacuation. Some reports suggest that whilst each of the Americans had four blankets, the porters were only given one each. Inevitably, three of the porters died from hypothermia on the descent. MacQueen wrote in his diaries, *In Wildest Africa*, 'Poor Mapandi, a carrier whom I had noticed shivering with fever for the last day or two stiffened, grew cold and died beside me in the mud.' Realising the hopelessness of the situation, he left his injured partner and went to fetch help alone. MacQueen reached a German mission station and raised the alarm. Dr Ahlboy and a colleague scrambled up the mountain and retrieved Dutkewich and the single porter that remained with him.

collecting phase reached its peak in **1908**, with many of the western world's premier scientific institutions sourcing specimens from the mountain.

The following year, in **1909**, the surveyor M Lange became the second person to make the summit. He went on to escape from Kilimanjaro without mishap.

Summiting Mawenzi

Kilimanjaro's second summit, Mawenzi, remained unclimbed for a further three years, until, in **1912**, the Germans **Edward Oehler** and **Fritz Klute** reached the highest point, which they christened Hans Meyer Peak, in tribute to their countryman. The pair then skirted Kibo and tackled the Drygalski Glacier. They reached the crater rim and descended via the Western Breach, becoming the first people to use this route.

As Kilimanjaro's reputation grew, and the number of people attempting to climb the now popularised Marangu Route increased, an enterprising German planter and hotelkeeper, **Dr E Forster**, set up two huts along the track on behalf of the German Kilimanjaro Mountain Club. The Bismarck Hut (now Mandara Hut) and the Peters Hut (now Horombo Hut) have been used ever since, although they have been modified and refurbished over the years.

In **December 1912** Dr Walter Furtwangler and Siegfried Konig became the fourth group to summit Kibo, and the first to descend the mountain on skis, using this unconventional mode of transport to drop off the mountain quickly. Kibo was conquered twice more before the onset of World War I, one of these ascents was the first full ascent by an Englishman, **W C West**. During the same era, the German Fran Von Ruckteschell became the first woman to reach the crater rim at Gillman's Point.

With the **outbreak of World War I in 1914**, climbing and exploration took a back seat. The Kilimanjaro region became the scene of sustained, ferocious fighting as German and Allied troops contested the border. Both sides relied heavily on recruiting local people to bolster their armies and these divisions inevitably bore the brunt of the fiercest fighting. African deaths as a result of the East African campaigns have been put as high as 100,000. The German army led by Paul von Lettow-Vorbeck adopted guerrilla-style tactics to tie down the numerically superior Allied army. Cut off behind enemy lines, one German patrol dug in on Kilimanjaro's slopes and held out for eight months, before eventually surrendering at Hans Meyer Cave.

Post-war Kilimanjaro

In **1920**, following the defeat of Germany in 1918, German East Africa became Tanganyika, a 'mandated territory' under the protection of Britain, and the region ostensibly reverted to British control. British rule was relatively benign in comparison to the regime that had existed before. Positive measures were enacted and the precious wooded lower slopes on and around Kilimanjaro were made into a forest and game reserve.

After some hesitation, climbers and explorers returned to the slopes, and in **1921 C Gillman** led a group to Kibo's crater rim, becoming the first climber to crest the crater since Kilimanjaro fell under British protection. Although Gillman didn't cover any fresh ground, he did provide much needed first-hand reports in English. Previously the only information had come from translations of material such as Meyer's reports. The first significant climb since the war occurred in **1924**, when the South African **George Londt** became the first man to summit Mawenzi's south peak, albeit by mistake since he was aiming for the highest point, Hans Meyer Peak, but became lost on the ascent.

Kilimanjaro's local climbers

At this stage it was still only the European climbers who received any recognition for their achievements on the mountain; but in **1925** East Africans were at last depicted as climbers on the mountain, when the Berlin film studio, UFA, made a film at high altitude. The resulting film showed local Chagga guides, including **Msameri** (who had accompanied Hans Meyer) and his

Plaque honouring the porters that accompanied Meyer on his first ascent

son **Oforo**, ascending the mountain. Oforo, who accompanied many of the European explorers at this time (including Londt, Reusch and West), was to later become the first Chagga known to reach the summit.

Leopard Point

A year later, in **1926**, another unusual sight was shown to the world. An English mountaineer, **Dr Donald Latham**, discovered the mummified corpse of a leopard on the crater rim, at a place that became known as Leopard Point. Latham took photographs of the leopard on a pile of rocks and being held triumphantly by a porter. He recorded his extraordinary find in an article entitled 'Kilimanjaro' for the *Geographical Journal* of December 1926, saying, 'A remarkable discovery was the remains of a leopard, sun-dried and frozen, right at the crater rim. The beast must have wandered over and died of exposure.' The leopard was later to become immortalised by Ernest Hemmingway, who wrote in the prologue to his classic short story, *The Snows of Kilimanjaro,* that, 'Close to the western summit there is the dried and frozen carcass of a leopard. No one has explained what the leopard was seeking at that altitude.' The leopard remained on the crater rim until the early 1930s, when it disappeared.

Kilimanjaro's continuing popularity

The Lutheran missionary **Dr Richard Reusch** made several ascents of Kilimanjaro between 1925 and 1927. On one such climb he came across the leopard that Latham had found and cut one of its ears off as a souvenir. In **1927** Reusch became the first climber to gaze down into the inner crater having forged a path across the inner cone. The ash pit at the centre of the crater was later named after him in recognition of his discoveries. During the same year, WC West, who summited Kilimanjaro in 1914, returned to the mountain and scaled Mawenzi and Kibo with Sheila MacDonald, who became the first woman to reach both of the two highest points on the mountain.

The slopes of Kilimanjaro were also graced by some of the celebrated climbers more usually associated with the Himalayas. The English mountaineers, **HW Tilman** and **Eric Shipton**, trudged up Kibo from Marangu in **1930** and reached Gillman's Point despite deteriorating weather. From here they circled to Stella Point in an impenetrable mist and abandoned the final push to the summit. By then Tilman was suffering from altitude sickness and vomiting regularly. Both of the climbers were also becoming snow-blind; Tilman wrote that his and Shipton's, 'eyes began to smart, then to hurt, until by evening they were firmly closed and exceedingly painful. We were completely snow-blind.' Despite this set back, they rested at Peters Hut (now Horombo Hut) and then tackled Mawenzi, becoming the first climbers to scale Nordecke Peak, having become disorientated on the way up to Hans Meyer Peak. They promptly descended and repeated the climb, this time successfully negotiating the way to the highest point.

In the same year, the rest of the world was also able to see exactly what lay at the top of the giant volcano, when the Swiss pilots, Walter Mittelholzer and Alfred

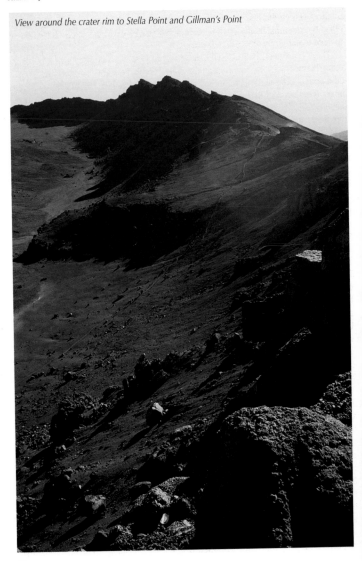

View around the crater rim to Stella Point and Gillman's Point

Kunzler, became the first to fly over Kilimanjaro. The photographs taken from their 200Hp Fokker airplane offered the first comprehensive views of the Reusch Crater and provided a unique perspective of Kilimanjaro.

Three years later, in **1933**, Tilman returned to make a solo ascent of Kibo, summiting the mountain and camping in the crater. He made some unusual observations and reported fumerole activity in the Reusch Crater. In his account of both his climbs, *Snow on the Equator*, he described the inner crater and reported that, 'At the top the diameter was about 400 yards across, at the bottom 200 yards. Sulphurous fumes rose from the lip and pieces of Sulphur lay about.' The report caused a great deal of concern amongst scientists and locals, who had previously thought that Kilimanjaro was extinct. Reusch immediately climbed to the summit again in search of the fumeroles. Failing to find them, he blithely and incorrectly announced that Tilman must have been mistaken and had allowed himself to be convinced that a 'certain kind of whirling little cloud' had resembled sulphurous steam.

During the 20th century, climbing on Kilimanjaro had become a much more popular pastime. Indicative of this was the **creation of the Mountain Club of East Africa in Moshi in July 1929**, which later became the Kilimanjaro Mountain Club. To supplement the Peters and Bismarck Huts, **Kibo Hut was built in 1932**.

Tanzanian Independence

The outbreak of World War II inevitably resulted in the cessation of climbing activity on Kilimanjaro and the end of the war in **1945** marked a major turning point in the history of Tanzania. Opposition to colonial rule was now widespread across Africa and the European powers realised that change was unavoidable. Recognising that, the United Nations appointed Tanganyika a trust territory, under British Guardianship, and vowed to secure self-government and independence for the people.

The independence movement was led by the Tanganyika African National Union (TANU), which chose **Julius Nyere** as its president in **1953**. Nyere won the begrudging respect of the British, who saw him as a trustworthy, peaceful man. In a speech to the Tanganyika Legislative Assembly in **1959**, Nyere pronounced that, 'We, the people of Tanganyika, would like to light a candle and put it on the top of Mount Kilimanjaro, which would shine beyond our borders, giving hope where there was despair, love where there was hate, and dignity where before there was only humiliation.'

Mounting tension in the wake of a series of rigged elections forced the holding of free elections in **August 1960**. TANU won 70 out of 71 seats in the Tanganyika Legislative Council and Nyere duly became chief minister. In this role, he spearheaded the drive to independence, which was officially proclaimed on **9th December 1961**. In a move that echoed Nyere's speech in 1959, the nation's new flag was raised on the top of Kilimanjaro. Unfortunately, exceptionally bad weather and heavy snow prevented the flag bearers from reaching the summit, and the flag was eventually hoisted at Gillman's Point. Exactly a year later, on Republic Day, Lt Alex Nyirenda planted the flag on the summit, which was renamed Uhuru Peak, meaning 'Freedom'. Two years later, in **April 1964**, Nyere persuaded the Sultan of Zanzibar to sign an Act of Union that merged Tanganyika and Zanzibar, and Tanzania was formed.

Measuring Kilimanjaro

During Tanzania's evolution from European colony to republic, climbing and scientific expeditions on Kilimajaro continued to occur. A great deal of geological survey work was also done. In **1952** the **British Ordnance Survey** mounted an expedition to determine the exact height of the mountain by taking a number of readings from predetermined triangulation points. Hans Meyer had claimed to reach a height of 6010m in 1889. This figure had been revised by the German colonial regime five years later and set at 5892m. The OS calculations resulted in Kilimanjaro being officially accorded an altitude of **5895m (19,340ft)**. This is the figure that is still displayed on the summit board that marks Uhuru Peak. Despite this pronouncement, written references to the mountain's height continued to fluctuate wildly.

A year later, in **1953**, a team from **Sheffield University**, working in tandem with the Tanganyikan government, became the first outfit to descend into Mawenzi's Great Barranco, the cavernous ravine on the north-eastern side of the peak. The audacious descent was part of a geological reconnaissance trip. In the course of the climb, the group found a plug of diorite at 14,000ft whose diameter measured approximately 300ft. After further investigation, Professor C Downie and Peter Wilkinson declared that this had been Mawenzi's main volcanic vent. The implication of this discovery was that the whole of Mawenzi's crater had been eroded over the years by the river gorges that now form the Little and Great Barrancos. After studying information gathered during the trip, the group later declared that Kilimanjaro was in fact a dormant volcano, which in all likelihood was virtually extinct. Their report contained the comforting pronouncement that, 'it seems highly unlikely that Kilimanjaro will erupt destructively in the foreseeable future.'

Opening the mountain to others

Success on Kilimanjaro became more commonplace during the second half of the 20th century. In **1955** an Outward Bound Centre was established at Loitokitok in Kenya, just to the north of the border with Tanzania. From here groups made regular ascents of the mountain as the culmination of their course.

These successes were tainted by the occasional tragedy. On 18th May 1955, an East African Airways Dakota became disorientated in thick cloud and flew straight into the south-eastern face of Mawenzi. Everyone on board was killed. Tragically, the plane was only about 10m lower than it need to be in order to scrape over the summit ridge.

Since the glory of reaching the summit for the first time had been captured by Hans Meyer, climbers felt obligated to undertake new and more challenging routes to the top of the mountain. One by one, the glaciers were climbed and Kilimanjaro's plum routes plucked. The Heim Glacier was broached in **1957**, the Great Penck Glacier in **1960** and in **1962** a difficult Grade 6 route was pioneered on the steep Kersten Glacier. Additionally, disinclined to reach the summit by walking or climbing, three French parachutists broke the world record for a high altitude landing by dropping into Kibo's crater. But the most fantastic was yet to come. In **February 1964**, **Barry Clift** and **Rusty Baillie** successfully climbed both Kilimanjaro and Mount Kenya within 24hrs. Beginning from the third cave on the then Loitokitok Route (now Rongai), they raced to the summit by 2pm. Using Outward Bound instructors as pace setters, they hurtled off the mountain and jogged to their car, which drove non-stop to Mount Kenya. Beginning at 2am they ascended the peak, crossing the Lewis Glacier at 8am before climbing and reaching the summit, Batian, at 11.40am, an incredible 21hrs and 40 minutes after they began the challenge. Perhaps unsurprisingly, this feat has never been repeated.

New routes were also being secured on Mawenzi. Two RAF climbers, **John Edwards** and **William Thomson**, made the first ascent of Mawenzi's grim, complex East Face in 1964. The face drops almost 3000m into two gorges, the Little and Great Barrancos. During the climb up innumerable dead-end chimneys and gullies that led to sheer cliffs of solid ice, the pair found the wreck of the Dakota that crashed on Mawenzi in 1955. They also came across the skeleton of a buffalo, improbably lying on a narrow ledge at almost 4800m. Four years later, **Ian Howell** and **Roger 'Fred' Higgins** forged a separate route up the stupendous East Face. The pair called off their first approach to the East Face when they realised that the Great Barranco they intended to follow had far too many waterfalls cascading down its sheer sides, causing Higgins to comment that, 'If it rained on the mountain we could expect to be flushed from the Barranco like rats from a sewer'. Their second, successful attempt approached the East Face via the Downie Ridge that separated the Little and Great Barrancos, before eventually merging with the East Face.

Using a more conventional route, a group of seven blind African climbers were led to the summit in **1969** in a bid to alert the rest of the world to the plight of blind people in Africa.

In a deliberate bid to prevent people approaching Kilimanjaro from Kenya, and in order to channel the tourists onto the Marangu Route, the Tanzanian government closed the border between Loitokitok in Kenya and the mountain in **1970**. Since then it has only been possible to start your climb from within Tanzania. Realising the potential revenue to be garnered from tourism in the area, the government also began the construction of Kilimanjaro International Airport during the same year.

During the 1970s, the massive Breach Wall on Kibo's western flank became the primary objective for talented mountaineers. After his tricky traverse of Mawenzi's eastern slopes at the end of 1969, the Swiss climber **Fritz Lortscher** was especially keen

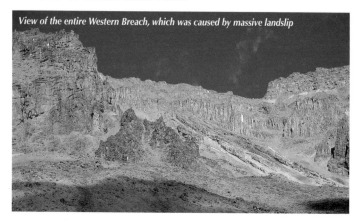
View of the entire Western Breach, which was caused by massive landslip

to secure the first ascent of this epic obstacle and tackled the Breach Wall in the early 70s. Although he managed to ascend an inner section of the Wall, the main section resolutely defied his advances.

Through the middle of the decade the stakes were raised as first **John Temple** and **Tony Charlton** forced a spectacular route at the eastern end of the Breach Wall and then Temple and **Dave Cheesmond** pioneered a new line up the Balleto Icefield and the series of gullies above it. A magazine published Temple's description of the breathtaking Breach Icicle that linked the Balleto and Diamond Glaciers in August 1976, fuelling the interest already shown in the Breach Wall. Elsewhere on the mountain, talented climbers (including Ian Howell, Bill O'Connor, John Cleare, Iain Allen and Mark Savage) were completing dramatic first ascents. Following his inspiring direct ascent of the precipitous Kersten Glacier in 1975, **John Cleare** wrote, 'We were level with the upper tier of the Great Breach Wall itself ... draped with fantastic icicles; one, a slim pillar linking the snow band to the tiny Diamond Glacier overhanging the Wall, was 500ft long! That was the line! But it would wait for the next generation.'

In **1978** the highly talented Americans **Rob Taylor** and **Henry Barber** approached the Breach Wall via the Umbwe Route. Bypassing the park authorities, they quickly trekked to the foot of the Wall and began to climb the face via the Window Buttress. Once on the icicle, Taylor realised the enormity of the climb ahead, later writing that, 'The ice on the icicle is the worst I have ever encountered ... I quickly find myself fully extended just trying to stay in contact with the decomposed vertical sludge.' 20ft into the climb, an ice pedestal Taylor was clutching snapped off and he fell heavily, smashing feet first into a sloping ledge at the base of the icicle and badly breaking his ankle. A broken ankle at this altitude, in such an isolated area, is often tantamount to a death sentence. Barber managed to manoeuvre and lower Taylor off the face and down the Heim Glacier in a remarkable display of skill. At the foot of the glacier he left the fading

Taylor and hacked across the mountainside to find help. Five days after the accident, the alarm was raised and after a further two days Taylor was found and evacuated from the mountain. Emergency surgery saved his gangrenous foot from amputation. After an horrific two months of hospitalisation in Tanzania, Taylor was flown back to America to eventually regain the use of his leg eight months later. Controversy followed the publication of Taylor's version of events in *The Breach*, as each climber blamed the other for the accident.

Despite its atrocious condition that year, the Breach Wall did eventually fall. The legendary South Tyrolean climber **Reinhold Messner** and his companion **Konrad Renzler** completed the first full direct ascent of the Breach Wall, including the ascent of the 300ft icicle, on the **31st January 1978**. The pair free climbed the route, without recourse to ice axes or screws, in an incredible 12hrs. The mountaineer **Iain Allen**, in the Mountain Club of Kenya's guide to Kilimanjaro, advises that, 'Future parties should allow at least 2 days.' The Wall was not climbed again for five years, until **Wes Krause** and **Scott Fischer** succeeded in **1983**.

Kilimanjaro National Park

Although the wooded lower slopes of Kilimanjaro had been made into a forest reserve by the British after World War I, and the Tanganyikan National Parks Authority had proposed that the mountain become a national park in 1957, it wasn't until **1973** that the **Kilimanjaro National Park (KINAPA)** was actually set up. The National Park was designed to incorporate all land above 2700m and preserve the flora and fauna found there. A major hut-building programme was launched, with a group of Norwegians lending development assistance and expertise; Mandara and Horombo Huts were constructed on the site of the old Bismarck and Peters Huts. Despite this pre-emptive step having been taken, the park was not officially opened until **1977**, when President Julius Nyere declared it as such. After much consideration, **UNESCO declared Kilimanjaro National Park a World Heritage Site in 1989**, in recognition of its extraordinary beauty and unique features. Since then, botanists and biogeographers have conducted extensive fieldwork on Kilimanjaro that has greatly added to the scientific knowledge of

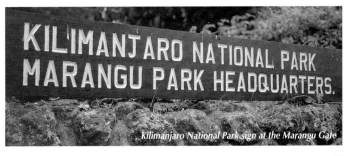

Kilimanjaro National Park sign at the Marangu Gate

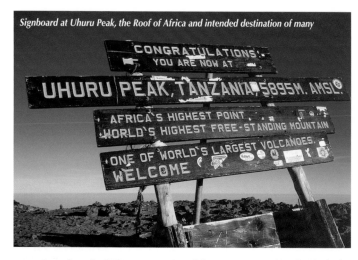

Signboard at Uhuru Peak, the Roof of Africa and intended destination of many

mountain ecology. In **1999**, a new survey of the mountain conducted with the latest Global Positioning System (GPS) and satellite technology by a joint German and Tanzanian geological expedition, concluded that **Kilimanjaro was in fact only 5892.55m (19,330ft) high**. This figure is some 2.5m (10ft) lower than the one long held to be correct. The debate as to the exact height of Africa's highest peak and the cause of the discrepancies still rages.

People have continued to climb Kilimanjaro in large numbers and in increasingly bizarre ways. In **1985** cousins Richard and Nicholas Crane mountain biked to the summit along the Marangu Route. By this time, cycling, motorbiking, paragliding and hangliding on Kilimanjaro had become an almost regular occurrence, frequently in conjunction with sponsored charity events. In **1995** the National Park took the unprecedented step of banning all high-risk stunts on the mountain to reduce the danger that these events posed to the public and to minimise the detrimental impact of such exploits on the mountain itself. Nonetheless, Kilimanjaro remains an enormous lure for people wishing to challenge themselves and is still the scene of innumerable charity climbs.

Kilimanjaro's popularity soared at the close of the 20th century, culminating in a mammoth, mass climb of the mountain to see in the new Millennium. Some 7000 people attempted to reach the summit in that week alone. The number of people who harbour a desire to reach the Roof of Africa shows no sign in letting up and the Millennium celebrations should have been the perfect justification for the authorities to give the mountain infrastructure a much needed boost, particularly if Kilimanjaro is to see out the next thousand years unscarred by human activity.

PART 3
NATURAL HISTORY

Geology and Vulcanology

The enormous base detracts from the apparent height, and this detraction is accentuated by the squat, pudding-like dome of Kibo, the highest summit. In fine weather Kibo can be seen from Nairobi, when the haze rising from the hot intervening plains blots out the lower slope, leaving the white dome suspended in mid-air like a cloud

HW Tilman

Mount Kilimnjaro is the highest mountain in Africa and one of the largest volcanoes in the world. The enormous volcanic massif rises 4876m above the surrounding savannah to a height of 5895m. Aligned in an east-south-east direction, it is situated 80km east of the rift valley. It is roughly 80km by 40km and covers an area of some 388,500ha.

This extraordinary apparition, which rises from the level plains unhindered by any adjoining mountain range, was born as a consequence of the cataclysmic movements of the earth's crust that formed the Rift Valley over 1 million years ago. Kilimanjaro itself is probably over 750,000 years old, making it a relative infant in geological terms.

In the course of the last 2 million years, the African plate, Arabian plate and the Somalian sub plate began to move against each other, rupturing and slumping as they did so. As the plates shifted, the Rift Valley was created, stretching 10,000km from the Middle East to Southern Africa. The deep fractures in the earth's crust allowed magma to surge along lines of weakness and erupt from beneath the surface of the buckled plains. The resulting volcanic activity was greatest where the original Rift Valley was deepest. The result was the eventual formation of a string of large volcanoes along 100km stretch of the Rift Valley. These included Ngorogoro on the Rift Valley itself and to the east, Mounts Kenya, Meru and Kilimanjaro.

The Rift valley is still technically active today. Geologically speaking, Kilimanjaro is the result of comparatively recent volcanic activity. This giant stratovolcano is actually comprised of three independent vents. The cones of Shira, Mawenzi and Kibo grew for thousands of years. The oldest peak, Shira, ceased to be active about 500,000 years ago, having reached a height of around 5000m: although the cone has since collapsed in on itself to form a caldera, it is still possible to make out the broad outline of the cone on the Shira Plateau. Mawenzi and Kibo remained active and continued to grow. Mawenzi became the second vent to become inactive, and was rapidly and dramatically eroded, not least by the subsequent eruptions of Kibo, whose growth continued unabated.

Kilimanjaro reached its most lofty point some 450,000 years ago when it probably grazed 5900m. Since then it has been in decline. Eruptions continued to occur sporadically though; the most explosive was 350,000 years ago when vast quantities of black lava spewed forth from the earth and filled the collapsed Shira cone as well as creating the Saddle linking Kibo and Mawenzi before fanning far down the northern and southern slopes. These prodigious extrusions of black rhomb porphyry lava are still clearly visible on the mountain, most noticeably on the Shira Plateau.

During periods of dormancy, erosion sculpted the mountain's surface. Shira became a gentle, rolling plateau; Mawenzi was almost completely eroded to leave just the hard core visible and Kibo was flattened and rounded.

Glaciers repeatedly covered and uncovered the peak, grinding the summit down and wearing it into its present shape. At one stage, an ice cap 100m deep covered Kibo, its fingers reaching far down the flank of the mountain.

As volcanic activity became more and more intermittent, a rash of parasitic, ash and cinder cones developed, running across the mountain in a north-west/south-east direction. A final burst of activity saw the formation of the flows in the inner crater and the creation of the Ash Pit. It is believed that this unusual volcanic feature was created within the last 300 years.

Sightings of volcanic activity by geologists and mountaineers and scientific studies have since led people to conclude that Kilimanjaro is currently dormant. Although virtually extinct, small fumaroles in the Reusch Crater continue to emit sulphurous steam, hinting at the enormous energy that once raged here.

Shira

The Shira volcano is the oldest part of the Kilimanjaro massif. It was the first to erupt and the first to become extinct. Consequently, from a height of over 4900m, Shira has been eroded and reduced to create a much lower caldera. The western and southern rims of the volcano are all that remain of what was probably a cone 3km in diameter.

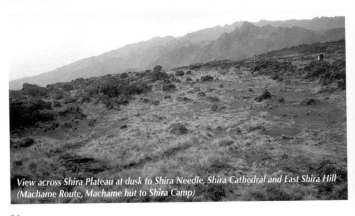

View across Shira Plateau at dusk to Shira Needle, Shira Cathedral and East Shira Hill (Machame Route, Machame hut to Shira Camp)

The Shira Ridge, which includes Johnsell Point and Klute Peak, and the steep-sided cliffs below the Shira Needle, Cathedral and East Shira Hill mark the western and eastern extremities of the caldera respectively. The Shira Plateau is now an expansive, rumpled plateau that peaks at Johnsell Point (3962m).

As the erosion progressed and the cone collapsed, smaller lava extrusions welled out onto the surface of the mountain. Streams have subsequently worn creases into the surface of the plateau and weathering continues to shape and mould the region.

There are a large number of rock types in the Shira area. A final eruption on Kibo caused the caldera to infill with black rhomb porphyry lava, a dark lava that is easily recognisable by the crystals of rhombic or occasionally diamond-shaped cross-section that stud its surface. There are also fragments of the green crystal olivine, which was forced to the earth's surface from a depth of almost 80km.

Mawenzi

The vertiginous, erosion-worn peaks of Mawenzi are the most visually impressive of Kilimanjaro's three cones. The blasted, shattered slopes rise to a high point, Hans Meyer Peak, at 5149m, making Mawenzi the third highest peak in Africa, behind Kibo and Mount Kenya.

The western face of Mawenzi, which is the one most commonly seen, is steep and rises over 600m from the Saddle. The face is craggy and has numerous pinnacles and gullies etched into it. However, the rarely seen East Face is substantially more dramatic. The face is sheer for over 1000m and the maze of gullies and chutes here has only partially been explored. The East Face drops into two deep gorges; the Little and Great Barrancos are sheer-sided gouges in the mountainside. A lake used to be held here by a rock wall; when it duly collapsed water flooded out and spread volcanic debris over an area of 1000sq km to the north and east of the mountain. The collapse of the wall resulted in the creation of the gorges and hastened the erosion of Mawenzi.

A local Chagga folk tale goes some way to explaining Mawenzi's broken, shattered appearance. Many years ago, whilst Kibo and Mawenzi were sat by their respective hearths, Mawenzi allowed his fire to go out. He approached his younger, but larger brother in order to beg a few embers in order to relight his fire. Kibo complied, but on his return journey across the Saddle, Mawenzi let the embers go out once again. He asked for a second set of coals and was in turn given them. These too he let grow cold. In a rage, Kibo attacked his younger sibling and battered him with such force that all of his features were scarred and damaged. The myth suggests (though there is no geological evidence to support this) that there has been volcanic activity on Mawenzi since the last phase of the ice age, during the time that the Chagga have lived on the lower slopes.

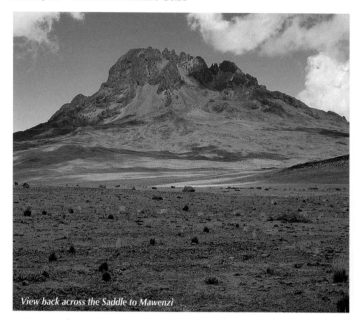

View back across the Saddle to Mawenzi

Erosion on Mawenzi is highly pronounced, and the peak is in an advanced sate of decay. Erosion is responsible for wearing away the main part of the cone and for producing the current shape of the peak. During the various volcanic eruptions, liquid lava was forced into gaps on the face of the cone where it cooled and set. The hardened lava is less prone to erosion than the surrounding rock and so remains after the rock has been worn away. These dykes are thus left as prominent pinnacles on the slopes of the peak; a host of dyke swarms make up about half the summit area of Mawenzi.

Mawenzi has a number of dramatically fluted rock faces. The rock that makes up these cliffs is brittle and prone to shattering, making it very difficult to climb. Since Mawenzi is strictly a technical climb, the peak is attempted far less frequently than Kibo. Only exceptionally experienced, talented climbers tackle the ascent to Hans Meyer Peak. Nonetheless, it is a very enticing proposition and represents a substantial prize. The mountaineer, HW Tilman, who was determined to conquer Mawenzi whilst tackling Kilimanjaro in the 1930s, described Mawenzi as, 'a fantastically weathered peak of red volcanic rock, 17,000ft high, separated from the higher but less interesting Kibo by a wide, flat saddle of shale.' In preparing to tackle the climb he noted that, 'It looked difficult, and if the climbing of Kibo was a duty, that of Mawenzi promised to be a pleasure.'

In addition, the technical difficulties are further complicated by the altitude, making the ascent of Kilimanjaro's second summit a real challenge. In his book *Kilimanjaro*, the photojournalist John Reader included the grisly story of two climbers who died on Mawenzi. Having successfully reached the summit, the two experienced climbers decided to try and pioneer a new descent route. Something went wrong on the descent and, having detached himself from the rope for some reason, one of the climbers fell to the foot of the slopes and was killed. In turn, the second climber fell and died as he tried to complete the descent. His rope snagged on an overhang as he plummeted and jerked him to a halt on the cliff face. Because of the extreme nature of the ascent, it wasn't feasible to try and collect the body by climbing the face and so a drastic alternative solution was devised. Reader recorded that, 'The body hung in such an inaccessible place that to retrieve it a marksman severed the rope with a bullet.'

Kibo

Kibo is the most recently formed of the three volcanic cones that comprise Kilimanjaro. Although now dormant, it is thought that Kibo may have been active as recently as a few hundred years ago.

As a result of this relative youthfulness, Kibo retains a more perfectly preserved shape. The upper part of Kibo is largely intact, but the crater wall has collapsed to create a caldera that measures 2km by 2¼km wide. On the southern side, this caldera is up to 180m deep. The summit has been flattened and rounded by erosion so that its upper slopes now incline at approximately a 30° angle.

Jagged North Ridge on lower slopes Mawenzi

Inside the caldera is a resurgent dome, an inner cone, which stands 150m higher than Gillman's Point but is currently still 60m lower than the actual summit of the mountain. Uhuru Peak (5895m) lies to the south-west of the cone on the crater rim.

In turn, the inner cone contains the Reusch Crater, which is over 800m wide. An ash cone containing a central ash pit made of shale and up to 130m deep and 360m wide is set within the Reusch Crater. The ash pit on Kilimanjaro is considered to be one of the most perfectly formed examples of this feature in the world.

The final eruptions on Kilimanjaro filled the caldera here with lava, which overflowed and ran down Kibo's north-eastern slopes. A smaller flow also followed the Western Breach and penetrated into the Weru Weru River Valley. The predominant rock types on Kibo, as on Mawenzi, are trachybasalts. However, the different flows have produced a variety of different rock types.

There are still frequent reports of fumerole activity in the Reusch Crater that suggest that the mountain is still only dormant and not yet extinct. However, these may represent the final death throes of the volcano. The fumaroles do however provide a unique microclimate for lichens in an otherwise inhospitable environment.

Around 100,000 years ago, an enormous landslip broke away a chunk of the crater rim. The gash in the uniformity of the summit is slightly less steep than the surrounding cliffs and now forms the Western Breach. The landslip proceeded to gouge a giant wound in the side of the mountain and created Kibo's Great Barranco Valley.

Kibo was once completely covered by an ice cap that would have stood 100m high and the glaciers extended far down the slopes. The brilliant white of the ice reflects the heat from the sun and enables the glaciers to survive at this latitude. Although Kibo still supports glaciers and permanent snow, these are much diminished and definitely in retreat. The only remnants of the glaciers at lower elevations are the numerous moraine ridges that are visible on the southern slopes around 4000m. The remaining glaciers are

Cloud and high winds over Kibo summit

Little Penck Glacier on Kibo

a shadow of the giant floes that dominated the summit previously and display little of the power that their predecessors must have shown.

Glacial Recession

At the height of the glaciated period, both Kibo and Mawenzi were completely covered by ice. The glaciers generally flowed down from the peaks to around 4000m although some fingers reached as low as 3000m. The heavy, powerful ice moulded and shaped the mountain and was responsible for levelling a number of the parasitic cones that had formed on the lower slopes.

In the 19th century, Hans Meyer encountered a glacial wall at 5500m on his first ascent. The glacial wall at that time encircled the summit and covered an area approximately ten times as great as today. When Meyer returned to Kilimanjaro in 1898, nine years after his first ascent, he was horrified to discover that the glaciers had retreated considerably on all sides. Furthermore, the crater floor was now more or less free of ice. At that time, Meyer speculated that all of Kilimanjaro's glaciers would have melted within 20 or 30 years.

By comparing photographs taken over the course of the last couple of decades, it is possible to readily determine the extent to which the glaciers have retreated. Views of the Southern Icefields and the Heim Glacier in particular as seen from Barranco Hut are markedly different in appearance. In the 15 years between 1984 and 1999, the glacier was seen to lose 300 vertical metres of ice.

However, whilst it is possible to detect that this is happening, it is hard to say why since there isn't a simple, conclusive explanation. The fact that Meyer first recorded

101

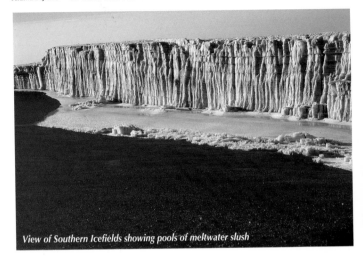

View of Southern Icefields showing pools of meltwater slush

glacial recession at the end of the 19th century suggests that global warming is not simply or solely to blame, and that recession is in fact part of a longer-term cycle of climatic change.

Studies of Kilimanjaro's ice fields by Sheffield University during the 1950s concluded that there has been a long history of glacial advance and retreat on Kilimanjaro. The current glaciers date from around 9700BC and have remained on the summit due to repeated ice ages during which time the glaciers were able to recover from melting. There have been eight separate glaciations. The current glaciers are thought to be the remnant of the ice cap that formed as a result of the worldwide drop in temperatures that occurred between 1400 and 1700.

However, the rate of retreat has accelerated rapidly over recent years as a direct consequence of a general increase in the earth's temperature. Lonnie Thompson of Ohio State University made an aerial survey of Kilimanjaro and stated that, 'comparisons with previous mapping showed 33% of Mt Kilimanjaro's ice had disappeared in the last two decades – 82% had gone since 1912.' There is less than 1sq mile of ice left on the summit. Although the warnings of the disappearing ice aren't new, the current rate of reduction is abnormally high. Separate ice tongues that used to exist have lost their definition and shrunk to form a continuous body of ice. Similarly, glaciers such as the Arrow Glacier or the Ratzel Glacier have ceased to be imposing landmarks and now remain only as vestigial ice floes.

Although the glaciers reflect much of the sunlight and consequently don't warm up and thereby melt, the dark coloured lava does heat up and this undermines the ice. As the ground's temperature increases, the ice begins to melt from beneath the glacier;

eventually the weight of the overhanging ice becomes too much and a chunk sheers off, exposing more of the glacier to the same phenomenon.

The melting glaciers are usually replenished by snowfall, but recently there has been a dearth of heavy snow on the mountain. This has been the case since the 19th century. Meyer wrote, 'It may have caused some surprise that all along I have continued to speak of ice, and not of snow, as might have been expected. But, as a matter of fact, at this season of the year there was hardly any snow on Kibo worth mentioning.' He went on to write that, 'In the great snowfields, which in July partially covered the slopes of Kibo from the ice-cap to the saddle plateau, the snow near the base was soft and slushy, whilst higher up it was dry and granular. In October, when all the snowfields had disappeared, there was likewise comparatively little snow to be met with on the ice-cap.' Thus, the glaciers are being melted by a natural phenomenon and not replenished by snowfall during rainy seasons because of the increase in the earth's general temperature.

A weather station has been set up on the Northern Icefields to monitor the situation and record any further developments. A number of ice-core samples were taken in 2000 and studied in a bid to try and ascertain the history of the climate over the years. The results of these studies will provide a unique perspective on the past and present global climate systems. The retreating glaciers are symptomatic of a larger,

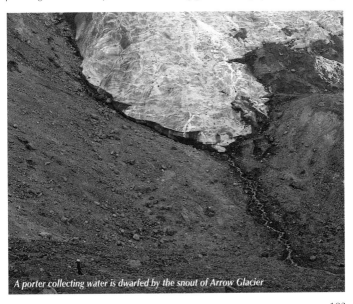

A porter collecting water is dwarfed by the snout of Arrow Glacier

more significant problem that is causing dramatic changes to the earth's environment during our lifetime. The results of the studies are still to be compiled and are eagerly awaited.

The findings on Kilimanjaro have massive implications. The potential ramifications of the loss of the ice fields on Kilimanjaro are immense; the local community will inevitably be affected since they rely on the ice as a source for drinking water, crop irrigation and hydroelectric power. Tourism will also suffer as the majority of people visiting the mountain do so in the hope of seeing the eternal snows that adorn the summit as Hemmingway saw them, '… great, high, and unbelievably white in the sun.'

Climate

Asifuye mvuwa imemnyea.
'He who praises rain has been rained on.'

Swahili proverb

It is very difficult to be precise about the climate on Kilimanjaro; as a result of its size, Kilimanjaro enjoys a number of climactic conditions and at any one time there are equatorial and arctic conditions present on the mountain. That said, the weather here follows remarkably regular patterns.

Although technically enjoying equatorial conditions, Kilimanjaro's climate is actually more tropical. On the warm, dry plains the temperature averages 30°C; as you ascend through the belt of tropical forest on the lower slopes, the temperature decreases, as does the level of rainfall, until you arrive at the permanent snows and freezing temperatures of the summit.

The weather on Kilimanjaro is the direct result of the seasons of the year. The conditions that you experience will also be directly affected by the side of the mountain that you are on and the altitude that you are at.

Kilimanjaro lies just to the south of the equator. As such it is affected by the passage of the Intertropical Convergence Zone, a band of rain that moves across the region between northern Uganda and southern Malawi. The rains cross Africa twice a year and consequently there are two distinct rainy seasons.

The highest rainfall occurs between mid-March and early May. These are the long rains, 'masika', and are brought by the south-east trade winds from the Indian Ocean. During this season clouds pile up over the mountain and drop snow on the summit and rain on the slopes. Even if no rain falls, a belt of cloud encircles the mountain and visibility is drastically reduced. Marginally less rain falls between early November and late December. These short rains, 'mvuli', are carried overland by the north-east monsoon winds and are charcterised by thunderstorms. However, rain and (higher up the mountain) snow can be encountered at any time of year, even during the driest periods of the year.

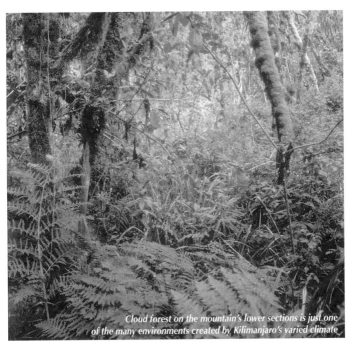

Cloud forest on the mountain's lower sections is just one of the many environments created by Kilimanjaro's varied climate

Rain occurs here because Kilimanjaro is a massive obstruction for the winds that bustle across the savannah. These winds hit the mountain and are deflected upwards. As the temperature and atmospheric pressure decrease with altitude, so the moisture condenses and becomes rain.

The heaviest and most sustained rainfall occurs in the forest zone on the south side of the mountain and can reach 2000mm/yr, giving these slopes the most favourable climate on the whole massif. Conversely, shorter and lighter rains fall on the northern and western slopes. The least rainfall lands on the summit itself.

The drier seasons between the two rains are associated with clear, dry weather. The middle of the year tends to be cold and dry whilst the end of the year is warmer, but similarly dry. These conditions can last for weeks at a time. January–February and September are the warmest, driest and most clear months on the mountain.

Regardless of the season, the best weather on Kilimanjaro is to be had during the morning. Cloud cover builds up during the day and convectional rainfall is more probable in the afternoon. The skies above the mountain will probably clear during the evening, ensuring that the summits are visible again come morning.

Animal and Plant Life

In 1893–94 the eminent botanist Georg Volkens spent a year on the Shira Plateau and northern slopes of Kilimanjaro, studying and identifying six separate vegetation zones. Beginning on the **lower slopes**, you pass through the **forest zone** and the **heath/moorland zone** before traversing the **highland desert** and entering the **summit zone**. These ecological bands occupy belts of approximately 1000m of altitude each and are distinguished from each other by the different association between altitude, rainfall, temperature, flora

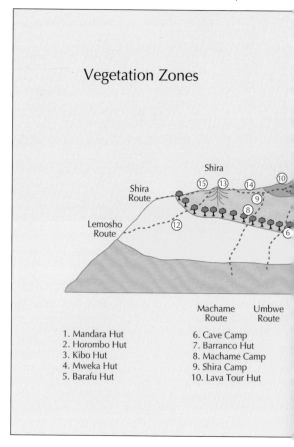

Vegetation Zones

1. Mandara Hut
2. Horombo Hut
3. Kibo Hut
4. Mweka Hut
5. Barafu Hut

6. Cave Camp
7. Barranco Hut
8. Machame Camp
9. Shira Camp
10. Lava Tour Hut

and fauna. A description of each zone and the plant, bird and animal life found in them is included at the end of the more general introduction to the region's wildlife.

Botanists have struggled over the years to apply a consistent nomenclature to the ecological zones and there has been frequent debate as to where they each begin and end. The uneven distribution of rainfall on the mountain means that the zones have formed an asymmetrical pattern. The northern side of Kilimanjaro receives far less rainfall than the southern half and consequently has a far narrower forest belt. Additionally, the trees found here are slightly different from elsewhere on the mountain.

Treeline
Lower Slopes
Forest Zone
Heath/Moorland
Highland Desert
Summit Zone

bo

Mawenzi

Marangu
Route

Mweka
Route

11. Arrow Glacier Hut
12. Big Tree Camp
13. Shira 1 Camp
14. Shira 2 Camp
15. Simba Camp
24. Uhuru Peak

N

0   5   10 km

The Impatiens kilimanjari, *unique to the slopes of Kilimanjaro, takes its name from the mountain*

As, in general, the temperature drops 1°C for every 200m of altitude gained and as rainfall also decreases with altitude, life is concentrated on the lower slopes. Plant life is most abundant in the areas of high rainfall and higher temperature, making the lower slopes and the forest zone far more habitable than the higher altitude zones. Since animal life is dependent on plant life being present, far fewer animals live at high altitude, congregating instead at lower elevations.

A huge number of plants thrive on Kilimanjaro, including a host of endemic species that can be found nowhere else in the world. Many of the plants don't have common English names, and so their scientific name, derived from either Latin or Greek, is given here. The scientific name comprises two parts: the first part is the genus and the second is the name of that particular species. Many plants on the mountain have the species name 'kilimandscharica' or 'kilimanjari', which means that the plant was named after the mountain. A number of others have the species name 'usambarensis', which is a reference to the Usambara Mountains to the south-east of Kilimanjaro and is indicative that some of the flora has spread from this range of mountains to Kilimanjaro. There are also a number of commemoratively named plants on the mountain. Many of the explorers, climbers and botanists who played a part in the discovery or study of the mountain have plants named after them; Meyer, Purtscheller, Johnson, Thomson, Decken and New all have species named after them.

At one stage, Kilimanjaro was heavily populated by animals, as is evident in the early writings about the mountain and in the mid-20th century animal count. In 1965 eyewitness reports of mammal sightings were correlated with contemporary fieldwork to create a checklist of 80 species found living in either the forest or heath/moorland zones. Nowadays, mammals are very rarely seen and you will have to be exceptionally lucky or incredibly patient to come across any of the shyer, larger game. Most of the animals simply slip away at the first sound of approaching foot traffic and vanish into the landscape. In some cases, the animals have quit the forest and retreated right off the mountain.

Early writings on Kilimanjaro that include descriptions of wildlife encountered and, in particular, big game sightings are usually confined to those reports that pre-date the second half of the 20th century. In 1964 a buffalo skeleton was found high on the east face of Mawenzi; elephant bones were also found as high as 16,000ft during the first half of the 19th century. Johannes Rebmann recorded seeing elephant on the day that he first sighted Kilimanjaro in 1848 and Hans Meyer wrote that he had seen elephants on the decent from his successful first summit in 1889. The frozen carcass of a leopard discovered on the summit in 1926 was the inspiration for Hemmingway's classic short story, while HW Tilman reported seeing 27 eland on the Saddle in 1933. Wilfred Thesiger was tracked during his push from Gilmman's Point to Uhuru by a group of five wild dogs in 1962; his discovery of a host of paw prints in the ice led him to suggest that the dogs were frequent visitors to Kibo. In another incident, in 1979, a porter was savaged by wild dogs in the moorland zone and was only saved by the timely arrival of a large group of walkers. Whilst you are unlikely to be as fortunate (or unfortunate, in some cases) as any of these individuals, you may still see monkeys, an array of birds and insects and perhaps the tantalising evidence of something larger living in the forest.

LOWER SLOPES

The first ecological zone on the mountain are the lower slopes, which stretch from 800–1800m. This zone receives varying quantities of rainfall; on the southern side of the mountain 500mm/yr falls on the plains that mark the lowest extremity of the zone. In contrast, the forest boundary at the high end of the zone receives up to 1800mm/yr.

These slopes were originally earmarked by British and German colonisers as potential sites for settlements and farms because of what they described as the ideal, 'European' conditions that they found there. There is now ample evidence of human use and activity on the lower slopes where local people graze livestock and grow subsistence crops including bananas, vegetables and coffee all around the mountain. This has had a negative impact on the natural vegetation and as a direct result, what was once bush and lowland forest is now largely grassland or farmland.

The lower slopes are nourished directly by rainfall and by rain falling in the forest zone; the water percolates down the mountain through underground channels to arrive on the lower slopes. The bountiful supply of water and the fertile, volcanic soils are the main reasons for the zone's successful plant and crop growth. The wealth of farmland in turn supports a number of densely populated settlements amidst Kilimanjaro's foothills.

Flora

The lower slopes are decorated with a host of small colourful flowers that exist amongst the **ferns and grasses** that populate this region. The local grass, *Pennisetum* *clandestinum*, forms thick, short lawns and is identified by its peculiar filament-like white flower. A number of clovers are found here, in the vicinity of water; the attractive, pink/white flowers of **Trifolium semipilosum** and the darker, purple flowers of **Trifolium usambarensis** are the most common examples. **Parochaetus communis** is a blue-flowered pea that is also easily found in damp, shady spots. The most attractive flowers here are the **African violet** (*Streptocarpus glandulossinus*), and the long, violet coloured blooms of **Coleus kilimandscharica**. A number of other plants grow in scruffy looking, tall clumps. These include all of the *Vernonia* species whose huge, shabby heads of small purplish flowers are very distinctive and the *Lippia* and *Lantana* species, which are most easily recognised by their lemony scented leaves and flowers. **Tangled vines** are evident in the trees: *Clematis hirsuta* has a host of pinkish flowers and the thorny *Pterolobium stellatum* displays a number of showy red seedpods that are frequently mistaken for flowers. The attractive blue *Ipomea* species, commonly called **morning glory**, is also found living on trees since it is a very fast growing, clambering plant. The seeds of the pink flowered **Erlangea tomentosa** adhere themselves to your clothes as you brush past and the recurved spines of the yellow-flowered Mauritius thorn, **Caesalpinea decapetala**, or the three-leafed **Toddalia asiatica** inevitably catch and snag your clothes or skin as you climb.

Birds

A great many birds thrive on the lower slopes of Kilimanjaro, particularly where the cultivated ground ends and the forest reasserts itself, since the forest provides good, secure nesting sites and the cultivated land an abundant supply of food.

The ubiquitous **common bulbul** can be seen over much of East Africa at altitudes up to 3000m. It is an unpretentious, small brown bird that has white ear patches and a mottled breast. Generally found on the edge of forests in bushy areas, it has a melodious, high, up-and-down chortle. The white-browed **robin-chat** is also common in shaded woodland and at the fringes of the forest. This shy, colourful bird has a black face streaked by a long white superciliary stripe, an olive-grey rump and rich, tawny-orange underparts. Its repeated rich whistle can usually be heard at dawn and dusk. Also frequently seen is the gregarious speckled **mousebird**, a smallish, stout brown bird with a very long, rigid tail, which makes it up to 30cm long. It has a brown crest, contrasting whitish cheeks and a thick bill. It whistles and chatters frequently, making a soft call except when alarmed, when the pitch becomes more insistent. The most attractive bird to inhabit this zone is the iridescent **bronze sunbird**. The male is generally black with gold, bronze and green reflections, and a long, curved bill; the female is a brownish olive colour and has a dusky facial mask. Found above 1200m, both sexes make an extended sputtering call that is interspersed with occasional louder notes.

Animals

The lower slopes host a few large game species, but these are much rarer than the smaller animals found here. Since you are most likely to start your climb towards the top of this zone and won't stay overnight within it, you probably won't see many of its inhabitants, a number of whom are nocturnal.

The tree-dwelling and vaguely catlike, silvery grey **galagos** (bushbabies) may be seen in the dense vegetation up to 1800m. They have large, leathery ears, enormous eyes and a bushy tail. Galagos are entirely nocturnal, emerging at night to forage for fruit, nectar, seeds, flowers, insects and larvae. Their baby-like cry can be repeated up to 100 times per hour, ensuring you are far more likely to hear than see them. **Tree hyraxes** also live almost exclusively amidst the trees. These rabbit-sized herbivores are distant relatives of the elephant and are identified by their brownish coat and short, coarse fur. Hyraxes are sociable and bond together in small colonies, and feed on leaves and shoots. For such small creatures they make a mighty din; the standard call begins with a series of groans and creeks and rises to a climax of eerie screams and shrieks – their alarm call is a high-pitched scream. Tree hyraxes are preyed upon by the **common genet**. This agile, feline predator is attractively marked with dark spots on its creamy fur and has a banded tail. It hunts alone at night in trees or along the ground. In some places, genets have learnt to scavenge off human rubbish and may be seen haunting camp or hut sites.

FOREST ZONE

The forest zone extends from 1800–2800m. It is the richest zone on the mountain because it receives so much rainfall. The southern slopes enjoy as much as 2000mm/ yr, whilst the drier northern and western slopes receive up to 1000mm/yr. Daytime temperatures reach 15–20°C, although the humidity makes it feel warmer. In contrast, the nights spent at either Mandara Hut (2725m) (along the Marangu Route) or Big Tree Camp (2790m) (on the Lemosho Route) can be very cold, especially if the sky is clear.

A wide band of lush montane forest encircles the whole of Kilimanjaro. The forest varies in width from a couple of kilometres to over 15, according to its position on the mountain, the steepness of the slope and the extent to which human activity has impacted on its natural state. When 19th-century explorers first attempted to ascend Kilimanjaro, it took them two or three days simply to traverse this zone. Tree clearance has nibbled away at the forest and reduced it dramatically; the wetter southern slopes are still the densest and most verdant whereas the western and eastern slopes have been cleared in places for softwood plantations. Although these plantations are economically productive, they have adversely affected the wildlife by disrupting the migratory routes of elephant and buffalo. The extent of the disturbance has caused the numbers of these animals on Kilimanjaro to dwindle. Those that are left are increasingly cautious.

It has been calculated that 96% of the water on Kilimanjaro originates in the forest zone. The heavy rainfall is absorbed by the thick carpet of leaves and detritus on the forest floor. The water then enters the soil and percolates through the porous lava and a series of underground channels to emerge as springs lower down the mountain. The humus and porous lava act as natural water filters, cleansing the water of most impurities as it passes through the soil. The resultant springs are then channelled into both ancient and more modern Chagga irrigation systems.

Owing to the dampness and altitude of the forest, a wide band of cloud frequently forms around the upper third of this zone, which prevents the moisture within the forest from evaporating. This leads to high humidity and ensures that the forest remains damp. The moist cloud forest is an ideal climate for mosses and lichens, which thrive here and give the whole forest belt a timeless, primeval air.

Flora

The tropical forest is dense, lush and alive. Overrun by plants, it is a steamy, sensuous place to walk through and elicits strong responses in most walkers. The mountaineer Rob Taylor wrote in his account of his assault on the Breach Wall that, 'These plants are the powerful life force here, and they appear to grow before my eyes. I sense that if one stopped and remained still too long in this place, he would be entwined and overpowered, claimed as one of their own.'

Most obvious of the forest plants are the **giant trees** that dominate the zone. As you start the Marangu Route, the trail passes a giant spreading *Albizia schimperiana*, supporting a signboard. The leaves of this tree are reputed to have medicinal properties when burnt. By inhaling the smoke from the singed leaves you are supposed to be able to soothe headaches and reduce a fever. The commonest tree in the forest is the wild poplar, *Macaranga kilimandscharica*. It has smooth grey bark and large heart-shaped leaves that are dark on top and lighter below. The leaves are used by local people to make a hot infusion that prevents diarrhoea. You will also encounter the hefty *Tabernaemontana holstii*, which has rhododendron-like leaves and white flowers that can grow up to 3cm across. *Xymalos monospora*, with its shiny dark leaves and orange berries, and the gnarled *Agauria salicifolia*, which has rough reddish bark, small shiny oval leaves and pinkish flower spikes, are the two other most prevalent trees. The giant trees often play host to a multitude of **mosses** and grey green streams of bearded **lichen** (*Usnea* sp.). The most common of these is *Usnea barbata*, which is more commonly called old man's beard. At times the forest tree trunks support so many epiphytes that they more closely resemble vertical gardens. **Moss-like plants** from the *Lycopodium* and *Selaginella* species also blanket the forest floor. These plants send out runners to rampage across the slopes and clamber over or up everything in their path.

Sycamore figs and **palm trees** are dotted throughout the forest, most usually in river gorges.

Beneath the spreading canopy, the forest sustains a myriad of **ferns**. Botanists have identified over 130 varieties of fern in the forest zone. The most noticeable are the giant tree ferns that grow up to 6m tall. The stalks of the tree ferns are highly valued as poles for use in houses and verandas.

Very little light penetrates to the forest floor and as a consequence, there is a dearth of wild flowers here. Those that do survive on the forest floor compensate

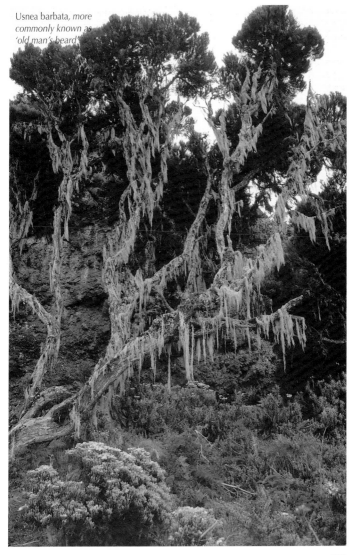

Usnea barbata, *more commonly known as 'old man's beard'*

The Chagga collect the aerial roots from the fig trees and boil them in water. Once the mixture has cooled, it is drunk to combat skin diseases and stomach upsets. The dracaena palm is also important to the Chagga, who use it to create a living fence around their homesteads. The palm sap has a medicinal value too.

by being especially striking. The most resplendent are the **Balsams** that make up the *Impatiens* species. These can be found in thick carpets around the buttressed roots of the great trees. The most exquisite is the endemic scarlet and yellow *Impatiens kilimanjari*. This delicate, tropical **busy Lizzy** is shaped like an inwardly curled spur and is found nowhere else in the world. Its shocking pink relative, the violetesque *Impatiens pseudoviola*, is also found in shady areas. Pink and mauve **orchids**, **violets** and the blue-flowered pea, *Parochaetus communis*, also grow here. **Vines** seen climbing over tree branches are most likely to be *Begonias*; the most common is the white flowered *Begonia meyeri-johannis*, which has a central clump of gold anthers amidst delicate petals.

As the forest is not uniform on each side of Kilimanjaro, the less dense, drier northern and western slopes harbour an entirely different collection of plant species. Of these, the tall, twisted cedar tree *Juniperus procera* is the most common. It grows to almost 40m tall and its fluted, shapely trunk is used commercially for the manufacture of furniture. Cedarwood oil is also used in soaps, whilst perfumes can be distilled from its sawdust. The **African olive trees** *Olea africana* and *Olea kilimandscharica* grow to 10m

Impatiens kilimanjari, *unique to the slopes of Kilimanjaro*

and 30m respectively. The taller species is particularly important as a timber tree. Another common forest giant is *Podocarpus milanjianus*, whose smooth trunk and narrow curling leaves most closely resemble a yew tree. The pale yellow, straight-grained wood is even and uniform in texture, making it an excellent timber tree and earning it the nickname 'yellow wood'. The **African holly**, *Ilex mitis*, also grows here, as does the immense camphorwood, *Ocotea usambarensis,* which grows up to 40m tall. In contrast, the brittlewood *Nuxia congesta* is a bulky, crooked tree with a spreading crown. Frequently festooned with moss and lichen, it produces round clusters of white flowers after rainfall.

Begonia meyeri-johannis

The forest zone on Kilimanjaro is unusual in one major respect: there is hardly any bamboo on the slopes, even though it is common on most other East African volcanic mountains, including Mt Meru just to the west of Kilimanjaro. **Bamboo** is usually found in a belt between 2100–2700m. Although very small clumps of bamboo exist on the northern and north-western slopes of the mountain, Kilimanjaro is essentially devoid of this species. The explanation for this dearth is that Kilimanjaro is higher and drier than other volcanic mountains and the transition from forest to heath/moorland happens much more abruptly. Instead of bamboo, Kilimanjaro supports vast quantities of **giant heath trees**, including the 3m tall *Philippia excelsa*, whose tiny white flowers nestle amidst short, needle-like leaves. In addition to the giant heather, there are a great many bushes of *Hypericum*, which are easily distinguishable by their large, bright yellow flowers, and in sheltered, moist areas the handsome **African rosewood** *Hayenia abyssinica*, whose drooping clusters of dark red flowers and large leaves catch moisture from the mist. In the higher reaches of the forest there are also a number of attractive **shrubs** that have brightly coloured berries. *Lasianthus kilimandscharica* has porcelain blue berries and white-mauve flowers, *Galiniera coffeoides* has red berries and *Pauridiantha holstii* has red berries and small white-yellow flowers.

At the very upper limit of the forest zone, the first endemic **giant *Senecio*** appear. *Senecio johnstonii* has an open, branched crown, cabbage-like leaves, small yellow flowers and grows up to 3m tall.

Hypericum revolutum

Birds

Because the forest is so dense, you may not see a great deal of birdlife here. However, the calls and choruses that ring out are testament to a number of species.

The largest of the forest birds are the silvery-cheeked **hornbill** and **Hartlaub's turaco**. The hornbill is black and white and in flight its dark upper plumage contrasts vividly with its white lower back and rump. Only the male has the distinctive silvery grey feather tips on its cheeks and ear-coverts. They make a very audible whoosh whilst flying in the forest and their raucous, braying call is equally distinctive. Whilst feeding, the hornbill makes softer grunting, quacking calls. The smaller turaco has a rounded bushy blue-black crest, white facial markings and a bright red ring around its eye. Its throat, breast and upper back are green, whilst its posterior parts are glossy violet-blue. When in flight, it displays a vibrant crimson underwing. It lives singly or in small groups and communicates using a gruff, harsh coughing sound.

The attractive bar tailed **trogon** is easily missed since it sits so still in the trees. The male has a scarlet chest, green back and black and white speckled wings. The throat and head are black. The female is similar, except her head and throat are brown and the chest plumage tends to be more orange. Both sexes have a very high, loud, crescendoing yelp. **Mountain greenbuls**, **brown woodland warblers** and **olive thrushes** are more lively but just as hard to spot owing to their drab green and brown plumage that camouflages them against the palette of forest colours.

Animals

The forest zone is home to most of Kilimanjaro's animals, both large and small. However, the vast majority are exceptionally shy, silent and very swift. The dense understorey keeps them hidden and the sound of your own passage will alert them to your presence far more quickly than you can detect them.

You are most likely to see monkeys, particularly **black-and-white colobus monkeys**. These incredibly acrobatic forest denizens have black fur, a flowing white cape and a long, white-tipped tail. They also have a highly distinctive, slightly sombre black face and white surrounding beard. They are gorgeous and graceful to watch. Colobus are sociable and tend to live in family groups numbering 6–10 individuals. They rarely venture out of the trees, obtaining water from hollows on the branches. They are strictly vegetarian and feed on leaves, fruits and seeds. At dawn and dusk the males can be heard uttering their guttural, purring territorial roar. **Blue monkeys** are also quite widespread. They are much less colourful than their name suggests, being mainly grey and black. They have a slender tail that helps them to move quietly through the trees whilst in search of fruit and leaves. Occasionally large troops of **olive baboon** are seen in the forests lower reaches. These large, greenish monkeys have a shortish tail and bare, dog-like muzzle. They are omnivores who have been known to hunt and kill as well as forage for fruit and grass. Their loud, 'wahoo' alarm call sometimes rings out across the forest.

The forest is also home to a host of antelope. Of these, various species of duiker are the most common. Duiker is the Dutch for 'diver' and is a reference to its tendency to plunge headfirst into the undergrowth when startled. **Abbot's duiker** is a very rare, small dark red-brown antelope. It has the hunched back common to all duikers and a small pair of horns hidden in a patch of long reddish hair on its forehead. The **red duiker** is smaller, more brightly coloured and is often seen in pairs. It is chestnut-red and has a black blaze down its face. The **bush duiker** is the largest of the three and the most adaptable. It is fawn coloured and has the same distinctive black blaze on its face, which helps to break up its outline against the forest background. Generally found at higher levels of the forest, it sometimes ventures onto the heath/moorland.

The **suni** is smaller than any of the duikers and is nicknamed the 'dwarf antelope'. It is dark brown and hides in patchy forest, most usually on the western slopes of the mountain, where it feeds on the leaves of the brittlewood *Nuxia congesta*. **Bushbuck** appear throughout the forest zone. Larger than the other antelopes, they are less secretive and more active during the day. The male tends to be darker brown than the female who is conspicuously red. Both sexes have large white throat patches and white stripes and spots along their flanks and face. The males can be distinguished by their medium-sized spiral horns. The compact, goat-like **klipspringer** used to be seen on the rockier stretches of the upper forest zone, but hasn't been sighted recently and is thought to now be extinct locally.

The antelopes share the forest with several other larger mammals. Nocturnal **bush pigs** range warily through the forest, feeding at night on shoots, roots and fungi. They have a large, distinct white stripe running from their face along a spinal crest the length of their back. The forest also houses **eland**, **giraffe**, **buffalo** and **elephant**, although the populations of these larger animals are unknown and probably transitory, passing through the forest on their way to other parts of the surrounding landscape. There have been no sightings of **rhino** on Kilimanjaro for many years and it's very unlikely that there are any resident in the forest.

As well as herbivores, the forest supports a number of carnivores, including **mongooses**, **civits**, **genets**, **lions** and **leopards**. Lions tend to simply pass through the forest on their way to the Shira Plateau, where they are recorded irregularly. The exact numbers of leopard living on the mountain are unknown and they are very rarely seen, preferring to hide in the forest and hunt rodents, antelopes and monkeys.

The forest also supports a huge range of **insects**. Safari ants and a range of attractive, showy butterflies offer an alternative wildlife viewing experience. Large, spectacular swallowtails can be seen in several forms; *Papilio rex* is black, cream and orange whilst *Papilio hornimanii* is black and turquoise. *Papilio sjostedti* is unique to the slopes of Kilimanjaro and Mt Meru.

HEATH/MOORLAND ZONE

The heath/moorland zone is in reality two intermingled ecological zones, which run from 2800–4000m and mark the transition from forest to low alpine desert. The edge of the forest receives more than 1300mm/yr of rainfall. This dwindles to 530mm/yr at the upper limits of the zone. The climate is usually cool and clear. Along the forest boundary there is frequently mist and low cloud, whilst above 3000m the sunshine becomes more intense and the plant life more sparse. The temperatures drop as the slopes become more exposed and during the evenings frost regularly occurs. Whilst the heath retains a number of plant species, the moorland is far more barren. In 1930 Eva Stuart Watt described the terrain in her book, *Africa's Dome of Mystery*, writing, 'The whole landscape as far as the eye could reach was a medley of dull grey lava slabs, dotted with the red-leaf protea shrub and stunted heaths, which became smaller and smaller as we rose higher. Not a sound disturbed the silence of this uninhabited mountain mystery; not a sign of life broke the stillness save a little ashy-brown bird that hopped about the boulders, flipping its tail up and down. And to add to the impression created by the eerie scene, huge senecios lifted to a height of 20ft their black stems and greyish-yellow crowns and stood spreading out their arms in the deep moist gullies, like ghostly sentinels of the untrodden wilds.'

There are several huts and campsites within this zone. At the lower levels of the heath/moorland zone are the Machame Hut (3015m) and the Mweka Hut (3100m). In the higher reaches of the zone are the Horombo Hut (3720m), Shira campsites (3850m), Barranco Hut (3965m) and campsites at Kikelewa Caves (3600m) and Third Cave (3935m).

Flora (Heath)

Heathers and shrubs dominate the heath. In the aftermath of the forest, the openness of the heath is a relief. The trees give way to **large shrubs and giant heathers**, the largest of which is *Erica arborea*, whose gnarled trunks grow to 10m tall in the upper forest, but only 3m on the moorland. The long slender trunks support tiny leaves and small white flowers clustered on the end of the branches. *Erica rossi* is a smaller, bushier heather,

Helichrysum, *more commonly known as everlastings, in bud*

The Helichrysum, *or everlastings, in flower*

distinguished by its flatter, cup-shaped white flowers. *Anthospermum usambarensis* is a cypress-like shrub that grows to around 3m tall and produces attractive clusters of green-white flowers. A similar sized shrub is *Stoebe kilimandscharica*, whose slender branchlets support tiny scale-like silvery leaves and minute dirty yellow flowers. *Kotschya recurrifolia* is a small shrub whose frequently forked branches support gold coloured flowers. *Myrica meyeri-johannis* is a diminutive shrub, adorned with catkin-like flowers. Mingled with all of the shrubs are quantities of spiny gorse, *Adenocarpus manii*, that reach 2m tall.

The heath is resplendent with attractive, brightly coloured, highly visible **flowers**. The most characteristic are **everlastings**. These simple, hardy flowers, which occur in a variety of colours, grow in clumps; *Helichrysum meyeri-johannis* has

Kniphofia thomsonii, *more commonly known as the red hot poker*

Gladiolus watsonioides, *one of the most attractive mountain flowers*

Dierma pendulum

simple pink daisy-like flowers with red tips; *Helichrysum argyranthum* has greenish white flowers, whilst *Helichrysum kilimanjari* produces yellow brown flowers and lemon-scented leaves. *Helichrysum cymosum* is taller than its relatives and produces tight clumps of yellow blooms. In the mid-20th century, the porters used to make garlands from these flowers for climbers who successfully made it to the summit. This practice has since stopped.

The heath is also home to various species of *Protea*. More common further south, it is the floral emblem of South Africa. The most widespread species found on the mountain is *Protea kilimandscharica*, which is more usually known as the 'sugar bush'. It stands almost 4m tall and has a large number of big, creamy flower heads, similar in appearance to a white globe artichoke, which consist of a mass of upright white filaments arising from a shallow, bowl-shaped rosette.

Amidst the grasses and shrubs are a plethora of vibrant flowers. The most distinctive is the **red-hot poker,** *Kniphofia thomsonii*, whose candle-like spike of red, orange and yellow flowers waves in the breeze. The most beautiful flower on the heath is the delicate red or salmon pink *Gladiolus watsonioides*, whose flower hangs gracefully from a curved stem. The gently arching, pink-flowered *Dierama pendulum* and the white flowered *Anemone thomsonii* are often hidden by clumps of grass, as is the small pink-flowered orchid *Disa stairsii*. The heath's phosphorous-rich volcanic soils support two types of clover, the blue-flowered *Trifolium cryptopodium* and the pink- and white-flowered *Trifolium burchellianum*. *Lobelia holstii* sometimes grow on the upper edges of the heath, although *Lobelia* in general are more common higher on the moorland.

Flora (Moorland)

The higher section of this zone, the moorland, is characterised by hardier plants. Clusters of giant *Lobelia* and *Senecios* are the archetypal symbols of African mountain vegetation and are found here in numbers, most often in valley bottoms and beside streams. There are two types of giant *Senecio*, *Senecio cotorii* and *Senecio kilimanjari*, each especially adapted to the rigours of living at altitude. They both have tall stems that act as reservoirs and collect water. The stems fork into two and then each branch forks again higher up; these support the large cabbage-like rosette of leaves that sits atop the stem. They are almost grotesque in appearance, and look misshapen and ungainly. The plants flower approximately once every 25 years; after this the parent branch forks again and grows for another 25 years before repeating the cycle. Therefore, by counting the number of forks that one branch makes and multiplying this by 25, you will be able to roughly determine the age of the plant. The delicate central growing shoot is protected from the sub-zero temperatures on the moorland by a dense leaf bud that insulates it. The plant retains these large leaves when they die, using them to form a shaggy skirt of dry material, which insulates and protects the trunk.

Senecio cotorii is the most widespread giant *Senecio*. It grows high on the moorland and can reach almost 5m tall. It has the classic *Senecio* shape and produces a 1m long spike of dull, mustard coloured flowers and has very thick, cottony leaves. *Senecio kilimanjari* is endemic to the mountain. Less common, it grows at slightly lower altitudes to a similar size, but has much brighter, lemon yellow flowers.

The moorland also supports two smaller, scrubby **Senecios**. *Senecio meyeri-johannis* and *Senecio purtschelleri* are similar to their relatives in shape, but are a fraction of the size.

The other visually striking plants on the moorland are the endemic **Lobelias**. The name *Lobelia* derives from the 17th-century botanist Mathias de L'obel. They are essentially giant overgrown herbs that have adapted to survive in this harsh environment. *Lobelia deckenii* stands almost 3m tall. It has a hollow stem and a pronounced flower spike that supports regular spiralling leaf-like bracts that hide small blue flowers. These flowers are frequently sought out by sunbirds hunting for insects and nectar. The *Lobelia* has a rosette of leaves at the base of the stem that fold over the central core of the plant at night to insulate and protect it from the cold. These rosettes exude a slimy, water-like secretion that freezes in the cold; the water below his layer of ice never freezes and consequently

Giant Lobelia *head, quintessential East African mountain flora*

Senecio kilimanjari *have adapted to survive at altitude*

The distinctive Lobelia deckenii *grows to almost 3 metres*

Carduus koniensis, *mountain thistle*

the sensitive leaf bud is protected from sub-zero temperatures. There have been suggestions that you could drink the fluid found trapped in the *Lobelia's* reservoirs: do not be tempted to do so since *Lobelias* contain lobeline which is highly toxic. The author and historian Audrey Salkeld reported that the mountaineers Ian Howell and Phil Snyder tried it when short of water and found it, 'viscous, tasteless, and home to colonies of little worms.'

The moorland also gives rise to the wiry shrub **Euryops dacrydioides**, which grows in clumps on rocky ridges. It has scale-like leaves and bright yellow flowers. As you climb higher, you will encounter especially adapted **everlastings**. These are even hardier than their lower altitude relatives and have evolved smaller leaves covered in dense, fine hairs that reduce moisture loss and safeguard the plant from the extremes of temperature. The most common everlastings are the yellow and brown flowered *Helichrysum cymosum*, the gaudy yellow flowered *Helichrysum splendidum* and the large white flowered *Helichrysum newii*. This final species is named after the missionary Charles New, who observed it whilst climbing Kilimanjaro in 1871 and described it as having, 'frosty-looking leaves and exceedingly pretty flowers.'

A number of species of **grass**, including blue-stem grass, unicorn grass and crested hair grass, grow in tussocks, intermingled with clumps of the minty herbs, *Satureia biflora* and *Satureia kilimanscharica*.

The moorland supports a number of **bogs**. These unique environments are incredibly fragile and delicate. Do not walk on theses habitats as this will damage and drastically alter them. **Bog sedge**, *Carex monostachya*, is the dominant plant here and is often accompanied by groups of **Giant Senecio**. Delicate flowers, including blue flowered **gentians**, *Swertia crassiuscula*, bright yellow **buttercups**, *Ranunculus oreophytus*, and pink-purple **thistles**, *Carduus keniensis*, hug the ground and take advantage of the bountiful water supply.

Birds

The higher you climb on Kilimanjaro, the fewer birds you encounter. At the lower reaches of the heath/moorland a number of smaller birds frequent the heathers and tussock grasses, whilst a number of larger raptors hunt small rodents and other prey.

The **alpine chat** is a widespread, companionable bird. Above 3400m it is the most common bird on Kilimanjaro. It is mostly brown and has a short, white-sided tail. It can frequently be seen standing bolt upright on rocks and boulders, where it surveys the lie of the land and utters its loud piping call. The **streaky seedeater** is another common moorland bird. Although generally brown, it has boldly streaked underparts and broad, pale streaks along the side of its face. It flits from boulder to bush in search of seeds and feeds on the ground. It has a high-pitched, long drawn cry. The **alpine swift** is a large, highflying swift. It has dark brown upper feathers, white underparts and a dark brown breast band across its pale chest. Its tail is deeply forked. The swift nests in colonies, high on crags. It has a strident rising and falling scream-like call. The only sunbird on the moorlands is the dazzling scarlet-tufted **malachite sunbird**. The long-tailed males are mainly metallic green and have bright scarlet pectoral tufts. The rump and upper tail feathers have blue-black reflections. The female has brown feathers on her upper body and is paler below. The feathers have orange-red pectoral tufts. It feeds on nectar from the flowers of the *Giant Lobelia* and has a rather mellow sounding song. The small montane **yellow-crowned canary** has a bright yellow head, yellow-olive rump and yellow wings. Its tail is discernibly forked. It makes a prolonged, bright jumble of trills that rise attractively.

Ground birds such as **Shelley's frankolin** and the **cape quail** are also found on the moorland. The shy, secretive frankolin resembles a western grouse and has a tawny head and a white-flecked neck. Its cream underparts are blotched and banded with brown streaks. It has streaked chestnut plumage on the rest of its body. When startled it rises from the ground with a great clatter, omitting a shrill squeal. The quail is pale brown and slightly squatter than the frankolin. It has a distinctive call that sounds like a series of short whistles.

The commonest bird of prey on the moorland is the **augur buzzard**. It is very broad winged and has a short, stubby tail. The feathers on its back are black and its underparts white. The buzzard soars on raised wings and is able to hover motionless. It relies on stereoscopic vision to judge the changing distance accurately as it dives on its prey. The augur buzzard has a loud clamorous cry. The smaller **mountain buzzard** is similar in colour and markings to the augur buzzard. It tends to hunt in pairs and is quite vocal, making a loud mewing cry. The **African crowned eagle** is another impressive bird of prey. This large bird proudly sits bolt upright. It is blackish brown above and has heavily mottled tawny cream underparts. It has broad rounded wings and flies remarkably silently. It feeds on large birds and mammals to the size of small duiker, but prefers colobus monkeys. It has a melodious, far-ranging cry. The largest bird of prey is the exceptionally rare **lammergeier**. This striking vulture has long pointed dark wings, a wedge shaped tail and a distinctive white head and black mask. Its underparts are pale and its neck is frequently rust coloured. It soars over the slopes with its wings held slightly below the horizontal and has a whistling call. The **white-naped raven** is a large scavenger that occasionally hunts in its own right. It has jet-black feathers and a broad white collar. It has broad wings, a short tail and a very large, tipped black bill. It has a series of short, guttural, harsh cries. It has learnt to scavenge from campsite and lunch stops along the various routes. It is bold and audacious and will confidently come close enough to pilfer food.

Animals

The most widespread animal on the heath/moorland is the **four-striped grass mouse**. This small, banded grey rodent has colonised the area around the Horombo hut and its numbers have risen steadily to almost plague proportions. Scavenging on scraps and benefiting from the wastefulness of people, these mice have prospered. Slightly less visible but still present are the **climbing mouse** and the **harsh-furred mouse**. Most extraordinary of the rodents found in this zone is the **naked-mole-rat**, an hairless burrower that lives in large underground colonies and attacks plant roots from below. Small mounds of earth along the paths indicate the presence of a colony and if you approach slowly and carefully you may see the workers digging near the surface, throwing up puffs of soil like miniature volcanoes.

The various species of mouse are important prey for small cats, such as the **African civet**, which hunt on the heath. This truculent loner is an aggressive nocturnal predator of small animals. It has white fur that is variously speckled, blotched, striped and banded with black.

East Africa's largest and slowest antelope, the **eland**, is a regular visitor to the heath. It is nomadic and journeys over the heath whilst traversing migration routes. It is about the size of an ox and has humped shoulders and a pronounced dewlap at the base of its neck. Both male and female elands have tightly twisted, spiral horns. The **bush duiker** also ventures onto the heath to feed and can be seen at the zones lower reaches.

Larger species, including **buffalo** and **elephant** are also very occasionally encountered on the heath, usually as they negotiate the mountain on their way to new territories. Their tracks and spoor are often the only indication of their passage.

Of the larger predators, the much maligned **African hunting dogs** (wild dogs) and **lions** have been known to frequent the Shira plateau, climbing out of the forest to hunt the open spaces. Hunting dogs work in packs and use their remarkable stamina to run

A Chagga legend maintains that there is an elephant graveyard high on the mountain. Elderly or dying animals climb Kilimanjaro in order to cast themselves into a pit high on the slopes, thereby thwarting the poachers and hunters who are after their ivory. The location of this legendary pit isn't recorded but may be the ash pit on the summit.

down prey. They are some of the most efficient predators on the savannah. Their fur is ochre, tan, black and white. They are slenderly built and have long legs, a prominent muzzle and powerful jaws. The famous, tawny coat and black and golden mane of the lion is a classic African symbol. They are the largest and most powerful big cat in Africa.

Reptiles don't usually frequent places as cold as the heath/moorland zone, but on Kilimanjaro you may see brown or grey **lizards** basking on the exposed rocks, using the sun's direct light and the absorbed heat of the rocks to warm themselves.

There are also a few **butterfly** species here, including the greenish white *Catopsila florella* and the bluish *Harpendyseus aequatorialis*.

HIGHLAND DESERT ZONE

This is a desolate, lunar-like landscape that stretches from 4000–5000m. It is much drier than lower sections of the mountain and receives as little as 250mm/yr. Professor Hedberg, an expert on Afro-alpine plant adaptation, described this alpine zone as enduring, 'summer every day, and winter every night'. The exposed landscape suffers from intense radiation and very high evaporation. Huge daily fluctuations in temperature, from 40°C in direct sunlight to well below freezing at night, ensure that only the hardiest plants can survive. Sudden cloud cover and an increase in wind speed can result in temperatures plummeting 20°C in almost as many minutes. Water is particularly scarce and the soil struggles to retain any moisture. To combat this, many of the plants have evolved to sieve water from the cloud and mist so that it drips down the leaves, to be absorbed by the roots.

Plants must also combat the process of solifluction. When ground water freezes, the soil water expands and disrupts the soil, potentially uprooting the plants.

Consequently, only the most enduring plants can exist here and the hut and campsites at this altitude, Kibo Hut (4703m), Barafu Hut (4640m), Lava Tower (4655m) and Arrow Glacier (4850m), are all set in bleak, inhospitable environs.

Flora

Botanists have calculated that only 55 species of plant survive above 4000m on Kilimanjaro, in contrast to the many hundred that exist at lower altitudes. The most common of these are the pale green and rust red **lichens**, which are able to avoid the soil entirely and choose to encrust the lava that is predominant here.

Rather than spread over rocks in the usual fashion, **mosses** at this altitude curl around soil nodules and form rootless spheres, known as grimmia, which are able to freely roll around the landscape. The moss feeds on the soil that it encloses and soaks up any available moisture that it encounters, like a sponge.

Flowering plants can't subsist in these conditions as readily because they rely on roots to stabilise and nourish them. Leaves and flowers are prone to damage by frost and the extremes of temperature. Those plants that do exist here are nearly all small **Senecios**, including *Senecio telekii, Senecio meyeri-johannis* and *Senecio purtschelleri*, or woody-stemmed, tough **everlastings**. Even these have had to adapt in order to survive. *Helichrysum newii, Helichrysum cymosum, Helichrysum splendidum* and *Helichrysum citrispinum* all exist in the highland desert as well as lower on the mountain. The higher altitude variations are smaller and hug the contours of the ground. They have developed leathery leaves, a thick skin and small stomata to aid water retention and prevent them drying out. Fine, silver hairs reflect solar radiation and trap air next to the leaves in a bid to reduce heat and water loss.

Small grass tussocks rely on clusters of dead matter to insulate their shoots and retain sufficient moisture for them to survive, but endure up to 4700m. The most common **grass** is *Pentaschistii minor*, whose narrow, wiry leaves reduce water loss. Where grasses manage to bind the soil together, other plants huddle and take advantage of the stabilised surface. These are almost universally ground hugging, cushion plants. Their leaf rosettes provide a degree of insulation and the shiny leaves reflect the harsh sunlight. The most unlikely plant in this zone is the small, delicate *Arabis alpina*. More commonly found in the Alps or Lapland, it is a surprisingly fragile plant to exist at this altitude.

Birds

In general, the air is too thin and the wind too strong for all but the strongest birds to fly here. **White-naped ravens** and larger birds of prey occasionally forage at altitude during the day but return to lower elevations to nest.

Animals

No large animals live in the highland desert zone, only ever passing through it on their way elsewhere. **Eland** are fairly regular visitors to these slopes and their tracks are common on the Saddle. The mountaineer HW Tilman encountered 27 eland there in 1933 and observed that, 'Their normal habitat is the open plains at heights of 5,000 feet to 6,000 feet, but so far as one could tell the eland up on the 'saddle' at 16,000 feet were in no way different except for apparently shaggier hair. This particular herd seemed to be subsisting very happily on a diet of little more than shale, and were very shy.'

Elusive predators including **serval**, **African hunting dogs** and **leopards** also occasionally pass through this zone.

The only other inhabitants of the zone are small, sedentary, wingless **insects**. The insects hide in tussocks and under the clumps of grass for protection. Little spiders living in the zone feed on small, ground-dwelling insects that have been caught on gusts of wind and carried here. These are probably the highest resident animals on Kilimanjaro.

SUMMIT ZONE

The summit zone comprises land above 5000m. It is very barren and hostile and is characterised by arctic conditions. It receives as little as 100mm/yr of rain and supports virtually no life. What rainfall there is, is immediately absorbed by the porous rock and lost. There is virtually no surface water present here, the vast majority of it being locked up as snow or ice.

The temperatures are burning hot by day and well below freezing at night. There is little atmosphere present to protect anything from the force of the sun's radiation and there is 50% less oxygen than at sea level.

Yet remarkably there is still life present in this extreme environment. The occasional **lichen** clings to exposed lava and grows at an excruciatingly slow rate, as little as 1mm/yr. Thus the red and grey lichens around the crater rim are very old. The highest recorded flowering plant on the mountain is an **everlasting**. A very compact version of *Helichrysum newii* was found growing inside the Kibo crater at 5670m. Fumaroles emit warm, sulphurous steam inside the crater and create unique micro-climates that, incredibly, provide just enough ingredients for life, enabling the everlasting to survive.

Lava rubble leading to the Southern Icefields – there is little life and little support for it in the summit zone

Summit wildlife sightings have been confined to the discovery of the frozen **leopard carcass** in 1926 at Leopard Point and the report by Wilfred Thesiger of five **African hunting dogs** that accompanied him and two companions to the top in 1962. Thesiger marvelled that, 'It was an amazing thing to have found wild dogs at 19,000 feet, about 10,000 feet higher than they normally ever go. They looked like wolves in the snow as they followed us, or sat and watched us. I have often wondered if there is any record of mammals having been found at a higher altitude.'

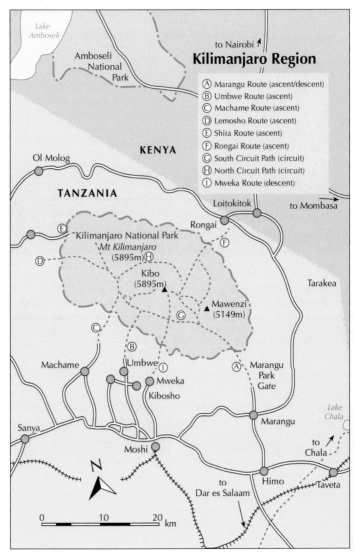

PART 4
CLIMBING KILIMANJARO

There are a number of ways to approach and climb Kilimanjaro. Six forest and heath/moorland routes begin on the lower slopes and ascend to 3500–4000m. These routes then usually merge with the South Circuit Path before linking to one of three final summit ascent routes. From the summit there are two separate descent routes that are affiliated to each of the earlier climbs. The easiest way to make sense of this jumble is to study the Kilimanjaro Region Map.

Typically, when you sign up with an outfitter to tackle Kilimanjaro, you sign up for a particular combination of routes; the most common uses the Marangu Route as both an ascent and descent route. If you sign up for one of the other paths, you will agree to tackle a particular combination of ascent and descent routes in advance of your departure. Thus you might wish to undertake the Machame-Mweka Route, which would climb the mountain along the Machame Route and then return to its foot along the Mweka Route.

Each of the **six initial ascent routes**, the Marangu, Umbwe, Machame, Lemosho, Shira and Rongai Routes are all detailed below (please see Appendix A for the route comparison chart). In addition, there are full descriptions of the **three final ascent routes** to the crater rim; the Normal/Marangu Route, Barafu Route and Western Breach Route are all outlined. Furthermore, there is a description of the **Summit Circuit Paths** that circle Kibo at around 4000m.

After a **full description of the summit**, there follow explanations of the **two descent routes** on Kilimanjaro: the Marangu, and Mweka Routes.

'IT WAS HELL. IT WASN'T FUN. BUT EVERYTHING TURNED OUT WELL.'

In June 2005 the American Sean Burch broke the record for the fastest ascent of Kilimanjaro. Burch, a fitness expert, completed the Marangu Route to the summit in 5hrs, 28mins and 48secs, shaving just under 8mins off the previous best time. Burch trained for this extreme challenge for more than a year and spent eight days acclimatising on the mountain, running laps around the crater and skipping on the summit. He commented 'By the time I reached the top, I immediately puked. So the feeling wasn't celebratory. It's now just starting to sink in as an accomplishment.'

There are two challenges that you might want to take up: the Kilimanjaro Marathon (www.kilimanjaromarathon.com), an impressive 26km loop from and to Moshi that doesn't actually climb the mountain; and the Kiliman Challenge (www.kilimanjaroman.com), which includes an ascent of the Machame Route, a circumnavigation of the mountain on bicycle and a quick lap of the Kilimanjaro marathon circuit. Only the last two elements are actually races as the organisers do not want to encourage people to race up the mountain itself. These challenges are, of course, only for very fit, fully acclimatised individuals.

ASCENT ROUTES

A: MARANGU ROUTE

Time on the mountain (ascent, summit ascent and descent):	5 days
Length:	65km
Altitude gain:	2903m
Grade:	Moderate/hard
Start:	Marangu Gate
Finish:	Kibo Hut
Summit ascent route:	Normal/Marangu Route
Optional extra days:	1 at Horombo Hut
Descent route:	Marangu Route
End trek:	Marangu Gate

The Marangu Route is the oldest and one of the quickest methods of ascending Kilimanjaro. It's also one of the easiest and most popular routes on the mountain, at one time drawing over 80% of trekkers on Kilimanjaro. As a consequence of its mass appeal and accessibility, it came to be known as the 'Coca-Cola route'. It is also somewhat unfairly referred to as the 'tourist route'.

Numbers on the Marangu Route have fallen with the improvement and promotion of alternative routes on the mountain. However, because it is also used as a means of descending the mountain, you are unlikely to ever feel truly alone or isolated in the huts or campsites along the track.

The Marangu Route ascends up the south-east side of Kilimanjaro through fine forest and moorland scenery. Though it is often harshly criticised for being overcrowded, and although this is far from a genuine wilderness experience, the route is still very beautiful and the forest sections in particular are attractive. The route passes to the south of Mawenzi before it crosses the desolate Saddle heading towards Kibo Hut. The summit ascent is then conducted via the Normal/Marangu Route on an arduous scree slope that culminates in the arrival at Gilman's Point on the crater rim. Uhuru Peak can then be reached from here.

The descent route for this particular trail is traditionally back along the Marangu Route. Steps are retraced from the summit to Horombo Hut, before you eventually walk off the mountain via the Marangu Gate.

Most people complete the route in only five days and as a consequence it has a surprisingly low success rate for getting trekkers to the top. Many people fail to acclimatise properly on the way up the mountain and as a result succumb to the debilitating effects of altitude on the final haul to the crater rim, or simply peak at Gillman's Point. In order to increase your chances of reaching Uhuru Peak, you should try to factor in an extra day for acclimatisation purposes. Ideally this should be taken at Horombo Hut, from where you can enjoy a number of fascinating side trips to explore various features of the mountain.

To the trailhead

The Marangu Route begins from the Kilimanjaro National Park Headquarters at the Marangu Gate. This is best accessed from the town of Marangu, on the south-east side of Kilimanjaro, some 40km from the town of Moshi. Most trekking companies will ensure that you are transported to the trailhead from where you are staying.

From Moshi, follow the sealed Arusha–Taveta road towards Dar es Salaam for just over 20km. At the small, bustling town of Himo, the road turns left and heads north for 13km to arrive at the sprawling, unkempt Marangu village. The fact that the road is paved all of the way to the village is a reflection of the economic impact that Kilimanjaro has had on the region in general and on Marangu in particular. In the centre of town, at the main junction, turn left again and follow the track uphill for 6km to the park gate. The journey from Moshi to the trailhead takes 45 minutes to an hour and represents a gain in altitude of almost 1000m.

At the park gate all of the formalities for entering the national park can be completed. This can be a laborious process and you should expect to spend up to an hour registering and paying the requisite park fees.

Huts and accommodation

The Marangu Route is the only route on the mountain to have sleeping huts provided at every night stop. A-frame buildings house communal dormitories, where basic bunks and sponge mattresses are supplied. The huts have solar powered lights and cold running water. Basic toilet facilities are also present at each hut. Groups dine together in a large

131

communal hut, resulting in a jovial, lively atmosphere and a great deal of interaction. It is often possible to purchase soft drinks, bottled water and even beer at the huts, although the prices increase as you climb higher up the mountain. Make sure that you carry small Tanzanian notes to pay for things bought along the route.

During the peak season, huts can sometimes be over full as a result of large groups altering their itineraries. As a result the facilities can become overstretched. ◄

The **first night stop is at Mandara Hut**. The lowest hut on the Marangu Route was originally constructed before World War I. It was christened Bismarck Hut, after the Iron Chancellor of Prussia in recognition of his significant role in the construction of the German Empire. The original stone hut has since been replaced by a series of comfortable wooden A-frame huts, built by a group of Norwegians as part of an aid programme. The largest hut comprises a communal dining area and an upstairs bunkroom. Smaller huts sleep up to eight people each. In total some 80 walkers can be accommodated here. There are flush toilets behind the main cabin. Water is retrieved from springs above the hut and is piped to the toilet block.

> Each hut has a number of tent pitches in the immediate vicinity and it is possible to camp at each site. Those camping can take advantage of the toilet and water facilities provided but are forbidden from using the hut dining or communal areas.

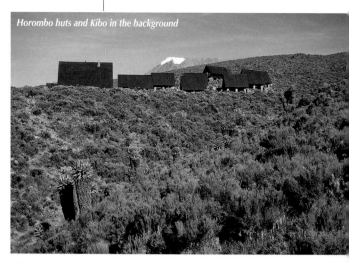
Horombo huts and Kibo in the background

The **second and fourth nights are spent at Horombo Hut**. This was originally named Peter's Hut, after Karl Peters, the German explorer and arch-imperialist. Similar to Mandara Hut, this vast complex comprises a number of wooden A-frame huts and resembles a small village. Horombo is designed to support up to 140 people, making it the busiest overnight stop on the entire mountain. Groups both ascending and descending the mountain use the site. There are flush toilets to the south-east of the main hut, down the slope a short distance. Water is piped from a stream to the north of the huts. It is forbidden to access the valley that contains the stream in a bid to ensure that the water supply remains clean and uncontaminated.

Kibo Hut, the third hut visited, is set at the foot of the final push to the summit. The original hut was built in 1932 and contained four bunks and a small stove. This has been replaced by a larger stone blockhouse that contains a small dining area and a number of dorm rooms that lead off a main corridor which sleeps around 50. A series of long-drop toilets are set to the south-west, behind the hut. There is no water available at Kibo Hut and all supplies must be carried here from the last water point on the ascent.

Stage	From–to	Distance	Time	Height Gain
1	Marangu Gate (1855m) Mandara Hut (2725m)	8km	3–4hrs	+870m
2	Mandara Hut (2725m) Horombo Hut (3720m)	12km	5–6hrs	+995m
3	Horombo Hut (3720m) Kibo Hut (4703m)	9km	5–6hrs	+983m

STAGE 1
Marangu Gate to Mandara Hut

This is a deceptively gentle introduction to the climb that may lull you into a false sense of security. The trail is clear and well maintained; consequently, you should be able to maintain a steady, gentle pace through the lower forest sections, ensuring that you arrive at Mandara Hut after 3–5hrs. If there have been quantities of rainfall, the going may be wet and slippery underfoot and the approach to the night's accommodation may take longer. You ought to aim to begin the route in the morning since the forest zone is prone to showers in the afternoons. Birds also tend to be more active first thing in the morning. This way you can enjoy a leisurely stroll through the forest and still have the afternoon spare to explore your surroundings.

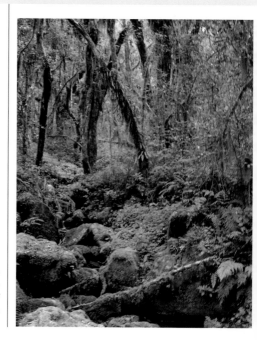

Typical montane cloud forest on early stage of Marangu Route

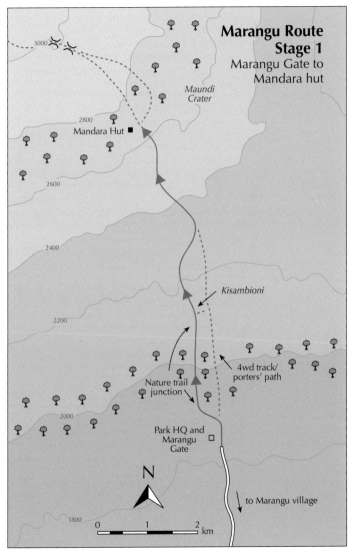

**Marangu Route
Stage 1**
Marangu Gate to
Mandara hut

3000

*Maundi
Crater*

2800
Mandara Hut ■

2600

2400

Kisambioni

2200

4wd track/
porters' path

Nature trail
junction

2000

Park HQ and
Marangu
Gate ☐

N

2 km
0   1

1800

to Marangu village

Near to the Marangu Gate is a **short detour** that visits a beautiful river gorge. Take the trail that leads to the left of the booking office and follow it west into a valley. Here there is a small waterfall, some tree ferns and a number of splendid trees whose huge oval leaves shade and shelter the smaller plants beneath.

The original 4WD track is still used by porters to help accelerate their ascent and to ease the footfall on the newly created route.

Away from the main gate you may see, or more likely hear, blue monkeys or black-and-white colobus monkeys moving through the tree tops as they search out and feed on fruits and leaves. Keep an ear out for the loud thrum of wings as Hartlaub's turaco flaps clumsily though the forest.

On the **drive to the Marangu Gate** take the time to observe your changing surroundings. At the National Park Gate you will be required to register and complete a series of formalities. Your guide ought to take responsibility for ensuring that you are registered correctly and that your park fees are paid in full. The process is protracted and slow and can take up to an hour to complete. In the interim, relax, stroll around the gate area and visit the small shop located here. If you find that you're missing a piece of kit, you can hire various bits (including gaiters and trekking poles) from the Kilimanjaro Guides Cooperative, who have a small hut at the gate. Admire the vast spreading *Albizia schimperiana* tree that supports the signboard at the trailhead and prepare yourself for the first stage of the ascent. ◄

Having completed all of the pre-trip preparations, the **ascent of Kilimanjaro begins** by following the broad, well-maintained path that leads north behind the booking office into the forest. Just beyond the gate, on the left-hand side of the path is an archway that marks the start of the trekker's path to Mandara Hut. A broad, 4WD track leads straight ahead. This used to be the main route up the mountain, but in response to overcrowding and erosion, the path has been re-routed slightly. ◄

The forest path, for walkers only, is a smaller trail that is nonetheless very clear. It provides more intimacy and interest as you pass through this beautiful, chaotic aspect of the mountain than the original Marangu Route did. The path climbs steeply but gently, passing beneath huge *Macarangu kilimandscharica* trees and on into denser, more verdant forest that limits the amount of light that penetrates to the forest floor. The path is well graded and has drainage channels cut alongside it. The trailsides are overgrown and the cascading vegetation hides quantities of scarlet and yellow *Impatiens kilimanjari*, violet *Impatiens pseudoviola* and the sweet-scented white *Begonia meyeri-johannis*. ◄

Shortly after the forest closes in there is a **signposted trail** to the left. This short nature trail loops to rejoin the main track about 2.5km further up. The main trail heads towards and then runs alongside a small stream. After an hour, the path passes a small pool to the right that is backed by a waterfall. If there has been any rain recently this can be a very attractive spot. There are also good views out over the plains to the west of Kilimanjaro here.

Crossing the stream on a small bridge, the path comes to a junction. The main trail continues straight on whilst a smaller path crosses a wooden bridge to **Kisambioni**, a picnic table and lunch area that lie adjacent to the 4WD track used by the porters. This site is approximately halfway between Marangu Gate and Mandara Hut.

The main trail continues its consistent climb, passing another side path and bridge as well as a couple of small waterfalls. As the path becomes a little rockier it bridges another small stream and steepens slightly. This marks the final ascent to Mandara Hut. The dense *Podocarp forest* becomes increasingly damp and bearded lichens, old-man's beard and other mosses become increasingly apparent, hanging from the trees like tattered lace. *Impatiens kilimanjari* continue to be visible amidst the tree roots and buttresses.

Half an hour after crossing the bridge, the forest gives way and you emerge into the clearing that houses **Mandara Hut** (2725m). ▸

The huts here are modern wooden A-frame buildings that have cold running water and flush toilet facilities. They can sleep up to 60 walkers. Surrounded by dense forest, they

This hut, or collection of huts, is named after the legendary local chieftain who terrorised so many of the early western explorers as they sought to access and ascend Kilimanjaro in the late 19th century.

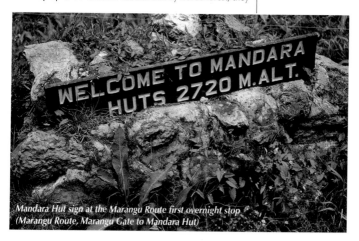

Mandara Hut sign at the Marangu Route first overnight stop (Marangu Route, Marangu Gate to Mandara Hut)

are frequently shrouded in mist during the afternoon and often have a peculiarly spectral air.

EXCURSIONS TO MAUNDI CRATER

If you arrive early and have the energy left to explore your surroundings, it is possible to stow your packs and clamber up nearby Maundi Crater (2800m). From Mandara Hut the path heads north through the last vestiges of forest and emerges onto the heath and moorland after 500m. Beyond a small bridge is a junction, signposted to Maundi Crater. This small parasitic cone on the south-east flank of Kilimanjaro is an interesting geological feature rich in wild flora.

The path climbs 500m to the top of the small grass and shrub-cloaked amphitheatre and affords you spectacular views on a clear day, both of the main peaks of Kibo and Mawenzi to the north and of Lakes Chala and Jipe to the south-east, as well as the distant Pare Mountains. The return trip to the top of Maundi Crater takes 1–1½hrs. (See Marangu Route Stage 2 map for outline of route.)

STAGE 2
Mandara Hut to Horombo Hut

This is an attractive day's walking that enables you to clear the confines of the forest and secure your first, inspirational views of Kibo and Mawenzi. The steady climb through the more exposed, bleaker heath and moorland is relatively gentle. The path is clear and even, ensuring that 5–6hrs of gentle walking should see you arrive at the village-like Horombo Hut complex.

From Mandara Hut the trail leads north though the remaining stretches of the forest zone. During this time the vegetation begins to change as *Podocarps* give way to giant heath trees (*Philippia excelsa*) and bushes of *Hypericum* and *Erica*.

After 500m the trail emerges from the forest, crosses a wooden bridge and forks. A **side path** leads right to Maundi Crater whilst the main trail curves north-north-west and heads towards the Saddle. ◄

It is possible to **detour to Maundi Crater** and then cut across the scrub to rejoin the main path 500m further up the trail.

The **main trail** skirts the base of Maundi Crater and progresses towards the higher reaches of Kilimanjaro. Crossing a further **two bridges** over frequently dry waterways, the path winds gently between a series of thickets

**Marangu Route
Stage 2**
Mandara Hut to
Horombo Hut

South Ridge

South-East
Ridge
Mawenzi

East
Ridge
Mawenzi

Horombo Hut

Numerous
small streams

Kambi Ya
Taabu

Kifunika
Hill

Mandara
Hut

Maundi
Crater

0   1   2 km

where the trees are festooned with lichen, before crossing several small bridges and ascending into the **open moorland**. The orangey-red path, visible between the tussocks of grass and heather, stretches into the distance enticingly. ◄

The trail undulates on its way to the Horombo escarpment, rising and falling as it negotiates a series of moorland ravines, which frequently have small streams running along the bottom. *Lobelias* can be seen growing in the damper, shadier parts of these ravines. As you drop into and then climb out of each hollow, the peaks of the mountain fall from view only to reappear fractionally closer as you clamber back up the other side.

The path climbs steeply onto a ridge and arrives at **Kambi Ya Taabu** 3.5hrs after leaving Mandara Hut; this is frequently used as a lunch stop. The picnic table and rickety shelter here mark the three-quarter point to Horombo Hut.

The section of track immediately beyond this point is exceptionally pleasant, especially if the weather is clear and

From here you will get your first proper views of Kilimanjaro's two main peaks, rugged Mawenzi in the foreground and snow-capped Kibo in the distance. Already looming large, the main summit is in fact still two days walk from this point.

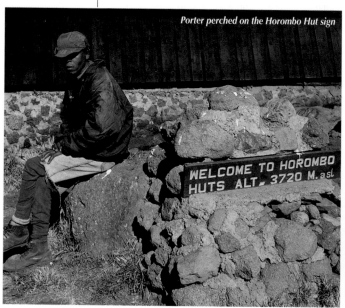

Porter perched on the Horombo Hut sign

warm. The gradient decreases and the path eases across the flank of Kilimanjaro through a very pretty stretch of grasses, heathers and wild flowers. The small, colourful flowers and the spikes of 'red hot pokers' stand out against the palette of greens, browns and yellows that constitute the moorland vegetation. ▸

The trail crosses a couple of **small streams** on little wooden bridges and climbs again to a point where you can see clearly up a *Senecio* filled valley. This valley lies to the north of the Horombo Hut and houses the stream that supplies the complex with water. Continuing to undulate, the path turns west to skirt a knoll and exposes the vast vista of plains and forest to the south of Kilimanjaro.

Having walked 1½hrs from Kambi Ya Taabu, the path rises sharply and enters a **rocky valley** at the foot of Mawenzi's southern lava ridges. The **Horombo Hut** (3720m) is situated here. As well as hut accommodation there are extensive camping sites. Mawenzi's craggy spires rise from behind a ridge to the north of the complex, while above the huts a clear stream runs through the flora-filled valley, allowing giant *Senecio* and *Lobelia* to flourish. You must not enter this valley for any reason since you risk contaminating the hut's water supply. ▸

Horombo Hut is a lively, noisy overnight stop, as a great many groups collect here. Both those going up the mountain on the Marangu Route and those on their way down from either the Marangu or Rongai Routes use the huts. In addition, those opting to spend an additional day ascending on the Marangu Route for acclimatisation purposes are likely to do so here, further adding to the press of bodies.

Directly below Horombo Hut are some interesting lava flows. The surface of these flows cooled more rapidly than their molten interiors, creating a tube-like crust. This crust sealed in the volcanic gasses and insulated the molten lava from the cool air, allowing it to continue to flow downhill, leaving behind a hollow tunnel. The hot interior lava re-fused some of the tube lava, which consequently re-crystallised as a glassy rock. Fragments of this can be seen all around the hut site.

A large section of the mountainside here was badly damaged by a series of massive wild fires. The evidence of these fires is still visible, with blackened shrubs, charred branches and ashy plants apparent along the path. However, there has been considerable regeneration in the interim period and new growth is flourishing.

As well as supporting a large number of walkers and their porters, the Horombo area is densely populated by four-striped mice. These opportunists have taken to scavenging for scraps and leftovers in and around the huts and during particularly mild seasons their numbers can reach plague proportions.

OPTIONAL ACCLIMATISATION DAY TO ZEBRA ROCK

If you choose to spend an extra day acclimatising on the Marangu Route, you are most likely to spend it based at Horombo Hut. On the extra day try to persuade your guide to climb above the hut with you to explore the lower section of the Saddle. Follow the path as it leaves Horombo Hut and walk north-west until you reach a junction. Take the right-hand fork, which heads north towards Mawenzi and the Mawenzi Hut.

After walking 1.5km from Horombo Hut, on the edge of the moorland zone, is a low, overhung cliff. Water seeping down the rock face from above has left pale encrustations deposited on the dark lava. The light and dark vertical bands on the cliff have led to this feature being known prosaically as Zebra Rock. From

The distinctively patterned Zebra Rock

here it is also possible to explore the area around the lower slopes of Mawenzi, admiring its dramatic fluted visage and many shattered ridges. (See the map for Marangu Route Stage 3.)

STAGE 3
Horombo Hut to Kibo Hut

By this stage the enormity of Kilimanjaro will begin to sink in; the 5–6hr ascent from Horombo Hut to Kibo Hut is a lengthy trudge across the very exposed, starkly beautiful Saddle that allows you to contemplate the great mound of Kibo rising ahead of you. As you plod across the barren highland desert you will be rewarded with great views of Kibo and Mawenzi, at least until the clouds boil in and obscure the summits.

The trail **leaves Horombo Hut** and heads north-west then north, climbing steeply through an area of changing vegetation. As you gain height, the variety and quantity of plants diminishes and they become smaller, hardier species. Heathers and everlastings replace the last of the *Senecio* as you wind between large boulder outcrops.

There are **two routes to the Saddle**, the Eastern Path and the Western Path that merge again at Jiwe Lainkoyo. The first junction that you encounter, which branches right from the main path, is the start of the less regularly used **Eastern Path**. This stony and badly eroded track veers north, past Zebra Rock, before curving north-west at East Lava Hill and bending left to pass by West Lava Hill and a pair of tarns. The path continues north, curving north-west past the junction with the North Circuit Path and crosses the Saddle to the north of Middle Red Hill before converging once more with the main Marangu Route at Jiwe Lainkoyo.

The **Western Path**, which is the most commonly ascended of the two, continues west from the junction with the Eastern Path briefly, before forking again. The left-hand fork here joins the South Circuit Path, which contours across the side of the mountain below the Saddle before curving around the southern side of Kibo to link up with the southern and western forest/moorland approach routes and the other summit access routes.

Take the right-hand fork instead and head north then north-west, gradually gaining height. After an hour's walking the path crosses the **Maua River**, where you can collect water. The path continues on this setting, rising and falling as

143

Marangu Route
Stage 3 Horombo Hut to Kibo Hut

it traverses the rumpled flank of the mountain, until it reaches the official, signposted **last water point** on this route. There are picnic tables adjacent to the stream. ▸

About an hour beyond the last water signpost, is another sign indicating that you are arriving on **the Saddle**. Hans Meyer recorded that when breaching the Saddle in the 19th century, he encountered six-foot drifts of snow on the southern slopes. This is likely to be an alien situation for most modern walkers since the Saddle is resolutely bare for much of the year now. Occasional blizzards do blanket the barren landscape in snow, but even without a white dusting, the expanse of sterile desertesque landscape is harshly beautiful.

The path continues to meander through this desolate place over orangey-red lava gravel, between small boulders and lava bombs and amidst tough tufty grasses and everlastings. The path passes to the south of **Middle Red Hill**, which provides some shelter from the gusting wind that bustles across the Saddle, and then bends to the north of the **Triplets**, some of Kibo's many parasitic cones.

Just north of the Triplets **the two approach routes from Horombo Hut merge at Jiwe Lainkoyo**, whose name translates as 'the painted rock'. This is reputed to be an old campsite once popular with local hunters. A third path that heads

This is the highest running water on the Marangu Route, though in reality it is a small, muddy stream that is generally inferior in quality to the Maua River. The explorer and mountaineer Hans Meyer named this point Schneequelle, meaning 'snow stream', since the stream he encountered here on his first ascent of Kilimanjaro emerged from a snow drift at that time.

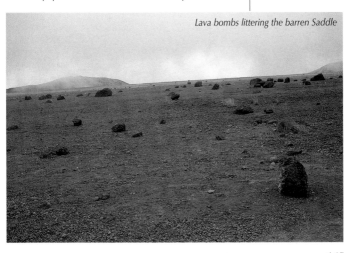
Lava bombs littering the barren Saddle

across the northern side of the Saddle from Mawenzi T.
Hut converges with the two from the south here as well.

The broad path then heads west directly towards Kil
Although the Kibo Hut is visible in the distance, it is stil
soul destroying hour trudge further on through an incre
ingly bleak landscape. Ascending past a large rocky outc
the path arrives at the wind blasted, basic stone blockhou
that comprise **Kibo Hut**. Sunk into the foothills of Kibo, **
is a fairly hostile place to wait and prepare for the ea
morning ascent to Gillman's Point and Uhuru Peak. ◄

There are fine
views to be enjoyed
though of Mawenzi's
austere, arresting
west face, visible
across the curving
slope of the Saddle.

Continuing on from Kibo Hut

From Kibo Hut the Normal/Marangu Route heads up Kib
eastern scree slopes to Gillman's Point on the crater r
amidst the eastern ice terraces (see Summit Ascent Rou
section). From here it is then possible to access the act
summit of the mountain.

B: Umbwe Route

Time on the mountain (ascent, summit ascent and descent):	5 days
Length:	44km
Altitude gain:	2800m
Grade:	Hard
Start:	Umbwe Gate
Finish:	Barranco Hut
Summit ascent routes:	Western Breach or Barafu Route
Optional extra days:	An extra day can be spent either at Barranco Hut or at Lava Tower on the Western Breach ascent, or Barranco Hut and Karanga Valley on the Barafu ascent
Descent route:	Mweka route
End trek:	Mweka Gate

The Umbwe Route is an exceptionally direct, beautiful method of scaling Kilimanjaro's western flank. The mountaineer Iain Allen wrote that, 'An ascent of Kibo by the Umbwe Route is one of the finest non-technical mountaineering expeditions in East Africa'. Lying between and parallel to the Machame and Mweka Routes, the Umbwe Route is a very steep, wild, exhilarating climb. As a consequence it is rarely used and should only be considered by more experienced, acclimatised walkers.

The standard version of the route, opened in 1963, provides the shortest ascent route to Kilimanjaro's Western Breach and summit ascent routes. The trail scales the thickly forested slopes beneath the Great Barranco Valley before climbing to Barranco Hut. Walkers then have the option of accessing the summit via the Western Breach or of detouring around Kibo via the South Circuit Path to approach the summit from Barafu Hut. Regardless of your eventual summit path, you will be required to descend via the Mweka Route.

The climb showcases some of Kilimanjaro's finest features and the views from Barranco Hut are outstanding. The sense of isolation and wildness on this route is the main lure for walkers. The downside to using the Umbwe Route is that the rapid ascent to altitude doesn't allow much time for proper acclimatisation.

The climb generally only takes five days to complete. However, there is scope to build in additional, vital acclimatisation days on the ascent; if planning to attempt the Western Breach there is the option to spend an extra night at Barranco Hut or higher at Lava Tower; otherwise, on the Barafu Route you may wish to consider spending an extra day at the Barranco Hut or stopping overnight in the attractive Karanga Valley.

To the trailhead

The Umbwe Route begins at the Umbwe Gate. The gate is amidst Kilimanjaro's western foothills at 1650m. Your outfitter will organise transport to the Marangu Gate (where you must register and pay the requisite park fees) and then on to the Umbwe Gate.

To reach the Umbwe Gate, follow the Moshi–Arusha Road west from Moshi for 15km. At the junction with Lyamungo Road, turn right and head north. When the road arrives at a T-junction, turn right and head towards the village of Mango. Before reaching the village take the left-hand turn signposted to Umbwe village. This track climbs to Umbwe village, mission and school. The Umbwe Park Gate is located several kilometres beyond the village up a dusty 4WD track. The drive to the gate from Moshi takes 1½hrs.

Huts and accommodation

There are no sleeping huts on this little-used ascent route though at higher elevations there are the traditional metal uniports at each campsite. Everyone ascending the Umbwe Route is required to camp.

The **first campsite, Cave Campsite**, is adjacent to a shallow cave that is in reality little more than an enlarged overhang. The **second campsite, at the Barranco Hut**, is next to the old, corrugated uniport. At both of these sites there are long-drop toilets. There are also obvious water sources in the vicinity of each site.

Above this point you will climb to either the **Lava Tower** or **Arrow Glacier campsites** to reach the Western Breach or cross to the Barafu Hut to begin the Barafu Route to crater rim. There are no huts below the Western Breach – the uniport at Arrow Glacier was destroyed by a rockfall a number of years ago and hasn't been replaced. There however two old uniports at **Barafu**. Built in 1968 these are now essentially only aged and dirty shells. There are long-drop toilets at each of these points. It is important to note that there are no water sources at Lava Tower, Arrow Glacier or Barafu Huts. All supplies must be carried to these points.

Stage	From–to	Distance	Time	Height Gain
1	Umbwe Gate (1650m) Cave Camp (2940m)	9km	4–6hrs	+1290m
2	Cave Camp (2940m) Barranco Hut (3965m)	5km	4–5hrs	+1025m
Onwards:	Barranco Hut (3965m) Barafu Hut (4640m)	8km	7–8hrs	+675m

STAGE 1
Umbwe Gate to Cave Camp

The first day on the Umbwe Route comprises a relatively short, sharp ascent up Kilimanjaro's western flank. The path climbs a ridge through thick, lush forest to arrive at Cave Camp on the upper limits of the forest zone.

Having registered at the Marangu Gate, your outfitter will convey you around the skirts of Kilimanjaro to the Umbwe Gate. **From the gate** the trail quickly enters thick forest and begins to ascend north-east along an increasingly narrow ridge. The vegetation is so tightly packed that it appears to surround and bear down on the trail and obscures much of the sunlight and certainly prevents you from enjoying any views of the summit ahead. In the gloom it is still possible to detect swathes of *Impatiens kilimanjari* and *Impatiens pseudoviola* nestled amongst the buttressed tree roots. Bright balsam flowers add vibrant splashes of colour to the myriad of greens surrounding the path.

149

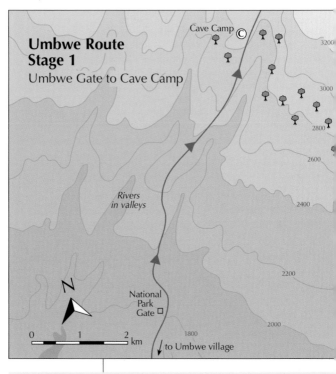

**Umbwe Route
Stage 1**
Umbwe Gate to Cave Camp

Cave Camp ©

3200

3000

2800

2600

*Rivers
in valleys*

2400

2200

N

National
Park
Gate □

2000

0   1   2 km

1800

to Umbwe village

The trail today is far more accessible than it used to be. The mountaineers Ro(
Taylor and Henry Barber used the Umbwe Route to access the foot of the Breac
Wall on their ill-fated attempt to be the first to scale it in 1978. Taylor recorde
the ascent, noting that, 'Side by side we begin together, groping our way up th
trail, a six–inch gap between two bushes, a slight crimp in waist-high weeds,
dimpled depression in the black peaty mud. It is not so much a path we follov
as our intuition'.

The path scrambles **up a ridge** between two vall
The **Umbwe River** flows to the right and the **Lonzo R**
to the left of the arête the path snakes along. Tree r

and ruts make the going uneven, but do ensure that there are handholds available to haul yourself up the steeper sections of path. The way is generally clear and obvious, but red splashes of paint on trail-side trees act as a reassurance that you are indeed heading in the right direction.

After 4–5hrs the path reaches a cave, just within the forest zone. The cave is ostensibly a large overhung wall made of slotted blocks that appear to be stacked perfectly and give the impression of a charred half igloo. This is **Cave Camp** (2940m). A flat area adjacent to the cave has a number of tent pitches cleared. Water is readily available here, probably most easily from a small pool 15m back along the approach trail.

STAGE 2
Cave Camp to Barranco Hut

The relentless climb towards Kibo continues, and as it does so, the path steepens and narrows before breaking out of the forest, weaving through the rampant heath and edging along the rim of the Great Barranco Valley before arriving at the Barranco Hut.

From Cave Camp, the trail climbs north-east once more. After ½hr the path breaks clear of the forest and passes onto the heath/moorland zone. Heathers and tussock grasses are abundant here. Shortly after leaving the forest the path arrives at the foot of a **10m high cliff**. There are a series of rocky steps, branches and roots here to help you scramble up this minor obstacle.

Above the cliff you will be able to see the western face of Kibo and the Southern Icefields for the first time; the initial view is immense and quite intimidating. Afternoon mist and cloud may obscure the summit though. The trail continues to climb and 1½hrs after leaving Cave Camp it reaches the **first of two higher caves**. These shallow overhangs at 3500m and 3780m offer little protective shelter. There are good water sources in their vicinity though and these can be reached by dropping down to a spring on the western side

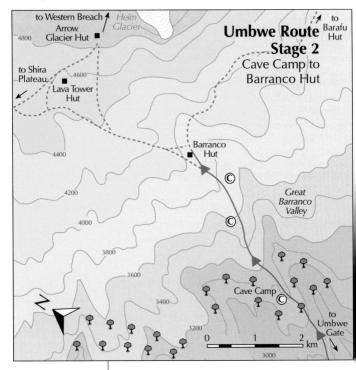

to Western Breach ↑ *Heim*
Arrow *Glacier*
4800 Glacier Hut ■

to Shira
Plateau 4600
■
Lava Tower
Hut

4400

4200

4000

3800

3600

3400

3200

3000

↗ to
Barafu
Hut

Umbwe Route
Stage 2
Cave Camp to
Barranco Hut

Barranco
■ Hut

©

©

Great
Barranco
Valley

Cave Camp ©

to
Umbwe
Gate

0   1   2 km

This deep valley was created as a result of an enormous landslip that gouged out part of Kilimanjaro's flank and created the Western Breach in the crater rim.

of the path. By now the track has begun to edge above the **Great Barranco Valley**. ◄

Alongside the path there are vertiginous drops of up to 400m to the Umbwe River at the foot of the valley.

Above the **second cave** the incline decreases slightly and the trail becomes easier and broader. The **path forks** 500m beyond the **third cave**; the left-hand fork veers north towards Lava Tower and Arrow Glacier. Ignore this and continue in a north-easterly direction along the right-hand fork for a further 500m until you arrive at the **Barranco Hut** (3965m).

There are numerous tent pitches and a couple of long-drop toilets located here near the hut, which is surrounded by *groundsel* and *Lobelia*. Water can be fetched from a stream 5 minutes further up the valley. The shabby green uniport is

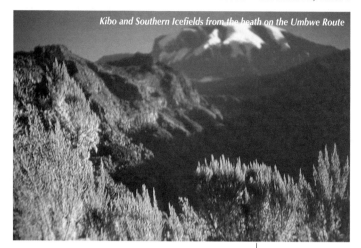

Kibo and Southern Icefields from the heath on the Umbwe Route

delightfully sited and is frequently adjudged to be the most dramatic campsite on the mountainside. ▶

The views ahead, beyond the scree and moraines, of Kilimanjaro's snow-capped summit are similarly dramatic. The rugged gash of the Western Breach disturbs the uniformity of the crater rim and the vast Heim Glacier hugs the curving dome closely. Kibo's bleak, savage beauty is encapsulated in this image.

The views back down the Great Barranco Valley, over the forest, or across to the looming Barranco Wall are especially impressive.

Continuing from the Umbwe Route

From here the trail now **joins the South Circuit Path**, from where you are faced with two alternatives. You can **either head north** towards the Lava Tower and approach the tricky **Western Breach** from Arrow Glacier, **or turn east** and cross the conspicuously rumpled slopes of Kibo's southern face to arrive at Barafu Hut (see Day 4 of Barranco Route, Barranco hut to Barafu hut) in order to make a final ascent to Uhuru via the **Barafu Route**. (See Summit Ascent Routes for summit route descriptions.)

OPTIONAL ACCLIMATISATION DAY

Whichever option you plump for, you would do well to consider building an additional day in to your itinerary to supplement your acclimatisation. This can either be taken en-route to your final nights camp or here at Barranco Hut. The advantages of taking an extra day at Barranco Hut are multiple; the hut is particularly attractive and magnificently located in an area of outstanding beauty that merits further exploration. From here you are ideally situated to explore the stunning Great Barranco Valley, scale the imposing Barranco Wall, revel in the heady views and even make an approach to the classic technical climbing route over the Heim Glacier.

To reach the Heim Glacier from the top of the Barranco Wall follow a faint trail marked by occasional cairns that leads in an easterly direction along a rocky rib directly towards the morraines and scree that litter the snout of the Heim Glacier. The scramble to the foot of the glacier takes over 2hrs from the top of the Barranco Wall. Allow at least 6hrs for the return trip from the Barranco Hut.

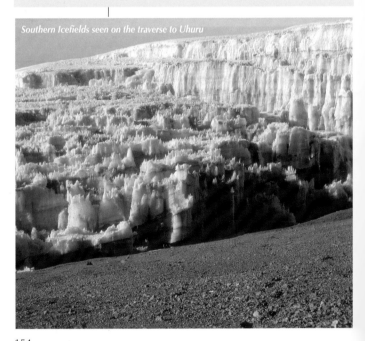
Southern Icefields seen on the traverse to Uhuru

C: Machame Route

Time on the mountain (ascent, summit ascent and descent):	6 days
Length:	61km
Height Gain:	2800
Grade:	Hard
Start:	Machame Gate
Finish:	Barafu Hut
Summit ascent routes:	Western Breach or Barafu Route
Optional extra days:	Karanga Valley on the way to Barafu hut if using Barafu Route to the crater rim. No obvious place on Western Breach final ascent route
Descent route:	Mweka Route
End trek:	Mweka Gate or Kidia Village

The Machame Route is the westernmost route to scale the southern slopes of Kilimanjaro. It is often considered to be the finest forest/moorland ascent route on the mountain. Hans Meyer wrote that, 'Without doubt Kibo is most imposing as seen from the west. Here it rises in solemn majesty, and the eye is not distracted by the sister peak of Mawenzi, of which nothing is to be seen but a single jutting pinnacle. The effect is enhanced by the magnificent flowing sweep of the outline, the dazzling extent of the icecap, the vast stretch of the forest, the massive breadth of the base, and the jagged crest of the Shira Spur as it branches away towards the west'.

When teamed with either an ascent of the Western Breach or more commonly with the Barafu Route to the crater rim and the Mweka descent route, this is one of the most lovely, complete outings on the mountain.

The route is slightly more challenging than some of the other forest/moorland routes but, like the other routes described here, it does not require any technical ability. Although the terrain is in parts tougher to negotiate than on other routes, the variety of vegetation, scenery and the stunning views of the Shira Plateau, the Western Breach and Kibo make this a highly attractive option.

The Machame and Mweka Routes used to simply be rough tracks used by the park rangers or groups of mountaineers looking to access the technical climbing

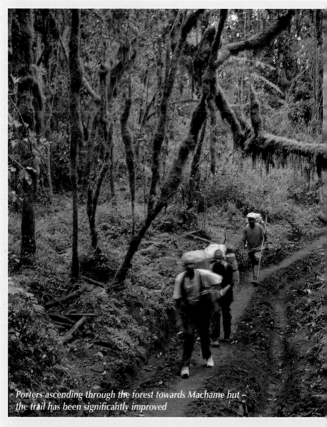

*Porters ascending through the forest towards Machame hut –
the trail has been significantly improved*

routes on this side of Kibo. Although improvements were made to the Machame
trail in the 1970s, it wasn't until the 1990s that it began to gain in popularity as
people recognised its myriad charms and began to appreciate that it offers you
a better chance to acclimatise whilst ascending. Subsequently, it has become
known as the 'whiskey route', since it is harder, more expensive and much more
intoxicating than the 'Coca-Cola route' (Marangu Route). A lot of work has been
done in recent years to improve the track conditions and promote this route as an
alternative to the Marangu Route, largely to reduce the pressure of numbers on

the main tourist path. The result has been a significant upgrade in the track quality, which in turn has ensured that there has been a marked increase in foot traffic on this side of the mountain. The route is at least as popular as the Marangu Route. As the total number of users has multiplied so the campsites have swelled under the wave of new interest, meaning this route is no longer the wilderness experience it once was.

The success rate for reaching Uhuru has traditionally always been higher on the Machame Route than on the Marangu Route. No doubt this has been at least partly due to the fact that it provides a longer ascent and that consequently you are allowed to acclimatise better ahead of the final summit bid. It is also likely that the greater success was also in part due to only more experienced groups choosing to ascend Kilimanjaro via this route. With the popularisation of the Machame Route, the percentage of people that successfully summit may fall as less capable groups opt to try this ascent route rather than the traditional Marangu Route.

The path begins climbing slowly through thick, leafy forest on the west flank of Kilimanjaro before emerging on the moorland. It then takes in the dramatic Shira Plateau, providing a glimpse of an unusual side of the mountain, before joining the South Circuit Path and contouring around the southern face of Kibo. The final summit bid can be made either via the perilous Western Breach, from Lava Tower and Arrow Glacier Hut, or, more usually, via the Barafu Route, which is reached by circumnavigating the peak beneath the spectacular Southern Icefields. Descent from the summit is then conducted on the Mweka Route, which drops quickly and steeply off the southern side of Kilimanjaro by way of the Mweka Hut to finish at the Mweka Gate.

To the Trailhead

The Machame Route begins from Machame Gate, adjacent to Machame village on the south-western side of the mountain. All of the registration formalities can be completed at the national park office here. Park fees are also paid at this point. Your outfitter will ensure that you are ferried to the gate by bus.

Machame village is 25km from the town of Moshi. To reach the village, follow the tarmac road from Moshi first west and then north for 45 minutes. Machame village itself is a straggling affair set amid fertile farmland. The final 3km approach to Machame Gate is through a series of banana and coffee plantations and via a small stretch of natural forest; it takes 15 minutes. The road that scales the final ridge to bring you to the gate is only a dirt track, but it is clear and well maintained. The gate itself is at 1800m.

There are toilet facilities at the gate. Local men are often stationed by the gate in a bid to sell walkers water, gaiters, trekking poles, some fashioned from tree branches.

Huts and accomodation

Everyone on the Machame Route is **obliged to camp**. Although there are a series of old corrugated metal uniports along the trail, walkers are not intended to use them. The uniports all old and generally in a state of disrepair. Adjacent to each these huts is an area cleared for camping. There are long-drop toilet facilities at each of the campsites, as well as, with the exception of the Barafu Hut, good water sources. Barafu is and all water supplies must be carried to this point.

The basic Machame Hut is a tatty uniport. There is park ranger stationed here who will require you to register once you arrive at the campsite. The Shira Hut is a similar basic structure that is in such a state that most groups actually choose to camp south of the hut by the Shira Cave even further south, at the Shira Camp. The Barranco Hut, erected in 1966, is idyllically located but it is nonetheless little shabby. There are two small uniports at Barafu that date from the 1960s. Set amidst a desolate lava landscape they are as inhospitable as they look.

Stage	From–to	Distance	Time	Height Gain
1	Machame Gate (1820m) Machame Hut (3015m)	11km	5–6hrs	+1195m
2	Machame Hut (3015m) Shira Camp (3840m)	6km	5–6hrs	+825m
3	Shira Camp (3840m) Barranco Hut (3965m)	10km	5–6hrs	+125m
4	Barranco Hut (3965m) Barafu Hut (4640m)	8km	7–8hrs	+675m

STAGE 1
Machame Gate to Machame Hut

This is a fairly gentle introduction to climbing Kilimanjaro, which passes through some of the finest forest scenery to encircle the mountain. Ascending steadily on a straightforward path, you are transported through lush montane cloud forest to arrive at the Machame Hut on the edge of the heath/moorland zone.

Having completed the requisite formalities and registration requirements at the gate, you **start the ascent by following a broad 4WD dirt track** as it loops around the warden's hut and begins to climb north and then north-east into the forest.

The 4WD track rapidly dwindles and within 3km is reduced to a single track. At the end of the 4WD track is a **signpost**. Reached 15 minutes after leaving the gate, it states that the Machame Route is only to be used as an ascent route. The path from this stage used to be a rough and unkempt way to access Kilimanjaro that involved scrambling over tree roots and up slippery, uneven sections of mountainside. However, a great deal of work has been carried out on this lower section of the route and the path is now well graded and even. Roots have been covered or cleared and drainage ditches dug alongside the track to ensure that it doesn't degenerate into a river channel during the heavy rains. In some places the new track crosses the remains of the older path and you can see just how different the two are. The transformation should make you appreciate just how much hard work has gone into creating the current highway. Although still ongoing at the time of writing, the path improvements are due to finish in early 2005 and should see the track up-graded all of the way from the gate to Machame Hut.

The path meanders through close, intensely green forest where lianas and mosses cover camphor, cedar, juniper and olive trees. ▶

The track rises along an increasingly vertiginous ridge, although the drops to either side are largely obscured by the thick vegetation. What breaks in the undergrowth there are reveal stunning views across forest-blanketed ridges. There

The endemic *Impatiens kilimanjari* is also prevalent here, as are *Impatiens pseudoviola* and *Viola eminii*. This stretch of the forest is particularly attractive. Birdlife here is abundant and vocal, although you will need to have quick eyes or boundless reserves of patience to actually see the turacos, hornbills and other avifauna that are creating the diverting sounds.

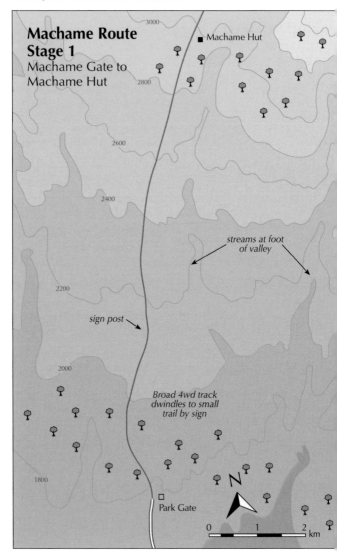

**Machame Route
Stage 1**
Machame Gate to
Machame Hut

■ Machame Hut

3000

2800

2600

2400

*streams at foot
of valley*

2200

sign post

2000

*Broad 4wd track
dwindles to small
trail by sign*

1800

□ Park Gate

N

0   1   2 km

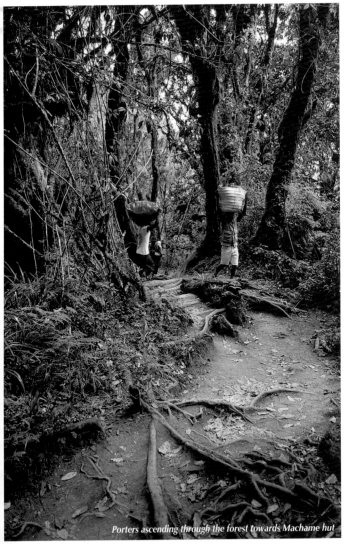

Porters ascending through the forest towards Machame hut

is a lot of interest here and you should walk slowly carefully, absorbing what's around you.

After 2½hrs the trail passes through a **large clea** in the forest that is often used as a lunch stop. There long-drop toilet here. After this point the gradient incre somewhat as the ridge steepens slightly. To the north you frequently hear the sound of water, rising from the stre which runs parallel to the track, at the foot of the ravine. also possible to spot a miniature waterfall to the right of track where another small stream passes close by the of the ridge. The path continues to ascend through the est on a clearly discernable path for a further 2½hrs. As track improvement had yet to reach this stage at the tim writing, there are still roots, ruts and other obstacles along path to be negotiated.

The forest then thins dramatically and changes c acter noticeably; the larger trees loaded with moss and man's beard merge with and then give way to giant heat and scrub. Scarlet *Gladiolus watsonioides* and red and low red-hot pokers lie amongst the grasses. A signpost a cent to the track warns of potential fire hazards and the ris dropping lit cigarettes in this often tinderbox-dry area.

After 15 minutes of this transformation beginning, path breaks cover and arrives at **Machame Hut** (3015

Trees festooned with Old Man's Beard at Machame hut

There are a handful of tent pitches along the approach to the battered uniport, but the majority of the pitches are on the higher ground above the hut. There should be a park warden resident in the hut who will require you to sign a register upon arrival. He can also sell you water or even beer at this point. There are long-drop toilet facilities in the vicinity of the hut and water can be retrieved from a small stream found 30m from the campsite to the north-west of the site, down a steep slope.

Unfortunately the campsite is frequently cloaked in mist and low cloud during the afternoon, so views of the mountain will be obscured. Early mornings are often clear though and you will be able to see the dome of Kibo rising above a ridge to the east. Looking the other way, out across the plains to the south-west, you will be able to pick out Mount Meru amidst the morning haze.

STAGE 2
Machame Hut to Shira Camp

Following an energetic start to the day and an aggressive ascent of a steep volcanic fin that juts out of the mountainside, the terrain levels and the path eases onto the Shira Plateau, an atmospheric, ancient part of Kilimanjaro.

As the early morning sun climbs above Kibo to the east of Machame Hut, **follow the path that heads north-east** towards a rocky ridge. The ridge protrudes from the mountain and is clearly visible from the Machame Hut. As you traipse up through the scrub, keep an eye open for glimpses of Kibo to your right, looming larger as you climb above the surrounding foothills. There are several clearings on the ascent, the first reached half an hour after leaving the hut site; from here you can gaze back over Machame Hut and the closely packed canopy of trees that stretch westwards towards Mount Meru.

The path loops from one side of the ridge to the other, crossing the crest of the ridge several times. As the path

Machame Route Stage 2
Machame Hut to Shira Camp

Large white-necked ravens often scavenge here and can be seen soaring above the area or hopping awkwardly from boulder to boulder in search of scraps. The route ahead is also visible from here and it is possible to make out the path as it skirts the head of the ▶

climbs, the vegetation around it alters and you find yourself leaving the skeletal trees to walk amidst hardy tussock grasses and *Senecio*. There are several large boulders on the ridge top that offer a superb view east to Kibo, although mid-morning cloud frequently mounts up and obscures the summit.

The path arrives at the foot of an **eight-metre-high semi-circular rock cliff** 2hrs after leaving Machame Hut. The ascent used to be relatively straightforward, amounting to nothing more than a scramble, but it has been further simplified with the recent creation of some cut steps in the rock face.

Having surmounted this obstacle, the path drops into a relatively sheltered, scenic **valley** dotted with *Senecio* and everlastings. This is usually the point where groups pause to have lunch. ◀

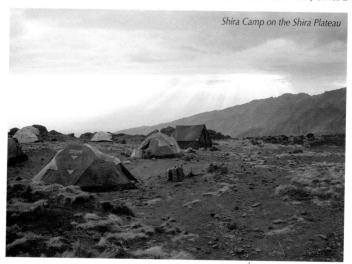

Shira Camp on the Shira Plateau

The path eases horizontally across a steep slope above the head of the valley. It crosses several small, smooth streambeds before clambering past a series of large boulders and rocky outcrops onto the flatter, easier ground of the **Shira Plateau**. The path then meanders over the plateau on an almost level gradient, winding around rocky patches of shale

◀ valley beneath the lip of the Shira Plateau, before rising north to access the plateau.

The plateau is exposed and barren, but has a number of fascinating features. From the campsite you'll be able to see the striking, jagged Shira Ridge edge to the west, about 1–1½hr walk away. The three high points on the sheer ridge, looking west to east, are the Shira Needle, Shira Cathedral and East Shira Hill. The Shira Needle has a small, precarious summit that can be reached by scrambling awkwardly up a serious rock face. The Shira Cathedral is a dramatic rock buttress set amidst a series of pinnacles and spires, with sheer drops of several hundred metres apparent on the southern face. The small rounded, grassy peak behind this ridge is the Shira Cone (3840m), which is also known as Cone Place. The highest point on the plateau is its far western extremity, where Johnsell Point (3962m) and Klute Peak are visible behind the Shira Cone. If you pan left from the end of the ridge, you'll get great views of Mount Meru to the south-west, particularly at sunset when the sun drops below the horizon adjacent to Meru's perfect cone.

Shiny black chunks of obsidian, formed by the very rapid solidification of lava, litter the Shira Plateau and act as potent reminders that this area is in fact the remains of the oldest of the three volcanic cones that comprise the Kilimanjaro massif. Indeed the final descent to the campsite, across the caldera, is on a giant solidified lava flow, clearly visible amidst the dust and gravel beneath your feet.

and clumps of everlastings. *Lobelias* also appear here for the first time. ◄

Continuing north, the path arrives at a rough cleared patch of ground an hour after the lunch stop. This is the overnight campsite for most groups. The **Shira Camp** (3840m) is just south of the Shira Cave and about 30 minutes south of the Shira Hut, which sits on the Shira Route to Kibo. At the campsite there are long-drop toilets, and a clean stream can be found some 10 minutes to the south-east of the site.

STAGE 3
Shira Camp to Barranco Hut

This is a superb day's walking that showcases some of Kilimanjaro's finest features. The path climbs across the Shira Plateau to a high point by Lava Tower, before dropping into the Barranco Valley to arrive at Barranco Hut, a mere 110m higher than the day's start point. This climb-high, sleep-low approach to scaling Kilimanjaro maximises your ability to acclimatise and improves your chance of successfully reaching the summit. The views of the Shira Plateau, Lava Tower and the western face of Kibo are sumptuous, and the final campsite affords you with some of Kilimanjaro's classic viewpoints.

From the Shira Camp, the path heads east across the Shira Plateau, aiming directly towards Kibo. As it negotiates the rocky plateau, the path intersects one that leads from Shira Cave. The path climbs gently east along a fin of petrified lava, undulating across the creases of the plateau.

After 2½hrs, **the track is joined** from the left by a small trail that leads from the Shira Hut and is part of the Shira and Lemosho Routes. Ignore the junction and continue on what is now technically part of the **South Circuit Path**. The path veers south-east, drops into a broad, rock-strewn valley and then regains the lost height, rising evenly and gently towards Kibo. To the left of Kibo, in the foreground is a line of hills; this is the Oehler Ridge. The path leads in a southerly direction and passes through an area of interesting rock formations.

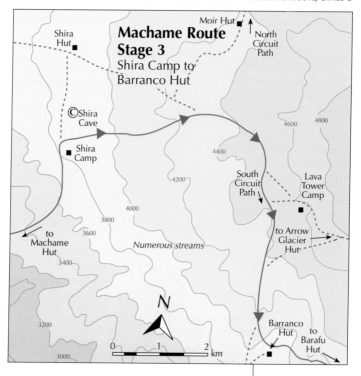

Large boulders are perched precariously on eroded plinths of smaller stones bound together by mud, providing surreal looking sculptures. The rocks are variously patterned with grey and orange lichens and provide scant protection for small clumps of everlastings. There is a very real sense of being in the wilderness here. The walk in towards Kibo is startlingly austere. Ahead the impressive ice-frosted cliffs of Kibo are visible as are the first views of the Western Breach.

If the weather is clear the views are astounding. Swirling cloud teases and tantalises you with glimpses of the summit. The high speed winds that race across the summit create unusual cloud formations and can cause a cloud cap to form that sits snugly atop the summit.

CLIMBING THE LAVA TOWER

Regardless of which ascent to Uhuru Peak you plan to undertake, most groups will follow the left-hand fork, which climbs slightly up to the Lava Tower. In order to get the best possible views of the Western Breach. Climb the tower itself and make the most of being at a higher altitude before descending to a lower height to camp at Barranco Hut. The scramble up the northern side of the Lava Tower is not clearly indicated at any point. Ask your guide to show you the way and take extreme caution whilst climbing the steep rock face. There are exemplary 360° panoramic views from the top of the tower. The sheer immensity of the landscape seen from here is staggering. The return trip takes half an hour from the foot of the Tower.

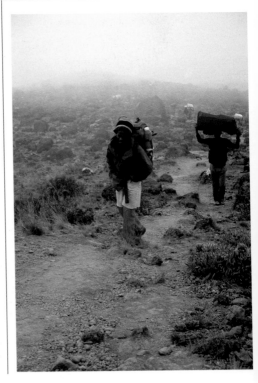

Porters approaching the Lava Tower

After half an hour the **path splits**, with forks passing either side of a distinctive, black wedge-shaped outcrop of rock. **To the left** of this landmark is the orange-black volcanic plug known as the **Lava Tower** (4655m). Those groups tackling the Western Breach ascent to the crater rim will camp in the lee of the Lava Tower overnight before climbing to Arrow Glacier Hut for their summit ascent attempt. **The Western Breach Route from Lava Tower to Uhuru Peak is described in the Summit Ascent Routes section.**

The right-hand fork, on the other hand, passes to the south of the Lava Tower, beyond the wedge-shaped rock outcrop. It is rejoined by the path descending from the Lava Tower after 1km. Whilst you will probably detour to the Lava Tower with your guide, your porters will almost certainly take this route, since it is a shorter, more direct route to the Barranco Valley.

There is a path from the far side of the Lava Tower that drops into a rocky valley, fords a small stream of meltwater and climbs a slope in order to crest a ridge before rejoining the path that leads to the Barranco Valley.

After the paths have rejoined to the south of the Lava Tower, the path drops down a loose scree slope in a series of zigzags. At the foot of the slope it crosses several branches of **Bastions Stream**. The path them scrambles back up a rock-strewn ridge and passes a **well-signposted junction** to the left that leads directly to Arrow Glacier and the foot of the Western Breach.

The path continues south for an hour, descending a stony ridge, before dropping steeply into the **Great**

THE GREAT BARRANCO VALLEY

An enormous landslip that occurred over 100,000 years ago gouged out the Great Barranco Valley. The slip broke away part of Kibo's crater rim, creating the less steep gradient of the Western Breach, and scored a deep gash in the mountainside. The views of this enormous gash, which is over 300m deep here, are superb and offer virtually unparalleled sights of the Western Breach and Southern Icefields. To the right of the Western Breach, the vast, vertical, Breach Wall and other sheer cliffs rise imperiously from the head of the valley to create an almost impenetrable rampart. On the far side of the valley, the 300m Barranco Wall stands, appearing to block the following day's progress around the southern face of Kibo.

Barranco Valley past quantities of *Senecio* and *Lobelia*. Perched on the edge of the final descent to the floor of the Great Barranco Valley is the dramatically sited **Barranco Hut** (3965m). The old uniport is battered and grubby, but there are very attractive sites to pitch a tent all around the area. There are long-drop toilets to hand and several streams from which to draw water.

STAGE 4
Barranco Hut to Barafu Hut

This is a potentially long and difficult day. The early stages are focused on traversing the attractive Great Barranco Valley and overcoming the stiff challenge posed by the ascent of the Barranco Wall. Having overcome this obstacle, the gradient relents as the path contours around the southern face of Kibo, under the massed ranks of the Southern Icefields, before making an arduous, tiring approach to Barafu Hut.

It is well worth waking early to catch the sunrise at Barranco Hut, since it can be spectacular to watch the light strike the dramatic slopes and catch the eternal snows.

There is a great sense of achievement to be had upon successfully cresting the Wall and the views of the bulk of Kibo from this vantage point are outstanding. The Heim Glacier, part of the Southern Icefields, ▶

◀ **From the Barranco Hut** the path descends into the Great Barranco Valley, passing tall *Senecio* and winding around tussock grasses as it goes. The path drops to the valley floor and crosses boggy ground and a stream. Be sure to mind your footing here since the ground is marshy and many of the rocks used as stepping-stones are unstable and may simply sink into the soft ground under your weight. On the far side of the stream, at the foot of the Barranco Wall, is a giant boulder with a small cave beneath it. Most groups pause here to regroup before tackling the Wall.

Although the Wall is imposing and looks to be very steep, it isn't actually very difficult to climb. The rock face is close to vertical in places, but a series of cairns and splashes of red paint highlight a diagonal line that zigzags up the face to avoid the sheerest sections. The rock is relatively exposed and can be very slippery after rainfall, requiring you to use your hands in order to scramble safely in some places. Whilst tackling the Wall, spare a thought for the porters as they attempt to scale the Wall, many carrying your kit on their heads or strapped to their own bags. The 300m climb to the top of the Wall takes 1–1½hrs. ◀

The path above the Wall crosses a **high alpine plateau** in a south-easterly direction, dipping and climbing to cross small gullies housing streams, whilst the Heim, Kersten and Decken Glaciers reveal themselves high above your left-hand side. The path drops into the **Karanga Valley** 1½hrs after scaling the Barranco Wall. This valley is windswept but hosts a variety of flora, including numerous Lobelia, in stark contrast to the rather barren surrounds that you have recently traversed.

The Karanga River at the bottom of this valley is the **last water point before the summit** for those climbing the Barafu Route to the crater rim. Your guide should ensure that there is enough water gathered to last until you retreat from the peak to Mweka Hut. Make sure that all the water collected from here is properly sterilised since there are a number of toilets adjacent to the stream and there is a slight possibility of contracting giardia from untreated water.

◄ is also clearly visible from here. A series of small cairns marks the indistinct path that leads to the snout of the glacier and the start of some of the technical climbing routes to the summit.

EXTRA ACCLIMATISATION

Some groups choose to camp in the Karanga Valley and use the additional day spent on the mountain to aid their acclimatisation. There are long-drop toilets and tent pitches on the valley floor for just such a purpose.

On the eastern side of the Karanga Valley the path climbs a series of switchbacks to escape the valley; this ascent takes 15 minutes. At the top the path skirts under an overhang and past an additional set of tent pitches. This sheltered spot is often used as a lunch stop.

The path from the Karanga Valley Wall continues south east, undulating across two gentle river valleys. The path contours around the mountain for 2hrs through a patch of moorland, before cresting a ridge and reaching a **crossroads**. The South Circuit Path continues straight ahead. The right hand path is the Mweka Route – the descent route that you will follow after your summit bid. The left-hand path is the final approach to the Barafu Hut, which is the final campsite before the assault on the summit.

Be careful when moving around the campsite after dark as the cliffs adjacent to the campsite are precipitous and the terrain underfoot is very uneven and unstable in places. There have been a number of serious and indeed fatal accidents here as a consequence of people loosing their bearings in the dark.

Turn left here and scale the broad ridge that climbs north-east towards Kibo. This final section follows a desolate, rock-strewn, wind-blasted path for 2hrs. The path curves to the north and rises more steeply for a further 30 minutes until it arrives at **Barafu Hut** (4640m), on the western lip of the South East Valley. Barafu is the Swahili for 'ice', and the exposed, hostile campsite here merits its moniker. A pair of old uniports are in reality little more than rusted shells and the tent pitches are scattered amidst outcrops of rough lava. Long-drop toilets are set on the edge of the ridge. There is no water available at Barafu or indeed anywhere in the immediate vicinity. ◄

By virtue of its elevated and exposed position, the views from Barafu are very good. Having approached from the western side of Kilimanjaro, this will be your first chance to examine the jagged outline of Mawenzi, now visible across the broad expanse of the Saddle. There are also expansive views of Kilimanjaro's broad southern flank, which reveal just how huge the mountain actually is.

Continuing on from Machame Route

The Barafu Route to the summit begins to the north of the campsite and climbs to Stella Point on the crater rim. (See Summit Ascent Routes, for route description.)

View across Kilimanjaro's crater to silhouette of Mawenzi. Uhuru Peak looms top right

D: Lemosho Route

Time on the mountain (ascent, summit ascent and descent):	7 days
Length:	72km
Altitude gain:	3250m
Grade:	Moderate/hard
Start:	Lemosho Glades
Finish:	Shira 2 Camp
Summit ascent route:	Western Breach or Barafu Route
Optional extra days:	Karanga Valley on the Barafu Route
Descent route:	Mweka Route
End trek:	Mweka Gate

This is a slight variation on the traditional Shira Route. The differences between the two are slight but significant and ensure that the Lemosho Route is a far more rounded approach to Kibo; it is slightly longer and begins much lower down the mountain than the Shira Route. This enables you to enjoy the forest sections on foot and to ascend gradually, acclimatising all the while and improving your chances of reaching Uhuru Peak.

The route is used significantly less than the more popular paths and is positively quiet in parts. The path approaches Kibo through unspoilt forest on the western flank of the mountain. Its remote, untampered nature means that much of the forest remains intact and the thick understorey shelters buffalo and other large game, although you are still highly unlikely to actually see any of the animals that live here. Once on the Shira Plateau, the path merges with the Shira Route and tracks towards Kibo, in turn intersecting with the Machame Route and then the South Circuit Path. The summit bid can be made via the Western Breach or the Barafu Route, whilst the descent is traditionally along the Mweka Route.

The length of time spent on the Lemosho Route can vary considerably. It is possible to complete the entire climb in as little as five days or stretch it to last as many as eight days. A reasonable compromise that allows you to ascend slowly and carefully whilst making the most of your surrounds is the seven-day trip outlined here. This incorporates two short days of walking but does ensure that you acclimatise well and enjoy a very comprehensive walk to the foot of Kibo.

To the trailhead

Though the trailhead is at Lemosho Glades, prior to starting the walk you must first register and pay all park fees at the Londorossi Gate. The journey from the town of Moshi to the Lemosho Glades, via Londorossi, is an interminable one. The 80km of poorly maintained roads take 2–3hrs to negotiate. Your outfitter will arrange all transport to the trailhead.

To reach Londorossi, take the Moshi–Arusha road west for 25km. At the village of Bomaya Ya Ng'ombe the road forks, the right-hand fork curving north around Kilimanjaro to the village of Sanya Juu, 22km away. Sanya Juu is the final place from which to stock up on provisions and foodstuffs. From here the road circumnavigates Kilimanjaro for a further 30km, until it reaches Londorossi. The gate is just beyond the small, ramshackle town.

Following registration and payment of park fees here, follow a 4WD track back south for 11km, until you reach a left-hand fork that is signposted to Lemosho Glades. At the junction you may be required to pay a toll fare before being able to progress to the trailhead. The journey from Londorossi Gate to the Lemosho Glades takes 45 minutes to an hour.

Huts and accommodation

As with all of the less heavily used routes on Kilimanjaro, there are no huts at all on the early stages of the ascent and **no accommodation other than in tents** on the entire route.

At each of the designated campsites there are long-drop toilets and good water sources. Once the trail merges with the South Circuit Path, each campsite is set adjacent to an old metal uniport. These corrugated metal structures are little more than shells, like the Barranco, Barafu and Mweka Huts. Mostly built in the late 1960s, they were originally used as basic shelters for early climbers on the mountain. They have long since fallen into a state of disrepair and are much too small to accommodate the heavy traffic that now uses the relevant trails.

Stage	From–to	Distance	Time	Height Gain
1	Lemosho Glades (2390m) Big Tree Camp (2790m)	7km	2–3hrs	+400m
2	Big Tree Camp (2790m) Shira 1 Camp (3505m)	7km	4–5hrs	+715m
3	Shira 1 Camp (3505m) Shira 2 Camp (3840m)	7km	2–3hrs	+335m
Onwards:	Shira 2 Camp (3840m) Lava Tower (4655m)	7km	3–4hrs	+815m
or:	Shira 2 Camp (3840m) Barranco Hut (3965m)	10km	5–6hrs	+125m
	Barranco Hut (3965m) Barafu Hut (4640m)	8km	7–8hrs	+675m

STAGE 1
Lemosho Glades to Big Tree Camp

After registering at Londorossi and then heading on to the Lemosho Glades trail-head, you will eventually begin climbing the mountain on foot. By this stage of the day there is only time for a brief foray onto the forested lower western slopes of Kilimanjaro.

From the trailhead the path begins to ascend through a swathe of thick cloud forest. It leads in a generally eastern direction as it weaves through the trees to the north of the Lemosho River. The forest is stunning and full of life. Birds and insects are particularly prevalent here. An armed park ranger often accompanies groups on this section due to a slightly higher likelihood of encountering big game. Buffalo do live in the forest around the Lemosho Glades although you are unlikely to encounter them, simply coming across tracks and piles of dung.

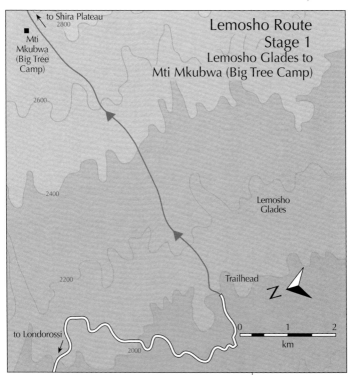

Lemosho Route
Stage 1
Lemosho Glades to
Mti Mkubwa (Big Tree Camp)

to Shira Plateau
2800

■ Mti Mkubwa (Big Tree Camp)

2600

2400

Lemosho Glades

2200

Trailhead

to Londorossi

2000

0   1   2
km

After 2hrs the path enters a small clearing in the upper reaches of the forest zone. This is Mti Mkubwa, or **Big Tree Camp** (2790m). The official name for the site is Forest Camp (as marked on some maps) but none of the outfitters or guides refers to it as such, preferring to use the nickname that is derived from the giant trees found in its vicinity. Water is available from a stream about 1.5km south of the campsite. The park ranger, who has been accompanying you from Lemosho Glades will not usually go beyond this point.

STAGE 2
Big Tree Camp to Shira 1 Camp

This is a longer day that sees you leave the confines of the forest and gain the edge of the Shira Plateau, from where exceptional views of Kibo, far to the east can be enjoyed.

The path leaves Big Tree Camp and continues to ascend smoothly and gently as the forest thins and the vegetation surrounding the path alters. As the taller trees give way and the thick understorey thins, you emerge on the heath/moorland zone, amidst giant heathers.

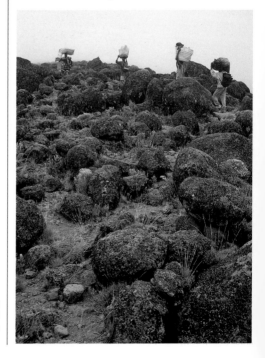

Porters climbing through Moorland above Shira Plateau

Lemosho Route Stage 2

Mti Mkubwa (Big Tree Camp) to Shira 1 Camp

Shira 1 Camp ■ / to Shira Plateau

Shira Ridge

Johnsell Point▲ ▲ Klute Peak

3800

3600

3400

Numerous streams

3200

3000

2800

Mti Mkubwa ■ (Big Tree Camp)

to Lemosho Glades

0 1 2 km

2600

▸ The gradient increases as the path progresses, only leveling or dipping slightly to cross one of the many small streams here. Most of the streams are dry throughout the year, unless there has been some recent rainfall. The path crests the **rim of the Shira Plateau** at almost 3700m. From here there are sweeping views of the entire rolling, crumpled plateau as it stretches south-east. To the right of the trail is the Shira Ridge and on it the highest points of the Shira Plateau, Johnsell Point (3962m) and Klute Peak.

Having gained the **Shira Ridge**, the main path drops slightly as it negotiates heathers, everlastings and small boulder outcrops on its way to the **Shira 1 Camp** (3505m). There are a number of tent pitches and long-drop toilets spread around here. Water can be fetched from a nearby stream.

The plateau is a relaxing, rewarding place to explore and there are a host of trails and indistinct tracks that criss-cross its surface.

There is a tangible sense of isolation and remoteness here on the edge of the plateau. Few people come this way and at this stage at least you can appreciate the enormity of the undertaking faced by early explorers as they hurled themselves against Kilimanjaro's ramparts.

STAGE 3
Shira 1 Camp to Shira 2 Camp

This is a very short, gentle day that transports you across the heart of the plateau but results in only a slight altitude gain. As such it is very good for acclimatisation purposes, allowing your body to adapt gradually to the sensation of being at altitude. There is an alternative route from the Shira 1 camp to the Shira 2 hut that has recently been opened up and goes via the Shira Cathedral and the southern rim of the plateau. Slightly tougher than the standard trek, it does however give you superb panoramic views from the top of the Cathedral and also aids your acclimatisation.

Keep an eye out for the sunrise which can be dramatic from here. As the sun rises behind the bulk of Kibo and climbs above the peak, it suddenly shifts and shoots brilliant beams of light from the snow-capped heights of the mountain.

◀ **From the edge of the Shira Ridge**, the path bends slightly to follow a south-easterly course across the plateau. As you set off you are walking straight into the sun and directly towards the mass of Kibo. Usually clear first thing in the morning, Kibo will rapidly become lost to mounding cloud that arises and shrouds the summit.

The path undulates across the surface of the plateau, hugging the lay of the land and following its every detail as it drops into small gullies containing tributary streams of the Engare Nairobi River and then climbs back up again. All

Strange Highland Desert sculptures; boulders perched on plinth of mud and pebbles

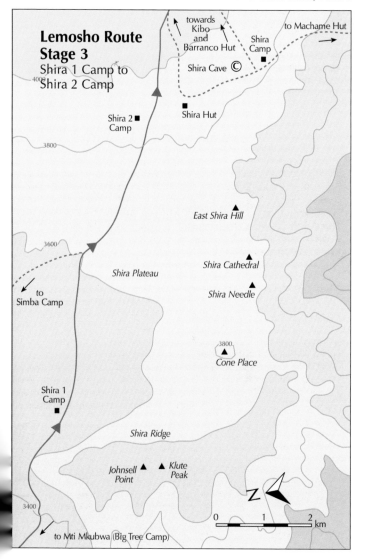

**Lemosho Route
Stage 3**
Shira 1 Camp to
Shira 2 Camp

towards Kibo
and
Barranco Hut

to Machame Hut

Shira Camp

Shira Cave ©

4000

Shira Hut

Shira 2 ■
Camp

3800

East Shira Hill ▲

3600

Shira Cathedral ▲

to
Simba Camp

Shira Plateau

Shira Needle ▲

3800
Cone Place ▲

Shira 1
Camp ■

Shira Ridge

Johnsell ▲ ▲ Klute
Point   Peak

N

0   1   2 km

3400

to Mti Mkubwa (Big Tree Camp)

EXPLORING THE PLATEAU

Because the walk into Shira 2 Camp only takes 2–3hrs in total, you should have an entire afternoon free to devote to the exploration and enjoyment of the Shira Plateau. Short forays will allow you to discover the strange and unusual flora of the heath/moorland zone, whilst longer, more energetic excursions will enable you to explore the further reaches of this impressive, ancient caldera.

To the right of the path are the prominent features that mark the southern reaches of the plateau. The Shira Needle, Shira Cathedral and East Shira Hill are all jagged points on a rugged ridge that runs along the lip of the plateau.

the while the path gains height subtlety, passing through an attractive high alpine meadow of heather and everlastings. ◀

The walk across this section of the oldest part of Kilimanjaro is gentle and can even be completed at a reasonable pace. As you yomp towards Kibo, the path **joins the Shira Route**. Together, the paths forge a route south-east for 4km towards **Shira 2 Camp** (3840m). The campsite is situated just to the north of the old Shira Hut. It is equipped with the standard long-drop toilets and is close to a good water supply.

Continuing on from the Lemosho Route

From Shira 2 Camp the Lemosho and Shira Routes progress together heading eastwards for 5km before merging with the **Machame Route** and **South Circuit Path** in turn. This opens up the summit approach routes of the Western Breach and Barafu Route, depending on your level of fitness and experience. (See Summit Ascent Routes for route descriptions.)

E: Shira Route

Time on the mountain (ascent, summit ascent and descent):	6 days
Length:	67km
Altitude gain:	3150m
Grade:	Moderate/hard
Start:	Londorossi Gate
Finish:	Shira 2 Camp
Summit ascent routes:	Western Breach or Barafu Route
Optional extra days:	Karanga Valley en route to the Barafu hut on the Barafu Route
Descent route:	Mweka Route
End trek:	Mweka Gate

This is an infrequently used ascent route that scales Kilimanjaro from the north and approaches Kibo via the Shira Plateau, climbing the mountain from almost the exact opposite direction as the Marangu Route. It is sometimes known as the Shira Plateau Route. The path begins above the forest zone and snakes across the Shira Plateau for two days. It then intersects with the Machame Route and joins the South Circuit Path. From here there are then two options for approaching the summit. Whilst some groups opt to tackle the Western Breach, most tackle the final climb along the Barafu Route. Descent from the summit is via the Mweka Route.

The Shira Route is quite an attractive route and the early stages are less frequented than many other sections of the mountain, allowing you to appreciate the isolation and wilderness all the more. Unfortunately, it has several drawbacks. The 80km approach to the Londorossi Gate (the trailhead) is a gruelling, lengthy drive on rapidly deteriorating roads. However, there are great views to be had of the mountains that dot the Great Rift Valley; Mount Meru and Longido are particularly prominent as you drive north around Kilimanjaro.

The early stage of this trek is essentially a driving route, and isn't much fun for trekkers. Because of this, the Shira Route is rarely offered and rarely tackled. However, for those so inclined, the trek begins with a drive along a 4WD track from the gate (2000m) to the Morrum Barrier (3100m) from where the walking starts. Cleared in 1968 by the Kilimanjaro District Forestry Department in order to improve access to this side of Kilimanjaro, the track is also occasionally used for emergency or rescue vehicles.

By driving this high on the mountain you will only see the forest sections through a car window as you bounce up a dusty track.

More pertinently, by beginning the walk on the heath/moorland zone, you impede your ability to acclimatise properly. The very rapid gain in altitude as a result of the distance driven, can lead to the equally rapid onset of altitude sickness. Even though the next two days are relatively short, you will not have given yourself the most solid start to your ascent.

The Shira Plateau itself possesses great beauty and is host to a number of fascinating geological features. The Shira Cone rises 200m above the plateau, but is shaded by the dramatic Shira Ridge to the west, which is up to 400m higher than the plateau. The prominent Shira Needle, Shira Cathedral and East Shira Hill mark the southern edge of the plateau.

DAY WALKS AROUND THE SHIRA PLATEAU

It is now possible to undertake a series of attractive day walks and an overnight hike from the Shira Route trailhead. This new hiking trail system has recently been established within the protected Shira Plateau Wilderness Area on the northernmost edge of the plateau. Park fees, and camping fees for the overnight route, must still be paid though. The day trips require a park permit only, whilst the overnight route requires you to book a campsite place and purchase a permit. Access is from the Londorossi Gate, although all of the routes actually begin at the Morrum Barrier clearing. Description boards detailing the routes are found along the way.

One of the day-trails provides access to a volcanic ridge that gives commanding views of the Shira Plateau and Kibo. To the north-east there are also distant views of southern Kenya and Amboseli National Park. The other day trip winds across the plateau to its northern extremities, over giant solidified lava fields. The route goes as far as Simba Gorge, where those only spending a day on Kilimanjaro can see giant *Senecio* and *Lobelia*. The overnight track forms a loop and links two designated campsites, enabling those not inclined to tackle Kilimanjaro's summit to spend a maximum of three days on the plateau, exploring its features and flat grasslands.

All of the tracks are clear, well signposted and in good condition, ensuring that with a little common sense, you can safely explore the area without the aid of a guide.

To the trailhead

The Shira Route begins at the Londorossi Gate on the northern side of Kilimanjaro. The Gate is 2½–3hrs from the town of Moshi. Park fees can be paid and registration formalities completed at the gate itself. Most walkers will be shuttled to the gate by their outfitter or agency.

To reach Londorossi, follow the Moshi-Arusha Road west from Moshi. After 25km the road passes through the village of Bomaya Ya Ng'ombe. There is a signposted junction right here that curves north around the flank of the mountain to West Kilimanjaro. The small town of Sanya Juu is passed 12km after the junction; this is the last point at which it is possible to pick up additional supplies or foodstuffs. From here it is a further 40km to Londorossi. This small, ramshackle town is almost exclusively constructed from wood. It has a frontier feel to it and provides no proper facilities for the casual visitor. Signposts indicate the Londorossi Gate, where there is a park warden's hut.

From the gate a rough 4WD track continues through the forest. This 11km stretch of pitted, rutted track leads all the way to the Morrum Barrier; at 3100m this is the highest point on the mountain readily accessible by vehicle. In dry conditions the track can be fairly easily used although progress is slow and awkward. The track climbs through the forest zone for about half its length, emerging onto the heath/moorland at around 2700m. From here the path bounces across the high alpine landscape to reach Morrum Barrier Gate, from where most groups start to walk.

Huts and accommodation

There are no huts on the lower sections of the Shira Route and **all overnight stops are taken at campsites**. Most groups don't even detour to the damaged uniport at Shira Hut anymore, opting to camp further north at the Shira 2 Campsite.

At each campsite there are clearly visible tent pitches and long-drop toilets. Water is readily available from streams in the immediate vicinity of each overnight spot.

After the Shira Route merges with the Machame Route and joins the South Circuit Path, you will either (if climbing the Western Breach) camp at Lava Tower and then at Arrow Glacier Hut, or (if ascending by the Barafu Route) camp adjacent to the uniports at the Barranco and Barafu Huts.

Stage	From–to	Distance	Time	Height Gain
1	Londorossi Gate (2215m) Simba Cave Camp (3650m)	15km	3–4hrs	+1435m
2	Simba Cave Camp (3650m) Shira 2 Camp (3840m)	7km	2hrs	+190m
	Onwards: Lava Tower Camp (4655m)	Shira 2 Camp (3840m) 7km	3–4hrs	+815m
	or: Barranco Hut (3965m)	Shira 2 Camp (3840m) 10km	5–6hrs	+125m
	Barafu Hut (4640m)	Barranco Hut (3965m) 8km	7–8hrs	+675m

STAGE 1
Londorossi Gate to Simba Cave Camp

This is a lengthy day, dominated by the drive from the village of Moshi to Londorossi Gate, where all of the requisite formalities for entering the national park are completed. From here you will then be driven for a further 11km to the Morrum Barrier Gate. Only at this stage will you actually begin walking, and then only briefly, since the day will already be drawing to a close.

There are picnic tables, long-drop toilets and a number of signposts and description boards for two short day trips and one overnight route in the area. (See box on Day walks around the Shira Plateau.)

The drive from Londrossi Gate to the Morrum Barrier take around 2hrs. If you set off late from Moshi or make especiall slow progress to the Morrum Barrier, it is possible to cam here overnight.

From Morrum Barrier Gate, the 4WD track contir ues for a short distance, before dwindling to a narrow track that heads out across the centre of the **Shira Platea** towards Kibo. This is the same trail for the day and overnigh walks. ◀

The track curves right and heads almost due sout through open heath/moorland, fording several small strean and tributaries of the **Engare Nairobi River**. After walking fc

**Shira Route
Stage 1**
Londorossi gate to
Simba Camp

Simba Cave Camp ■

to Shira 2 Camp

*Morrum
Barrier Gate* □

*Numerous
streams*

to Shira 1
Camp

3400

3200

3000

2800

2600

2400

to Londorossi
Gate

Mti Mkubwa
(Big Tree Camp) ■

to
Lemosho
Glades

N

0   1   2
km

187

4km (it should take 1½hrs) the path arrives at **Simba Cave Camp** (3650m). Here there are tent pitches and long-drop toilets; water is available from the nearby streams.

The views and sense of open space on the Shira Plateau are remarkable and quite unlike any other aspect of Kilimanjaro. Take the time to savour them before you join the busier stretches of track in the forthcoming days.

STAGE 2
Simba Cave Camp to Shira 2 Camp

This is a second short day that sees you ease further onto the Shira Plateau. Following the dramatic gain in altitude the previous day, the gentle nature of the short ascent to the next campsite should be welcome. The short day also means that you are left with plenty of spare time to explore the surrounding ridges and conspicuously rumpled surface of the plateau.

From the Simba Cave Camp the path is clearly visible and well signposted. It heads south-east, climbing gently past boulders and clumps of tussock grasses and everlastings. The walk is deceptively simple. Although the gradient is gentle and the terrain not unduly tough, your body is unlikely to have adjusted to the altitude gained the previous day and consequently progress is likely to be slower than you might anticipate.

After 3km the **Lemosho Route joins the path** from the right. Together the Shira and Lemosho Route continue south-eastwards for a further 4km until, a mere 2hrs after leaving Simba Cave Camp, you arrive at **Shira 2 Camp** (3840m). This new campsite lies to the north of the old, dirty Shira Hut. There are long-drop toilet facilities and a readily accessible water supply here.

Continuing on from the Shira Route
The following day's route from Shira 2 Camp is determined by which final ascent route you will tackle. Initially, you will follow the path from the campsite and ascend over 5km to join the South Circuit Path. As on the Machame Route you will then be able to access the Western Breach via Lava

Shira Route Stage 2 Simba Camp to Shira Camp 2

to Londrossi Gate

Simba Cave Camp

Shira Plateau

Shira 1 Camp

Shira 2 Camp

Shira Hut

East Shira Hill ▲

Shira Cathedral ▲

Shira Needle ▲

Cone Place ▲

Johnsell Point ▲

to Mti Mkubwa (Big Tree Camp)

Klute Peak ▲

0   1   2 km

Tower and the Arrow Glacier, or the Barafu Route via the Barranco and Barafu Hut. (See Summit Ascent Routes section for descriptions.)

EXCURSIONS AROUND THE SHIRA 2 CAMP

Having arrived by late morning, you have the option of exploring the area, weather permitting, during the free afternoon. Simply being able to stroll on the rolling plateau is a relaxing experience. For the more energetic, there are good side trips that can be undertaken in the vicinity; one attractive option is to explore the area to the west of the Shira 2 Camp that boasts the Shira Needle, Shira Cathedral and East Shira Hill.

F: Rongai Route
(including Alternative Five-day Rongai Route)

Time on the mountain (ascent, summit ascent and descent):	6 days (Alternative Rongai Route: 5 days)
Distance:	54km (Alternative Rongai Route: 48.5km)
Altitude gain:	2750m (Alternative Rongai Route: 2800m)
Grade:	Moderate/hard
Start:	Naromoru village
Finish:	Kibo Hut (Alternative Rongai Route: School Hut)
Summit ascent route:	Normal/Marangu Route
Optional extra days:	0
Descent route:	Marangu Route
End trek:	Marangu Gate

This unusual and less-heavily used method for ascending Kilimanjaro was set up in the 1960s to act as an alternative to the Marangu Route, which was at that time the only real walking route on the mountain. The local chief, Salakana, set up facilities on his tribal land and charged walkers to use the huts and facilities there. The money raised was then ploughed back into the local community, which thus benefited directly from the presence of tourists.

A number of small routes sprang up, all of which began on the northern flank of Kilimanjaro and tended to converge at the Second Cave before progressing either towards Mawenzi or heading directly towards Kibo, depending on the speed of the chosen ascent. The polarised nature of relations between Kenya and Tanzania and the proximity of the start points for the Rongai, Loitokitok, Outward Bound and Naromoru Routes to the border between the two countries meant that they fell into disuse for many years. However, during the last decade, this means of ascending Kilimanjaro has begun to gain in popularity once more. This is as a response to overcrowding on the other routes and because people are again recognizing that its relative quietness, unspoilt nature and spectacular views make this a very pleasant way to climb Kilimanjaro.

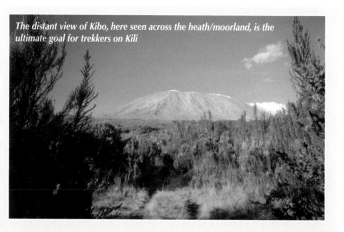

The distant view of Kibo, here seen across the heath/moorland, is the ultimate goal for trekkers on Kili

Unfortunately the revival has been constrained to just one route; the Rongai Route. What is now known as the Rongai Route, is actually something of a misnomer, since the path followed runs parallel to but slightly east of the original Rongai Route, on a path akin to the Loitokitok Route that started from the village of Loitokitok in Kenya. The perceptive walker may also spy a couple of way signs on the early stages of the route that are labelled 'Nalemoru Route', further adding to the confusion.

Regardless of what you call it, this ascent of Kilimanjaro is quite extraordinary. Taking advantage of the drier northern slopes, you are able to approach the Saddle relatively easily. The views north over the arid, flat Masai Lands in southern Kenya reveal the sheer scale of your endeavour and make the ascent seem very grand indeed. By opting to complete the walk in six days rather than in five (for the **five-day route see Alternative Five-day Rongai Route directions**), you are able to detour to Mawenzi Tarn Hut, situated just below Mawenzi's North Corrie. This is a truly stunning campsite that allows you to admire the jagged peaks and to explore the foothills of Kilimanjaro's second summit more effectively than on any other route.

The only drawbacks to ascending this route are the lengthy drive around Kilimanjaro to the start point and the disappointing early stages of the first day's walk. Much of the lowland forest has been cleared for farmland and as a consequence you only climb through a small section of genuine forest before reaching the heath/moorland zone. This is in some way recompensed by the fact that you traditionally descend via the Marangu Route, which has some attractive forest scenery on its lower sections. The grueling final ascent to the crater rim is conducted from either School Hut or Kibo Hut and is via the Normal/Marangu Route.

Nonetheless, the scenic variety, emptiness and technically very easy nature of the walk more than compensate for the drawbacks, making this an excellent method of ascending and enjoying Kilimanjaro.

To the trailhead

Plans to create a national park gate at Naromoru have been mooted, but at present it is still necessary to register and pay the requisite park fees at the Marangu Gate. Your outfitter will ensure that you are shuttled to the gate and then transported on from here, around the eastern side of Kilimanjaro to the actual trailhead.

The trailhead is 50km from the Marangu Gate. The tarmac ends just after Marangu and the road then deteriorates rapidly as you circumnavigate the mountain. The road passes through a series of Chagga towns and villages, becoming increasingly dusty and difficult, whilst after rain the road surface can become incredibly muddy.

After driving for 1½hrs you arrive at the town of Tarekea, 40km from Marangu, on the north-eastern side of Kilimanjaro. Here the road forks. The right-hand fork crosses the border and heads into Kenya, whilst the left-hand fork curves north-west around the mountain, following the border on the Tanzanian side. Half an hour from Tarekea is the village of Naromoru. A small junction heading up a bumpy track leads to a motley collection of huts adjacent to the Snow Cap campsite.

Huts and accommodation

Although there are a couple of uniports along the Rongai Route, you will need a tent for each of the overnight stops on the ascent. **Camping is the only option on the early stages of the climb**, but there is the **possibility of staying in the hut at Kibo and again at Horombo on the descent**, although you are almost certain to camp throughout your time on the mountain.

There is a corrugated iron uniport at the First Camp and at Mawenzi Tarn Hut. Though there are structures at Mawenzi Tarn, which dates from the early 1970s, and

chool Hut neither are suitable for walkers to stay in and they
ren't used for this purpose. School Hut used to be known
s the Outward Bound Hut, but the park authorities are now
eferring to it by this new moniker.

The larger stone blockhouse at Kibo Hut accommo-
ates a number of people, but is primarily designed for
hose ascending the Marangu Route. The same is true for the
-frame complex at Horombo. In either case, camping may
vell provide you with a more peaceful, better night's sleep
han you would get in a communal bunkroom.

Stage	From–to	Distance	Time	Height Gain
1	Naromoru (1991m) First Camp (2635m)	8km	3hrs	+644m
2	First Camp (2635m) Kikelewa Camp (3680m)	6km	5–6hrs	+1045m
3	Kikelewa Camp (3680m) Mawenzi Tarn Hut (4300m)	5km	3–4hrs	+620m
4	Mawenzi Tarn Hut (4300m) Kibo Hut (4703m)	8km	5hrs	+403m

Alternative five-day Route

Stage	From–to	Distance	Time	Height Gain
2	First Camp (2635m) Third Cave (3935m)	8km	4–5hrs	+1300m
3	Third Cave (3935m) School Hut (4715m)	6km	3–4hrs	+780m

STAGE 1
Naromoru to First Camp

The first day on the Rongai Route is a fairly inauspicious start to the ascent of the largest mountain in Africa. After a 2–2½hrs drive from Marangu Gate, the climb begins by ambling gently through an area of heavily deforested land that is now being used for cultivation. Fortunately it improves rapidly and before too long passes into a small copse of natural forest. Beyond this it emerges amidst some scrub and heather close to First Camp, from where you have the first exceptional views of Mawenzi's serrated outline and Kibo's snow-capped dome.

The trailhead at Naromoru is fairly nondescript. The dusty, pitted road branches into a level area in front of a clutter of huts. A wide signposted track leads away from here, skirting the edge of a small pine forest above a stretch of fields and cultivated lands. Once your guides and porters have divided up all of the equipment and food, you'll need to register your name and party in one of the rickety huts. You are then free to begin the climb; **head south-west** along the dusty 4WD track ahead of you. The trail circles a pine forest and then sets off across a series of small, cultivated plots of land. ◄

This whole area used to be lightly forested, but the pressures of human encroachment have resulted in the destruction of most of the natural forest in this area.

Continue along this fairly shabby track as it winds between plots of maize and potato and past pitiful shacks, gradually gaining height. Gangs of raggedy boys and raggedy girls shouting 'Jambo, Chocolate!' will most likely accost you here.

The path **passes two signposts** marked 'Naremoru', which refer to a previous incarnation of the route, and after 1hr bends right and dips to cross the Nare Moru River before entering a stand of forest. ◄

As you enter the forest you may see a resident troop of black-and-white colobus monkeys in the treetops, making huge leaps of faith and moving agilely from branch to branch in search of fruit and seeds.

Once inside the forest, the track curves left and climbs **past a third 'Nalemoru' sign**. There is a makeshift picnic table and long-drop toilet here. The gradient then increases and the going underfoot becomes more uneven. Jumbled roots and fallen branches lie on the path in untidy heaps. Small, brightly coloured flowers lurk amidst the overwhelming palette of greens.

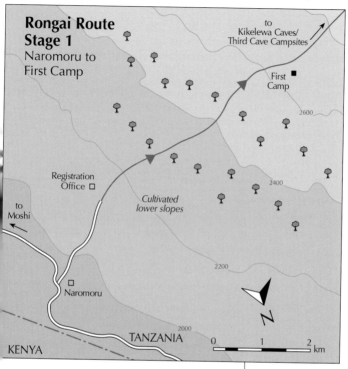

Rongai Route Stage 1

Naromoru to First Camp

to Kikelewa Caves/
Third Cave Campsites

First Camp

2600

Registration Office

to Moshi

Cultivated lower slopes

2400

2200

Naromoru

2000

TANZANIA

KENYA

0   1   2 km

N

The forest, which is quite small, shelters a variety of birds and animal life. All too quickly the trees thin and the undergrowth recedes as you enter an area of giant heathers and scrub. The forest briefly reasserts itself but quickly gives way once more to the rampant heath. The path continues to gain height gently, undulating through the pleasant scenery. Having dropped to cross a frequently dry riverbed, the path climbs once more to reveal views north-east. Kilimanjaro's foothills taper into the dusty, wheat-coloured Kenya plains. The path picks its way across a second stream on polished blue-gray rocks and reenters the scrub. ▸

Quite suddenly, a little over an hour after leaving the forest, the path comes to a number of cleared patches of scrub. This is the site of **First Camp** (2635m). The grassy

There is often evidence of larger wildlife here, even though you'll be lucky to actually see any. Although you may come across an elephant skull beside the path and quantities of spoor, you are more likely to have to content yourself with spotting birds and insects.

195

pitches afford reasonable camping opportunities and th tall scrub hides a number of the pitches, making the site fee smaller than it really is.

Upon arrival you will have to register your group wit the warden stationed in the uniport here. There are severa long-drop toilets in the area, but little else. Water is availabl from the stream you crossed about 50m back along the track Kibo and Mawenzi are both visible, weather allowing, an make for a stirring and inviting view.

STAGE 2
First Camp to Kikelewa Caves

This is a fairly long day that sees those completing the climb in six days separate from those who will only take five days to summit and drop off the mountain again. All walkers start together and follow the same trail to Second Cave. At this point the paths diverge, those taking five days heading to Third Cave (see directions in Alternative Rongai Route section) whilst those taking six days turn towards Kikelewa Caves.

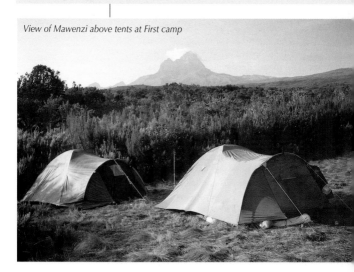

View of Mawenzi above tents at First camp

irst thing in the morning there are glorious views of Mawenzi to the south and Kibo to the west. The peaks are visible through and above the scrub for the first part of the day, until early cloud drifts over the Saddle and smothers the summits. **Leaving First Camp**, the trail continues on a westerly heading, rising steadily onto the heath/moorland zone, aiming for Kibo's northern flank. The trail coils between tussock grasses, sweet-smelling herbs and small garish flowers that stand out against the ubiquitous yellows and browns of this part of the mountain. Trees are stunted, skeletal or non-existent at this altitude.

The track passes a rocky outcrop and begins to rise a little more sharply, climbing onto a small plateau. ▸

To the left of the trail is a shallow canyon, carved by mountain runoff that flashes down from the higher slopes after heavy rain. For much of the year it is dry though. From here the path ascends alongside the riverbed via a rocky outcrop and another level stretch of terrain. As it gains the lip of this second level patch of ground, the trail passes a faint **junction to the right**. This used to be the point at which the original Rongai Route joined the main track up the mountain. 1–2hrs after leaving camp, the path reaches a **small cave**. The cave is a small, low-ceilinged affair that has previously been used as a campsite although it doesn't have a readily accessible water supply (you are no longer permitted to camp in any caves on the mountain). The roof of the cave is charred and blackened from countless old campfires.

The path above the cave climbs up the valley between two ridges before scrambling onto the shoulder of one of them as it curves south-west across the track. Here the terrain becomes rockier and steeper. Several false summits offer false hope before you finally reach the top of the ridge. The path then crosses a flatter area, liberally dotted with feathers and wild flowers. Half an hour after passing the small cave, the path comes to **Second Cave** (3450m), which is clearly signposted. This is often used as a lunch stop. Second Cave is a much larger hollow, whose more substantial overhang provides some cover for those cooking or eating. There is a long-drop toilet just in front of the cave. ▸

From Second Cave the paths diverge. Those heading to Third Cave for their overnight stop on the five-day route

Looking back there are good views of where the fingers of forest reach down Kilimanjaro and flatten to form the yellow, broad Kenya plains. It is also possible to see the shine of Lake Chala on the border, to the east.

From the rocky mouth of the cave you can see out across the northern flank of Kilimanjaro. The pudding bowl dome of Kibo and the Eastern Icefields on the crater rim are also visible to the west, as they have been in the approach to the cave.

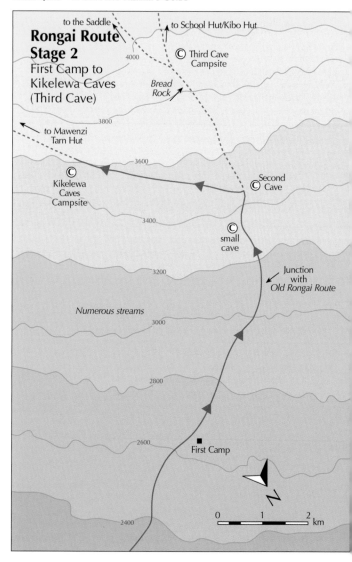

**Rongai Route
Stage 2**
First Camp to
Kikelewa Caves
(Third Cave)

to the Saddle

4000

to School Hut/Kibo Hut

ⓒ Third Cave
Campsite

*Bread
Rock*

3800

to Mawenzi
Tarn Hut

3600

ⓒ
Kikelewa
Caves
Campsite

ⓒ Second
Cave

3400

ⓒ
small
cave

Junction
with
Old Rongai Route

3200

Numerous streams

3000

2800

2600

■
First Camp

N

2400

0   1   2 km

Second Cave signpost

continue south (see **Alternative five-day Rongai Route**) whilst those progressing to Kikelewa Cave follow the path that leads south-east, directly towards Mawenzi.

Having climbed over a small knoll, the path drops to cross a riverbed. It then rises again on the far side of this waterway, albeit on a gentler gradient since you are now essentially traversing the contours of the mountain; you only gain around a further 150m height in the final 3km section.

The path rises and falls repeatedly, skirting above a series of gullies and ravines and crossing two further, frequently dry, streams. After the second of these, the track edges around a rocky promontory and 1½–2hrs from Second Cave drops into a valley that contains the **Kikelewa Caves campsite** (3600m). The valley, just below the Saddle, is full of *Senecio* and is an attractive spot to stay overnight with all of the usual facilities and further fine views.

STAGE 3
Kikelewa Caves to Mawenzi Tarn Hut

This is a shortish day that elevates you quite quickly on a relatively steep trail. The effort is well rewarded by sumptuous views and an exceptional campsite beneath the jagged spires of Mawenzi that will leave you with a tangible sense of wilderness and isolation.

Mawenzi Tarn campsite seen from higher on Mawenzi

The **path heads south** from Kikelewa Caves and climbs steadily on a ridge through an area of *Senecio*. On either side of you other ridges rise as well, making the whole place appear rugged. The path climbs fairly steeply and you ascend towards Mawenzi rapidly. After 1½hrs the gradient

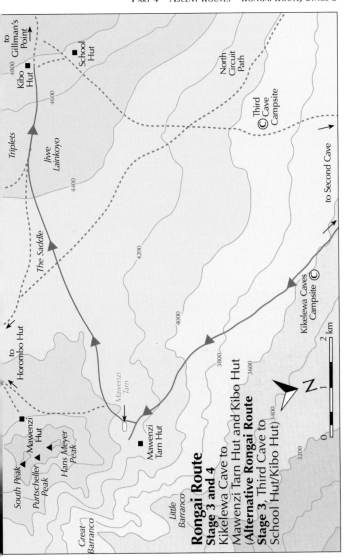

Rongai Route
Stage 3 and 4
Kikelewa Cave to
Mawenzi Tarn Hut and Kibo Hut
(**Alternative Rongai Route**
Stage 3, Third Cave to
School Hut/Kibo Hut)

eases slightly. At this point the vegetation begins to alter as the heath plants give way to everlastings and hardier species.

Relentlessly the path continues to climb for a further half hour before it crests a false summit and temporarily levels. Beyond here the path climbs more steeply and negotiates a 5m section of slope that you may have to use your hands to scramble up. Cresting a ridge you enter the **north-east valley on Mawenzi**. The path eases around Mawenzi's edge, contouring across the mountain and hugging the rumpled lie of the land.

Dropping slightly, the path squelches across a boggy section bisected by a stream. As the trail gains height once more, the vegetation fades away and the area becomes more barren and exposed, seeming to only support everlastings. The trail rounds a rock outcrop to suddenly reveal Mawenzi Tarn set beneath the blasted, shattered slopes of Kilimanjaro's second summit. Allegedly the tarn never runs dry, although it can shrink considerably during periods of sustained dry weather. On the far side of the tarn are a small, corrugated tin shack and a signpost announcing the site of the **Mawenzi Tarn Hut** (4300m).

MAWENZI TARN HUT

This is one of the most dramatic campsites on the mountain. Much less heavily used than others, it is a quiet, ethereal place to stay overnight, one where, 'Dark and threatening the shattered bulwarks of Mawenzi rise sternly into the upper air.' (Hans Meyer). The tarn and campsite are set in a cirque at the foot of **Mawenzi** and the walls immediately above the campsite have the appearance of an organ vault. On either side of the valley containing the tarn are serrated ridges. The one to the west barely conceals **Kibo**, which can be seen from some vantage points peering over the crest.

To the east is a further ridge, beyond which is a scooped slope that leads to a sudden, dramatic drop. Further east are the stunning, chilling gouges in the mountainside that comprise the **Little and Great Barrancos**, two abyss-like river gorges that fall away from the summit. These two features have been described as being 'Himalayan' in scale and are too deep to see into. Hans Meyer recorded his impressions of the gorge from high on Mawenzi, writing, 'On this its eastern side, from an altitude of about 16,830ft, the mountain sinks sheer downward into a gigantic cauldron, the sides of which are scarred with innumerable, rugged ravines. As we gazed from our dizzy height upon the hills and valleys, the streams and bushes, the endless proliferation of gullies and gorges 6000 or 7000 feet below, it seemed as if we had a birds-eye view of earth from a balloon.'

The sunrise from Mawenzi Tarn Hut is also spectacular. As the sun creeps up behind the jagged, silhouetted spires, the shadows shorten before the light bursts from behind the peaks and floods the rest of the mountain. From vantage points above the campsite it is just possible to see over the western ridge to the sparkling snows atop Kibo.

EXCURSIONS FROM MAWENZI TARN HUT

Since this a fairly short day you ought to arrive here with much of the afternoon spare. Use this time to rest and rehydrate. After that make sure to explore the area. Clamber up onto Mawenzi's foothills, scour the cirque and marvel at the sheer edifices and damaged rock slopes that make Mawenzi such a challenge to climb. Use the opportunity to climb higher before dropping to sleep at a lower elevation, thereby aiding your acclimatisation. Be careful whilst doing so though, as the slopes here are unstable and can be prone to rock falls.

STAGE 4
Mawenzi Tarn Hut to Kibo Hut

This is a simple day that culminates with you being in a position to tackle the final summit bid. Little additional height is gained as you forge across the lunar-like Saddle landscape between Mawenzi and Kibo, allowing you to prepare physically and psychologically for the challenge ahead. If the weather is bad or the winds are high, this highly exposed section of the mountain can become tough (see Stage 3 map).

The strong morning light picks out a myriad of colours and creates a truly beautiful picture. Even by this early time of day, cloud is often boiling up the lower slopes and preparing to storm the Saddle. The wisps and tendrils of cloud make the object of the days walk seem even more remote and grand than previously imagined. Make sure that you don't break camp too late in the morning otherwise the view may already be hidden from you.

Retrace your steps from the previous day, passing back past Mawenzi Tarn. Then **ascend the scree and lava ridge** to the north-west of the campsite. After 15–30 minutes the path crests the ridge to reveal extraordinary views of the Saddle and Kibo. The views from this outstanding vantage point are particularly potent if poor weather or afternoon cloud obscured them on the walk in the previous day. Kibo's squat dome and eternal snows are clearly visible across the vast spreading Saddle. ◀

The path descends from the ridge, slip-sliding down the loose lava pebbles for half an hour. At the foot of the descent the path **passes the junction** with the trail that leads to Kikelewa Caves. Follow the left-hand fork and veer west towards the Kibo massif.

The path climbs sharply for 30–45 minutes, regaining the lost height, passing past heathers and everlastings until it plateaus out at the start of **the Saddle**. It continues to rise on a slow, steady incline as it progresses across this featureless moonscape. The terrain is flat and barren, supporting little life as it is so exposed. Small outcrops of hardy grasses and everlastings can be spotted sheltering under orange-red lava bombs and rock fragments. The narrow path snakes ahead.

In the distance Middle Red Hill and the Triplets, some of Kilimanjaro's parasitic cones, can be made out to the south-west – they appear to remain distant though you inch closer. The journey across the northern section of the Saddle takes an age since there are few landmarks to gauge your progress.

View of Kibo massif above cloud band from Mawenzi's North West Ridge

by. This is particularly true if the cloud has swamped the Saddle or the weather is bad, in which case visibility can be dramatically reduced. The constant buffeting by the wind and the searing cold can take their toll. Make sure that you are properly dressed in warm clothes.

Eventually Kibo Hut comes into view, settled on a rise at the foot of the Kibo crater wall. The path continues to ascend towards this point. Adjacent to the Triplets, at a point known as **Jiwe Lainkoyo**, an old local hunters' campsite, the path intersects with the Marangu Route and then makes the final push to the hut. Rising past a rocky outcrop, the path arrives at the stone outhouses of **Kibo Hut** (4703m). Cleared tent pitches surround the basic buildings. There is no water here so make sure that everything that you'll need for the night and the following climb to the summit is carried with you to this point. The views back across the Saddle towards Mawenzi are dramatic, especially at dusk, when the blue and violet colours in the sky and the sinisterly shadowed silhouette of the second summit are most striking.

Continuing on from the Rongai Route

You are now poised for the final climb to the peak. The Normal/Marangu Route starts from behind Kibo Hut and climbs to Gillman's Point, from where it is possible to access Uhuru Peak, ideally in time to witness the sunrise over Africa. (See Summit Ascent Routes for route description.)

ALTERNATIVE
FIVE-DAY RONGAI ROUTE

(For Stage 1 of Alternative five-day Rongai Route please see
the description in Rongai Route Stage 1.)

STAGE 2
First Camp to Third Cave

This Alternative five-day Rongai Route diverts from the more leisurely Rongai
Route, offering a faster and more direct route to Kibo. Having ascended to First
Camp on the same path as those following the normal Rongai Route, this second
stage begins in the same fashion for both branches of the Rongai Route. It isn't
until Second Cave, the usual lunch stop, that the paths diverge and this is where
the route description for the Alternative Rongai Route begins. (Please see the map
for Rongai Route Stage 2 when following this route.)

Please see Stage 1 and Stage 2 route descriptions in th
Rongai Route for instructions as to how to reach this point
Just above the Second Cave the path splits. For Third Cav
follow the right-hand fork as it leads straight ahead. The path
ascends steeply and steadily, crossing several dry stream
amidst increasingly rocky terrain. A number of clearly visible
cairns highlight the way ahead and help you to negotiate the
tributary streams of the Nare Moru River. As you near Third
Cave, the trail passes a large, distinctive rock on the left-hand
side. **Bread Rock** is about 12m high and is often adorned with
a sizeable cairn. Other large rocks now become apparent
around the trail, sheltering everlastings.

The path crosses a broad river bed 1½hrs after leaving
Second Cave, and brings you to the large, shallow **cave** tha
the site is named after (3800m). There are long-drop toilet
here. The small stream just below the campsite is the las
water point on this particular ascent route.

STAGE 3
Third Cave to School Hut

This brief section leads you up a steady incline of increasingly loose scree to either School Hut or Kibo Hut, from where the summit attempt will be launched. (Please see the map for Rongai Route Stage 3 when following this route.)

The **path leads south-west** from Third Cave, climbing steadily all the while. The trail is fairly obvious and clearly marked by cairns. Half an hour after leaving the camp, the track reaches an indistinct crossroad. The path heading roughly north-south is the North Circuit Path. Ignore this and **continue straight ahead**, climbing south-west slowly through the increasingly desolate landscape where everlastings and red lichen provide the only colour relief from the interminable browns and grays of the rock and lava.

After an hour of snaking through this barren place the path crests a false summit. It then descends briefly in a series of zigzags, crossing a number of solidified lava tracks. All too soon it begins to climb again and proceeds to do so for the next hour before arriving at **School Hut** (4715m). School Hut is a large, shabby metal uniport with a wooden floor, set beneath a large rocky outcrop. There are long-drop toilets adjacent to the hut, but no water source. ▸

Continuing from the Alternative Rongai Route

The final ascent from School Hut begins by **scrambling west of the hut** on a faint trail marked by cairns. The path then follows a southwesterly direction over solidified lava flows, before it zigzags up the loose scree that follows. Rather than heading to the crater rim though, the path **merges with the Normal/Maranagu Route** from Kibo Hut. The two meet between William's Point (5000m) and Hans Meyer Cave (5151m). The junction comes after a slight descent, 2hrs from School Hut. You are then faced with a 15 minute climb to Hans Meyer Cave and a subsequent 2½hrs of slogging up loose scree to Gillman's Point and the chance to climb to Uhuru Peak. (See Summit Ascent Routes, Normal Marangu Route.)

There is a trail from School Hut to Kibo Hut, which heads south from one of the toilet shacks for 30 minutes before arriving at the Kibo Hut site.

CIRCUIT PATHS

One of the least used routes on Kilimanjaro is the Circuit Path that surrounds the base of Kibo. Although sections of its southern half are frequently used in conjunction with the Shira, Lemosho, Machame and Umbwe Routes, very few people

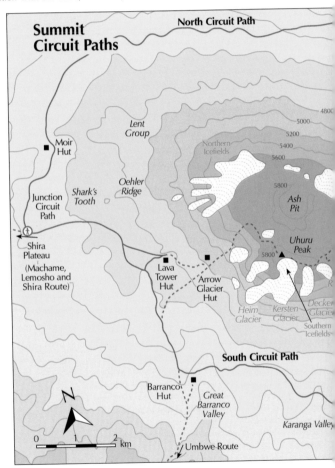

Summit Circuit Paths

North Circuit Path

4800
5000
5200
5400
5600
5800

Lent Group

Northern Icefields

Moir Hut

Oehler Ridge

Shark's Tooth

Ash Pit

Junction Circuit Path

Uhuru Peak
5800 ▲

Shira Plateau (Machame, Lemosho and Shira Route)

Lava Tower Hut

Arrow Glacier Hut

Heim Glacier

Kersten Glacier

Decken Glacier

Southern Icefields

South Circuit Path

Barranco Hut

Great Barranco Valley

Karanga Valley

N

0   1   2 km

Umbwe Route

access the northern part of the loop or indeed complete a full circuit of Kilimanjaro's crater mound.

The first full circuit of Kibo was completed in 1912 by Oehler and Klute, who spent 10 days in September 1912 carrying out a photogrammetric survey as they skirted the massif. The second full circuit was then not completed until 1969, when a party circumnavigated Kibo in 3½ days. With the further development of the South Circuit

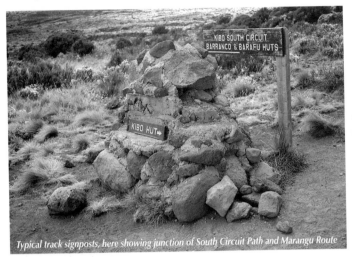

Typical track signposts, here showing junction of South Circuit Path and Marangu Route

Path, the route can now readily be completed in just three days. However, a compromise, taking five or six days is much more realistic and enjoyable. The full circuit amounts to nothing more than a stiff walk and although it rises to 4600m, it is not unduly taxing, particularly if additional days are built into your itinerary.

The path is largely clear and eminently walkable, particularly on the southern half. The main difficulty is the lack of water on some sections. To counter this, sufficient supplies must be carried to prevent you becoming dehydrated at any point.

All overnight accommodation is in tents as the battered old uniports that can be found on some stretches of the circuit are unappealing and unsuitable places to sleep. Along some parts of the circuit, even uniports haven't been constructed. At each campsite there are long-drop toilets provided.

The Circuit Path can be **accessed from any number of points**, mostly along the southern section. It can then be tackled using a variety of combinations, depending on how long you intend to spend on the mountain. For the sake of simplicity and to reflect the disparity in numbers using each half of the circuit, it is described here in two parts, beginning with the more popular **South Circuit Path**, followed by the less frequented **North Circuit Path**.

G: SOUTH CIRCUIT PATH

If you tackle Kilimanjaro by any route other than the Marangu or Rongai Route, you will inevitably end up using part of the South Circuit Path to complete your ascent. The path circumnavigates the southern section of Kibo, passing beneath the glorious icefalls of the Heim, Kersten and Decken Glaciers.

At its western end, the path connects to the Machame Route above Shira Hut. This point can also be reached from the Shira and Lemosho Routes. The South Circuit Path then runs around Kibo, linking the Shira, Lava Tower and Barranco Huts before connecting to the Marangu Route above Horombo Hut at its eastern end. Along its length it is joined by the Umbwe Route and in turn gives rise to the Western Breach and Barafu Routes to the crater rim and the Mweka descent route.

Most groups will travel the South Circuit Path from west to east, and as such it is described below. The beginning of the circuit above the Shira Plateau is indistinct and not at all well marked. The path officially begins just east of the junction of the Shira Route and the North Circuit Path. This junction is marked by a splash of red paint on a rock and a sign that points north towards Moir Hut on the North Circuit Path. After this point and unbeknownst to most walkers, they are traversing the South Circuit Path.

At the beginning of the circuit, above the Shira Plateau, **the path heads** east, aiming directly for Kibo. It undulates towards the massif before curving right and bearing south. Arriving at a distinctive black wedge-shaped rock outcrop, the path splits. The **left-hand fork** climbs to the foot of the Lava Tower, from where you can access the Arrow Glacier and scale the **Western Breach** or drop down a rocky trail to rejoin the South Circuit Path. ▸

The right-hand fork winds down a rocky slope and passes to the south of the Lava Tower. After 1km the paths rejoin.

From here the route continues to undulate, gradually losing height as it approaches the Barranco Hut (3965m). It takes 2¼hrs to amble from the Lava Tower to Barranco Hut, passing a clearly signposted junction that leads directly to Arrow Glacier after an hour. **Barranco Hut** is idyllically

Most groups use this route as it allows you to climb a little higher and aids your acclimatisation. It is also privy to some of the most outstanding scenery and views of the Lava Tower and the breathtaking Western Breach.

View of Western Breach and summit amidst cloud

situated on the western side of the Great Barranco Valley and is a very attractive campsite.

From the Barranco Hut, the South Circuit Path continues east, dropping into the Great Barranco Valley and weaving between giant groundsel and Lobelia. It crosses the Umbwe River tributary at the bottom of the valley and passes a giant boulder at the foot of the **Barranco Wall**. The 300m high Barranco Wall is a rough, craggy volcanic cliff. Although visually imposing, it isn't too difficult to negotiate. A series of tight switchbacks clamber up the steep face for 30 minutes and lead to a level area at the top of the Wall. The views from here are simply breathtaking.

This is the last water for many kilometres and you should take advantage of this to collect as much as possible. The valley is narrow and steep-sided, and is a pleasant place to camp.

Having crested the Barranco Wall, the South Circuit Path enters an area of high alpine desert. It continues to skirt Kibo, contouring around the mountain, rising and falling as it negotiates the valleys and ravines that are scratched into the mountainside. The path descends into the picturesque **Karanga Valley** where a stream runs between ferns and heathers. ◄

A steep zigzag path brings you to the top of the eastern side of the valley. From here the path undulates beneath the looming slopes and Southern Icefields of Kibo. The Heim,

212

Kersten, Decken and Rebmann Glaciers bear silent witness to your passing as you struggle onwards.

The South Circuit Path reaches a **crossroads** atop a ridge 7km after leaving the Barranco Hut. The left-hand trail rises steeply through an exceptionally bleak landscape to the Barafu Hut (4640m) on the edge of the South East Valley. The right-hand fork drops smoothly and swiftly off the mountain along the Mweka Route.

The South Circuit Path itself **continues straight on**, rippling across the vast expanse of moorland that lies beneath the Saddle.

From here it descends gently across rumpled slopes until it **joins the Marangu Route**, at its eastern end. The South Circuit Path–Marangu Route junction is poorly marked and unclear. The faint South Circuit Path simply fades into the larger Marangu Route 1km above and to the north-west of the Horombo Hut (3720m).

H: NORTH CIRCUIT PATH

Kilimanjaro's North Circuit Path is one of the loneliest, least used stretches of track on the entire mountain. To walk this section of path is to be truly isolated and to enjoy the mountain undisturbed. You will also get to enjoy some unusual views of the peaks and be able to appreciate a different aspect of the mountain. The route has great, untapped potential.

The North Circuit Path stretches from the Shira Plateau in the west around Kibo, beneath the massed steps of the Northern Icefields, to the Saddle. The path is relatively straightforward to follow, although it is rocky, uneven and in places indistinct.

At its western extreme, the **path begins above the Shira Plateau**. A red splash of paint daubed on a rock and a signpost angled north and inscribed 'Moir Hut' are the indications that the North Circuit Path is about to begin. The path contours around the north western side of Kibo at around 4300m. It begins by climbing slowly for an hour to the west of the Oehler Ridge rock projection that stretches out from beneath the Credner, Drygalski and Pengalski Glaciers. Three kilometres after the Moir Hut signpost the path enters

Moir Hut lies 2km to the west of a number of parasitic cones that collectively form the Lent Group.

the Lent Valley and reaches the aforementioned Hut. **Moir Hut** (4300m) comprises a dirty, shabby uniport that has ten pitches adjacent to it and long-drop toilets nearby. Water is also available in the vicinity, from a stream about 100m below the hut. ◄

From the Moir Hut, the path continues to circumnavigate Kibo, contouring clockwise across numerous gullies, rocky lava ribs and gashes in the northern slopes. The path is uneven and littered with rubble and fragments of lava that make the going slow and exhausting.

There is no other hut or obvious campsite on the remaining section of the North Circuit Path. There have long been plans to construct one on the north-eastern side of Kibo, but as yet nothing has come to fruition. Water is also scarce on this section, although the path does stumble across a number of small streams during its traverse of the northern slopes. Unfortunately, at certain times of year these may well be dry.

On the eastern side of Kibo the path climbs up toward the Saddle. It **crosses** the Rongai Route's direct approach to School Hut above Third Cave and continues to head south, climbing onto the back of the **Saddle**. Once on the Saddle, it **crosses the other branch** of the Rongai Route as it tracks from Mawenzi Tarn Hut to Kibo Hut. Cutting across the austere landscape between Mawenzi and Kibo, the North Circuit Path fuses with the **Marangu Route** 1km north of West Lava Hill. From here it descends gently from the Saddle, passing East Lava Hill, Zebra Rock and the junction with the South Circuit Path, to arrive at **Horombo Hut** (3720m).

SUMMIT ASCENT ROUTES

There are three ways that walkers can access the crater rim on Kibo from the high huts on the lower approach routes. Those people who have climbed via the Marangu or Rongai Routes will make their summit bid via the **Normal/Marangu Route** and access the crater rim at Gillman's Point. If instead you climbed either the Umbwe, Machame, Lemosho or Shira Routes, you will have been asked to make a choice ahead of your departure as to which final ascent route you would like to tackle. Most people will have opted for the longer but substantially easier **Barafu Route**, which accesses the crater rim at Stella Point. Those more experienced, fitter and better-acclimatised groups that chose to tackle the alternative route will access the crater via the **Western Breach**.

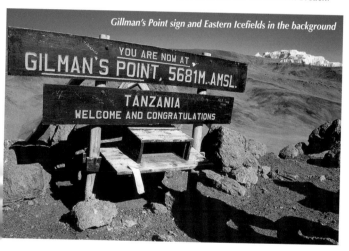

Gillman's Point sign and Eastern Icefields in the background

I: NORMAL/MARANGU ROUTE

Time on route:	6–8hrs
Length:	6km
Altitude gain:	+1192m
Start:	Kibo Hut (4703m)
End:	Uhuru Peak (5895m)
Descent route:	Marangu Route

This is the standard ascent route for the majority of climbers on Kilimanjaro. First climbed by Lange and Weigele on July 6th 1909, it is essentially a continuation of the Marangu Route. As such it is frequently known as the Marangu Route to the summit. The push to the crater rim from Kibo Hut is a steep, endless slog on loose scree that frequently gets the better of aspiring summit groups. It is the easiest approach to the crater rim of all the routes on Kibo, yet its tedious, monotonous grind can cause even the hardiest walkers to turn back. The ascent to Gillman's Point generally takes 4½–6hrs and the push to Uhuru Peak then takes a further 1½–2hrs. If the weather is bad, this final section may take much longer or even be impractical to attempt. The summit bid is usually timed to coincide with sunrise. However, slower moving groups may well arrive on the summit long after the sun is in the sky. You must keep an eye on the time though, since this marks only the halfway point for your day's exertions – you must also descend to Kibo and most usually beyond, to Horombo Hut, the same day.

The path to the summit lies directly behind Kibo Hut. Most groups will aim to leave at around midnight–1.00am, in order to maximise their chance of being on the summit for sunrise just after 6.00am, depending on the time of year. Furthermore, by setting off in the dark, the scree is more likely to be frozen, making passage easier. You will also be unable to see the sheer scale of the task ahead. Besides, sleep for any length of time at this altitude is hard to come by. Try not to arrive on the crater rim too early as you may have to wait in very cold, windy conditions for the sunrise to take place, and there is no shelter on the summit of a mountain.

Having been shaken from your fitful sleep, try to drink something before setting off. When you do begin, follow your guide as the path curls behind the Kibo Hut and begins to

THE TORTUOUS TRUTH

The photojournalist John Reader made a series of chilling calculations regarding the ascent from Kibo To Gillman's Point. In his book, *Kilimanjaro*, he wrote that, 'Gillman's Point is 980 metres above Kibo Hut, that is almost the equivalent of three Empire State Buildings standing one on top of another. The horizontal distance between Kibo Hut and Gillman's Point is roughly 3000 metres, so the gradient averages about 1:3.3 and the distance covered on the way up is about 3300 metres – the equivalent of nine Empire State Buildings laid end to end up the incline. The climb is not difficult in mountaineering terms; you could say it is equivalent to scrambling up a staircase rather more than three kilometres long. Or you could say it is equivalent to clambering up the side of nine Empire State Buildings laid end to end at about sixteen degrees. But then at 4710 metres, where the final ascent of Kilimanjaro begins, there is little more than half the density of oxygen which occurs on Manhattan or at the foot of most staircases. So in effect, the aspiring climber attempts the equivalent of those feats with the equivalent of only one lung.' He goes on to conclude that, 'The result is agonizing, there is no other word for it.'

climb. The track winds away from the huts and begins to scale the slopes.

▶ After 2hrs the trail climbs to Williams Point (5000m) and then on for 30 minutes to Hans Meyer Cave (5151m), which marks the approximate halfway point in time spent climbing, although you have gained less than half the requisite height by this stage. Hans Meyer Cave is much less grand than its name suggests and is a rather shallow hollow, marked by a plaque that commemorates the Hungarian Samuel Teleki's stay here in 1887. After the cave, the trail steepens considerably as it begins a series of demoralising switchbacks over small scree and gravel. This is by far the hardest part of the climb.

The zigzags tighten as you gain altitude and pass between two rocky ridges. You are now required to focus on the endless and enormous task of stepping into the footprints of the walker ahead of you. Set yourself small goals and continue to march on. Use trekking poles for balance and support, especially if the wind picks up on this very exposed section. Small kick steps will reduce the likelihood of scree slipping back and carrying you down the slope. The pure drudgery will dull even the most resilient spirit and the sheer exertion means that there is very little spare energy for

The early sections are uneven and rocky and care should be taken as you find a suitable, comfortable rhythm. A slow, steady pace is less tiring than taking a lot of short breaks and moving too quickly between them. It is imperative that you stick to the Kilimanjaro mantra, and ascend 'pole pole', slowly, slowly.

talking. Equally, there is nothing in the repetitive nature of the climb to hold your attention, bump your thoughts from snippets of song on heavy rotation or disturb the incessant reiteration of snatches of conversation in your head.

Although the looming ridge seems to refuse to get any closer, your progress up the slope is fairly rapid. Just below the crater rim, some 2½hrs from Hans Meyer Cave, the switchbacks and scree give way to larger boulders and jumbled rocks. The path here becomes even less distinct and you may have to scramble the last section onto the **crater rim**. Gaining the rim, you arrive at a small, level area, sign-posted **Gillman's Point** (5680m). From this point (named after a celebrated climber and prominent early member of the Mountain Club of East Africa) you can see down into the crater, across to the massive, stacked Eastern Icefields and out across the Saddle to the silhouetted outline of Mawenzi.

If you arrive at the crater rim and there is no signpost, you are most likely to be just to the right of Gillman's Point, at Johannes Notch. This spot is named after the then District Officer in Moshi, who reached here in 1898. Catch your breath and clamber left for 5 minutes, along the rim of the crater, until you arrive at the appropriate place.

Gillman's Point is a small access point and it isn't really possible to loiter here for long. Unless unable to carry on you ought to move on fairly swiftly in order to make space for other climbers coming up behind you. However, do take a moment to catch your breath and marvel at the sheer beauty of the place.

From Gillman's Point, walk along the crater rim, teetering between the steep drop into the crater itself and the outer slopes as they fall away smoothly. The views in every direction are exceptional and as the sunrise unravels then bursts from behind Mawenzi, you will be privy to one of the most spectacular, moving sights in Africa.

The haul from Gillman's Point to Uhuru Peak typically takes 1½–2hrs and is riddled with false summits. Although not especially steep, it is exceptionally draining and you may need to rest regularly before you arrive at the signpost that marks the **highest point in Africa**.

J: BARAFU ROUTE

Time on route:	6–8hrs
Length:	4.5km
Altitude gain:	+1255m
Start:	Barafu Hut (4640m)
End:	Uhuru Peak (5895m)
Descent route:	Mweka Route

A version of The Barafu Route was first used in the opening half of the 20th century to access Kibo's crater rim; today it is usually tackled in association with the Machame Route, though it can also be accessed from the Umbwe, Lemosho and Shira Routes. Regardless of the approach route, this is the most strenuous part of the climb. The ascent to the summit takes around 6–8hrs. The climb to Stella Point on the crater rim usually lasts 4½–6hrs and the push from here to Uhuru Peak will take a further 1½–2hrs.

The Barafu Route is a steep, tough ascent on loose scree and small rocks that crests the crater rim alongside the Rebmann Glacier at Stella Point. The climb is only a stiff walk, except in the aftermath of heavy snow when it may become much more of an effort. During the driest months from December to March the whole route is usually free from snow. In the remainder of the year you may encounter snow as low as 4600m. However, the altitude and cold add to the overall hardship on the climb.

As on all of the final ascent routes, the climb to the crater rim begins shortly after midnight in order to take advantage of the frozen scree and ensure that you arrive on the crater rim or at the summit in time for sunrise. A headlamp is vital and walking poles may also make your progress easier on the unstable, shifting surface. By setting off early, you will also guarantee that you have sufficient time to descend from the mountain to the Mweka Hut, the overnight campsite on the way down the mountain from here.

From the Barafu Hut the path winds up the western side of the South East Valley. The path scales two short, rocky cliffs to the north of Barafu Hut before levelling as it approaches the final steep climb to Stella Point. The path bends left and begins to zigzag up the slope on a series of tight switchbacks These switchbacks persist for the next 3hrs. The climb is ir no way technical, but the tedious slog on loose and enervat ing scree and shale is disheartening. Kick your feet into the scree and plant your walking poles firmly into the slope to help you edge your way up the slope and prevent yourself from slipping unduly.

The gradient increases yet further as you arrive a the **final incline**. The switchbacks peter out and the fina 30-minute direct ascent is done on fine, loose gravel. As you approach the snout of the Rebmann Glacier, the path jig right to climb between this and the remains of the Ratze Glacier. Follow the gap up until the gradient relents and you gain the crater rim at **Stella Point** (5700m). ◀

By this stage the sun is probably set to rise from behinc Mawenzi and the thin band of red and gold on the horizon is likely to be expanding rapidly. Pause at Stella Point and revel in your achievement as the light fills the sky and the sun bursts from behind the horizon, illuminating the glacia snows and the blanket of clouds lying far below you. Behinc you, to the north, is the crater. The view across the inne Reusch Crater to the Northern Icefields is similarly powerful

The route from Stella Point to Uhuru Peak is the same as that from Gillman's Point (the access point on the crate rim from the Marangu and Rongai Routes). Gillman's Poin

Stella Point is named after the wife of Kingsley Latham, a member of the Mountain Club of South Africa. They both reached this point in 1925.

Silhouette of Mawenzi from Stella Point at sunrise

lies 30-45 minutes to the right of Stella Point. For the summit, turn left and head west around the crater edge, passing above the stepped Rebmann Glacier, ascending slowly for 1–1½hr until you arrive at the celebrated signpost on the **'Roof of Africa'**.

Rebmann Glacier at sunrise as seen from Stella Point

221

K: WESTERN BREACH ROUTE

Time on route:	5½–7½hrs
Length:	4km
Altitude gain:	+1045m
Start:	Arrow Glacier (4850m)
End:	Uhuru Peak (5895m)
Descent:	Mweka Route

Following the deaths of three US trekkers close to the Arrow Glacier Hut in January 2006 the Western Breach was temporarily closed. The route has been modified slightly since and reopened, with the proviso that all trekkers tackling it take a protective helmet. Even so some agencies steer clear of it entirely and others insist that you sign a waiver form clearing them of any fault should an accident occur.

This is the hardest, most impressive non-technical route to the crater rim. The Western Breach is a rugged gash in Kibo's flank, which disturbs the uniform shape of the summit. Created by a massive landslip around 100,000 years ago, the gradient here is marginally less steep than the sheer cliffs that surround the route. The climbers Oehler and Klute first descended the route in 1912. The date of the first ascent is not recorded, but it is known that the Sheffield University scientific survey party ascended the Western Breach in August–September 1953.

The views are breathtaking and the fact that the route is so much less popular than either the Normal/Marangu Route or the Barafu Route means that you will have a far greater sense of isolation and wildness. The reason for this lack of popularity is readily apparent. Although there is no technical climbing involved, this is a classic scramble route involving some very steep sections and some quite exposed areas. Exertion is high and the route should only be contemplated by fit and highly acclimatised groups.

The Western Breach can be accessed from the Machame, Umbwe, Lemosho and Shira Routes, most usually via an overnight stop at Lava Tower. The descent from the summit after this route is traditionally done along the Mweka Route.

The Western Breach is in some respects a one-way ticket, since there is little option of retreat once you have started up the face. A little after your departure, the porters will strike camp and race around the bulk of Kibo in order to meet you in time to pitch camp at Mweka Hut. Thus, if you turn back, there will be no shelter, food or water at Arrow Glacier for you. Your only real option is to then descend all the way to Mweka Hut yourself, in pursuit of your porters.

STAGE 1
Lava Tower to Arrow Glacier

The Western Breach is best tackled in two stages. The first sees you ascend from Lava Tower to Arrow Glacier, from where you are ideally poised to begin the final ascent. If coming from the Umbwe Route or via the South Circuit Path there is the option to skip Lava Tower and progress straight to Arrow Glacier. Unless you are exceptionally fit and well acclimatised, this is not recommended. Rather, detour to Lava Tower and use the additional day to prepare yourself physically and psychologically for the challenge ahead.

The ascent from Lava Tower to Arrow Glacier is very short and will only take 1–1½hrs. However, the additional 200m height gained and the extra 24hrs exposure to altitude is invaluable.

From the campsite in the shadow of the orange-black volcanic plug of the Lava Tower, the path is clearly visible, winding across a set of desolate ridges. The track descends slightly and crosses a small stream of meltwater before beginning to climb on fine, loose gravel. A series of small tight switchbacks carry you to the top of the first ridge after 20–30 minutes. From the top of this ridge there are great views of the Lava Tower and across the northern flank of Kilimanjaro towards the Shira Plateau.

The path dips briefly in order to descend into a small valley and ford a further meltwater stream. It quickly picks up and rises again, crossing slightly larger obstacles as it regains the lost height. Use walking poles and carefully placed steps to keep your balance here. After 30 minutes the path crests the ridge and enters a small, level area at the foot of a vast, natural amphitheatre. This is the **Arrow Glacier campsite** (4850m).

Campsite at foot of Lava Tower

Arrow Glacier itself is visible east of the campsite o[n] the far side of a creased plateau. The imperious glacier is i[n] retreat and what was once a significant mass of ice is now [a] rather grubby shadow of its former self. Arrow Glacier H[ut] was destroyed by a rock fall in the mid 1980s and hasn['t] been rebuilt since.

There are few obvious tent pitches here, but when selec[t]ing a site, try to place yourself in the lee of the rocky prow th[at] rises on the western side of the plateau and affords some sma[ll] shelter from the raging winds that hustle across the plateau. I[n] the midst of the plateau are rather exposed long-drop toile[ts]. Water is usually fetched from meltwater streams flowing fro[m] the Arrow Glacier 200m east of the camp.

The wind often picks up later in the day and can b[e] heard whipping across the summit. Cloud will often mou[nt] up in the afternoon as well, obscuring the way ahead. Havin[g] explored the area, retreat to the relative comfort of your te[nt] to eat and sleep, and await the early morning summons [to] tackle the climb to the summit.

The Arrow Glacier campsite is a particularly inhospitable, barren place to camp. However, the views are sensational. The camp is set right at the foot of the Western Breach. Ahead of you an enormous amphitheatre rises from the boulders and scree. To the east of the Western Breach itself stands the massive, sheer cliffs of the Breach Wall. This 1400m cliff features some of the hardest technical mountaineering on Kilimanjaro and indeed the whole of Africa. Legendary mountaineer Reinhold Messner, and Konrad Renzler first climbed the direct route on the Breach Wall, which includes an improbable ascent of a 90m icicle that links two glaciers, on 31 January 1978. The route has been likened to the north face of the Eiger in terms of technical difficulty.

There are several sobering reminders of the severity of the climbing in the area. Whilst exploring the immediate slopes you may well come across a brass plaque commemorating the death of a young American climber in 1972 from AMS. However, it's not just climbers that must beware here, trekkers too are at risk. In January 2006 three tourists were killed close to Arrow Glacier Camp and a further trekker and three porters seriously injured when a sudden change in weather and the onset of stiff winds caused a rockslide as the group were preparing to tackle the Western Breach. The Park authorities subsequently closed the route temporarily. This tragedy serves to reinforce the need for caution in this area at all times.

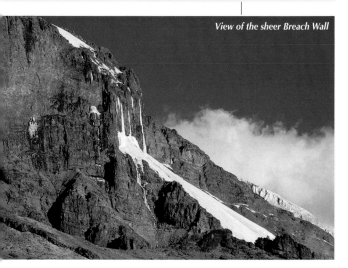

View of the sheer Breach Wall

STAGE 2
Arrow Glacier to Uhuru Peak

This final approach to the crater rim and on to Uhuru Peak is the toughest non-technical climb on Kilimanjaro. In less than ideal conditions, the Western Breach has epic potential. The ascent is steep and exposed, requiring you to use both hands to scramble upwards in places. On the plus side though, the climb is exhilarating and the sense of achievement enormous. The ascent is akin to a series of steep stairs with sections of ladder thrown in for good measure. Once you begin the ascent proper, the climb is free of the scree and loose material that characterises the climb to the crater rim on either the Normal/Marangu Route or the Barafu Route. The Western Breach ought to be clear and viable most of the year round. Although this is a non-technical trekking route, if there has been heavy snowfall then it may become impassable without the aid of an ice axe and crampons.

Most groups depart from Arrow Glacier camp around 1.00am, allowing themselves to climb through the night and take advantage of the frozen scree and more stable underfoot conditions. In turn, this should ensure that you arrive on the summit in time for sunrise.

If you are lucky and the night sky is clear, then you will **begin by picking your way across the lower scree slopes** beneath a star-studded, black obsidian sky. Use a headlight to illuminate a path over the rocks as you begin to ascend east of the small talus and scree hill above Arrow Glacier campsite, past overhanging cliffs and pale patches of snow and ice. Above this is a **rock rib**. Skirt this, climbing alongside it for 500m until the path arrives at the foot of the wall ahead. Here the path cuts right onto the rocky rib and becomes steeper. A section of abrupt scrambling follows, which will require you to stow your walking poles in order to be able to use both hands to stabilise and balance yourself. The Arrow Glacier camp shrinks far below you as you gain height, edging between the patches of residual snow and ice.

Unlike the other two walking ascents to the crater rim, you can not simply drift up the slope in a trance. On the Western Breach you must focus and concentrate closely on what you are doing. There is little margin for error and a fall here could be very serious indeed. Nonetheless, the haul to Uhuru is a sensational skywalk.

If the moon is full, or even if the night is clear, then you will have unprecedented views over the Shira Plateau and western flank, allowing you to gauge the sheer physical size of the mountain and get a real feel for its enormity.

The ascent to the **crater rim** takes 4–5hrs. The final climb to access the crater is via a series of steep cliffs and intricate buttresses above airy drops, which require you to take large vertical steps and hold yourself in place with both hands. Having zigzagged from one cliff to another, you will arrive at a depression in the crater rim, occasionally referred to as the **Great West Notch** (5650m).

Once inside the crater, you will be faced by the **Furtwangler Glacier** at the western foot of the central ash cone. To the right the crater rim rises approximately 250m and away to the south-east Uhuru Peak is visible. The path is indistinct, but circumvents the crater floor between the Furtwangler Glacier and the edge of the Western Breach. Furtwangler Glacier is named after a climber who summited in 1912 and then became the first man to descend Kilimanjaro on skis.

Approach the peppermint snout of the glacier. Keep the glacier on your left as you crunch across the level interior of the crater. As you pass by the glacier, feel the icy chill that hums off the white-blue wall like electricity. On the far side of the crater, some 2km away, Stella Point is visible.

After 15–30 minutes the path brings you to the foot of a steep gully. A clear track zigzags up the slope to the left of a prominent buttress. As you gain height on the switchbacks, pause and look back over the Furtwangler Glacier to the Reusch Crater and beyond to the massed steps of the Northern Icefields.

After 1–1½hrs of ascending these strenuous final switchbacks, the path bends left one more time and climbs onto the **edge of the crater rim**. Away to the west, Mt Meru is often hazily visible. From here the path follows the edge of the crater rim south for 15–30 minutes, climbing slightly to reach **Uhuru Peak** (5895m). As you approach the signpost that marks the summit, Mawenzi will be silhouetted across the crater and the sun will rise from behind its jagged peaks to signify the beginning of another glorious day.

THE SUMMIT

'Kilimanjaro is a snow covered mountain 19,710ft high, and is said to be the highest mountain in Africa. Its western summit is called 'Ngaje Ngai', the House of God.'

(Ernest Hemmingway,
The Snows of Kilimanjaro)

The summit of Kilimanjaro is a remarkable, otherworldly place. The crown of Kibo is a vast crater that contains an inner crater and an ash pit. The blasted rock and shattered slopes give it a harsh air, whilst the improbable icefields and glaciers decorate the rim and upper slopes. The landscape here is akin to a still raw wound, redolent of the earth's violent and explosive past.

Having scrambled up the Normal/Marangu Route, Barafu Route or the Western Breach, you find yourself on the rim of this vast volcano. The highest point on the crater rim is Uhuru Peak (5895m). This is unsurprisingly the focus for the majority of walkers. However, whether they make it to the summit is still open to question since it is some distance from any of the crater access points. HW Tilman observed that, 'Between the point at which the crater wall is first reached and this highest point, a distance of perhaps 600 or 700 yards, are three other peaks, points, or bumps of varying heights, all slightly lower than Kaiser Wilhelm Spitze [now Uhuru Peak] itself. These several points were always the cause of much heart burning.'

For many people simply gaining the crater rim is sufficient reward. Gillman's Point is the lowest point on the southern rim. Accessed from the Normal/Marangu Route, it is still 1.5km from Uhuru Peak. The summit is a further 210m higher than this point and the arduous approach is often too daunting for exhausted walkers. Tilman himself and his companion Eric Shipton, failed to reach Uhuru Peak on his first attempt in 1930, admitting that beyond Stella Point, 'Yet another top loomed vaguely through the mists some distance ahead, but I am obliged to confess that its challenge aroused little interest in us, and, after debate, we turned in our tracks.'

Those that do have the strength to push on to the summit will be richly rewarded. The view from Uhuru is utterly breathtaking. The whole summit looks unfinished. In the thi

Jubilant celebrations at the summit

CONGRATULATIONS! YOU ARE NOW AT **UHURU PEAK, TANZANIA, 5895M. AMSL.** AFRICA'S HIGHEST POINT, WORLD'S HIGHEST F... ...TANDING MOUNTAIN ...ONE OF WORL... ...VOLCANOES. ...ELCOME...

and freezing air every line and every colour is sharp. Everything is jagged. There are no curves, no fading, no blurring. It is beautiful. From the summit you will be able to see across the outer crater and over the resurgent inner cone to the remarkable Northern Icefields and beyond to the sunblushed clouds below. Inside the inner cone is the **Reusch Crater** and the 360m wide, 120m deep **Ash Pit**.

For those wishing to **access the Reusch Crater** and see into the heart of the volcano, there is an indistinct trail that leads from the top of the Western Breach. The climb itself is relatively simple, allowing for the fact that you are at extreme altitude and takes 45 minutes to an hour to complete. It is also possible to drop into the crater from Gillman's Point or Stella Point and cross to the foot of the cone. The path is virtually invisible, but your guide should be able to find his way.

Make sure that you arrange the trip to the Reusch Crater well in advance of your climb. This unusual addition to an ascent of the mountain will require additional preparation and will certainly incur extra cost. Similarly, it is possible to camp in the crater although this is rarely done and not widely recommended (unless you are very well acclimatised and rather wealthy, as it is exorbitantly expensive).

KILIMANJARO'S FABLED HIDDEN TREASURE

A well-known legend alludes to the burial place of Menelik I, the great emperor of Ethiopia and the son of Solomon and Sheba, on the summit of Kilimanjaro. A popular and successful monarch, Menelik I expanded his territories to include the lands to the south of Ethiopia, as far as Kilimanjaro. As the elderly king journeyed home after these conquests, he passed over the Saddle and determined to die on the mountain. Gathering a number of his warlords and his personal slaves, Menelik I collected his finest treasures and set off up the slopes. The warlords later returned unaccompanied and reported that the king and his slaves had descended into the crater in order to sleep forever. The legend maintains that an heir to the throne will climb Kilimanjaro and discover the fabled treasures and the Seal of Solomon, the mystical ring responsible for his great wisdom. Armed with this discovery, the heir to the throne would help Ethiopia to reclaim her exulted status.

DESCENT ROUTES

In order to reduce the potential damage to the mountain and to channel people descending off the summit, there are several dedicated descent routes on Kilimanjaro. Having ascended slowly to the summit over the course of several days, you will drop off the mountain quickly, taking a fraction of that time to return to a lower elevation.

National Park regulations stipulate that particular ascent routes are affiliated with particular descent routes. Those people who climb the Marangu or Rongai Routes will be required to descend along the Marangu Route. Those who used the other ascent routes will have to come off the mountain on the Mweka Route. The Alternative Mweka Route is described here as well; opened whilst the Mweka Route was being renovated, it is currently closed, but could be called back into service if further renovation to the stipulated descent route is required in the future.

L: MARANGU ROUTE

Time on route:	2 days
Length:	29km
Altitude loss:	–2848m
Start:	Kibo Hut (4703m)
End:	Marangu Gate (1855m)

STAGE 1
Kibo to Horombo Hut

Having ascended via the Normal/Marangu Route, whether in conjunction with the Marangu Route or the Rongai Route, you will descend the mountain along the Marangu Route. For those who used the Marangu Route on the ascent this is an unfortunate retracing of your steps that is one of the drawbacks to using this particular climb. For those who approached Kibo from the north along the Rongai Route, this is a chance to see an entirely different aspect of the mountain and to enjoy some of the forest sections that have been cleared on the lower northern slopes. Your path on this descent route can be traced on the maps in the Marangu and Normal/Marangu Ascent route descriptions.

Having loitered on the summit, reveled in your achievement and taken the obligatory photographs, **turn back and begin to retreat** around the crater rim to Gillman's Point. The return journey is equally slow and tiring due to the altitude. After an hour of shuffling and stopping the path arrives at Gillman's Point.

It is essential to be back at Gillman's Point around 3hrs after sunrise, since the top layer of snow is by now beginning to become wet and slippery, complicating your descent. Equally, the rising sun is very strong and can be harsh to spend too much time under.

From Gillman's Point, lower yourself over the large rocky outcrops until you reach the beginning of the scree slope. By now you can see just how large and horrific this gravel slope is. It is likely that it is also no longer frozen, making the surface much less stable. Every step will be accompanied by a sink and slide, making the descent to Kibo Hut almost as tough as the original climb. Many of the zigzags are indistinguishable, but try to avoid simply running down the scree, as this can cause large amounts of disturbance to the mountainside, forcing tons of rock down the slopes. It also causes a lot of fine, irritating dust to be kicked up and will increase your chances of having a potentially dangerous fall.

The descent to Kibo takes 2hrs, although it will feel much longer since the huts are visible from high on the mountainside and don't appear to get any closer despite your exhausted, sleep-deprived body's best efforts in steadily rising temperatures.

Eventually the path careers past **Hans Meyer Cave** and **Williams Point** before coiling across the foothills and back to **Kibo Hut**, where, dusty and sweat-streaked, you'll receive your congratulations or commiserations. Try to rest here for 1–2hrs, drinking and rehydrating your body.

Leave Kibo Hut as you arrived and drop back down to the Saddle. Beneath the prominent rocky outcrop at the entrance to the Kibo Hut area is a fork in the path. Ignore the path to the left, which traverses the Saddle on its way to Mawenzi Tarn Hut, and follow the larger, clearer **track on the right-hand side of the Saddle**.

Having most likely ascended from Horombo Hut onto the Saddle via the Western Path, try to persuade your guide to take you back via the Eastern Path, which will prevent you from simply seeing the same features again.

Descend through the vast, featureless alpine desert for 45 mintutes to an hour to **Jiwe Lainkoyo**. Beyond here, the path continues east towards Mawenzi on a faint trail that branches off from the main track. Some 20 minutes later the trail passes a **sign** indicating the intersection with the North Circuit Path. Ignore this and bear south past a **pair of tarns**, undulating as you work your way across Mawenzi's lower slopes. ◄

An hour beyond the junction you reach the highest point on this section of path and are afforded excellent views by looking back across the expanse of the Saddle towards Kibo's eastern face.

The path then drops gently past a series of low cliffs towards **Zebra Rock**. Once past this unusually stripped cliff face, the path reconnects with the alternative, Western Path and then descends between rocky outcrops, boulders and groundsel to arrive at Horombo Hut (3720m).

STAGE 2
Horombo Hut to Marangu Gate

This final section is a very satisfying end to your Kilimanjaro experience. The descent is gentle and steady and passes through some very pleasant stretches of scenery. Walk slowly, enjoy the downhill gradient and look at the minutae along the trail. You'll also be able to see both Kibo and Mawenzi slip away from you.

Retrace your steps across the heath/moorland through the tussock grasses and heathers. Inevitably, a multicoloured tide of humanity flowing uphill will pass you on its way towards Kibo's ramparts. The path re-enters the forest and drops swiftly to **Mandara Hut**, arriving here after 2½–3hrs. This is usually used as the last lunch stop on the mountain.

Having finished your snacks, continue walking by joining the path as it snakes though the forest. Make the most of your final moments on this monolith, since the **Marangu Gate** is reached after only a further 1½hrs. At the end of the trail, the path passes under an archway and swings round to finish before the National Park offices, where you conclude your trip by registering your success and collecting your certificate.

M: Mweka Route

Time on route:	2 days
Length:	17km
Altitude loss:	–3000m
Start:	Barafu Hut (4640m)
End:	Mweka Gate (1640m)

The successful attainment of the summit is only the first part of what will seem like an endless day. Having reached Uhuru Peak, or even just the crater rim, you will still need to descend. What's more, you must drop not only to Barafu Hut, but then also onto Mweka Hut for the overnight camp. The descent is steep and you lose height rapidly. It is consequently very tough. The slopes leading from the crater rim are unstable and the slipsliding descent means that your knees will take a pounding.

The Mweka Route is the stipulated descent route for the Umbwe, Machame, Lemosho and Shira ascent routes. It is used having climbed to the crater rim via either the Barafu or Western Breach routes. First opened in 1965, the Mweka Route is the easternmost route on the western flank and provides a very fast, direct descent from the mountain.

Originally, park regulations only permitted a small number of people to use the various forest and moorland ascent routes, which meant that the authorities could control and regulate the number of people descending on the Mweka Route. Thereby they were able to restrict the damage that was being done to the mountain. With the removal of the cap on the numbers of people walking the various routes and the general increase in popularity of the Machame Route, it was inevitable that the extra wear on the path would result in massive track damage. The Mweka Route as it was simply couldn't cope with the additional volume of traffic. Consequently the route was closed for a while in August 2001 so that essential track maintenance could be carried out and the surrounding environment could recover and regenerate. The Mweka Route was reopened at the end of 2002 and once more became the nominated descent route for the western and southern approach routes.

STAGE 1
Barafu Hut to Mweka Hut

From Uhuru Peak, initially follow the crater rim south and then east, passing above the Southern Icefields, until you reach **Stella Point**. The circumnavigation of the crater takes an hour. From here drop off the side of the crater and zigzag down the Barafu Route to the summit. By this stage of the day, the scree will have unfrozen and the ground underfoot will be even less stable than it was during the ascent to the top. Retain your balance by using trekking poles and by not rushing. **Do not feel pressured into descending too quickly as there is a real risk of a serious fall here.** The more energetic or nimble may find scree running a quicker alternative to following the switchbacks. **However, this can kick up quantities of irritating, fine dust and the slope suffers more erosion as vast amounts of scree is pushed downhill by the passage of running feet.**

At the foot of the scree slope the path regains more solid ground. It winds across a flatter stretch before descending two short, steep, stepped cliff sections to arrive at **Barafu Hut** after 1½–2hrs. Rest and recuperate briefly on the barren, lava-strewn ridge here, taking the time to rehydrate and reflect on the earlier mornings achievements.

Kibo looming above the forest as seen from the Mweka Hut

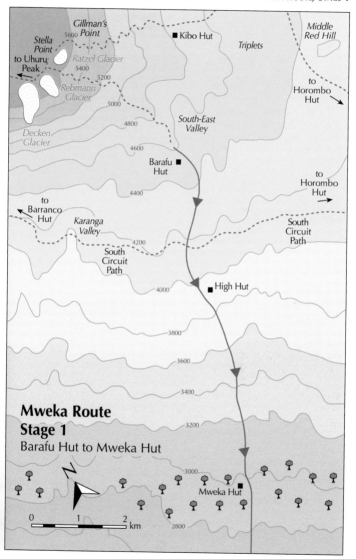

**Mweka Route
Stage 1**
Barafu Hut to Mweka Hut

Shortly after the crossroad you will be able to make out the roof of a uniport in the distance amidst a grove of trees. This is a deceptive vision though, since although the hut has a campsite next to it, it is usually only used by those descending late or too slowly to make the Mweka Hut.

From Barafu Hut, the path drops south and then south-west for 45 minutes along a prominent ridge above **South-East Valley**, through a thoroughly bleak and benighted landscape. The path tumbles out of the desolate, highland desert and into the moorland, where it arrives at a **cross-roads** that marks the intersection of the descent route with the South Circuit Path. The crossroads is well signposted, with directions to Barranco or Horombo Huts via the South Circuit Path and to the Mweka Hut. Continue **straight ahead**, descending in a roughly southerly direction. Vegetation begins to reassert itself as you drop lower and heathers and grasses reappear alongside the path as you enter the moorland. ◄

Thirty to forty-five minutes after the crossroad, the path drops through light forest to this hut and high campsite. There are long-drop toilets here and water can be collected from a stream close to the path.

The path continues to descend steadily south through giant heathers and patchy grasses. Other plants begin to reappear as you get lower, including *Protea* and *Erica* bushes.

A great deal of work has been done to improve the quality of the track here, and many of the worst sections of the track have been re-laid and levelled. Steps have been built to ease the slope and drainage channels have been cut alongside the track to prevent the soil from washing away during heavy rains. However, in some places the stones laid to level the track are unbalancing and awkward to walk on.

There are good views to be had looking north over the treetops towards the glistening snowfields atop Kibo.

The path broadens and runs to the west of a wide, shallow valley, through an area rich in *Protea* and *Erica*. After an hour the trees gain height and the understorey becomes thicker. Fifteen minutes later the path dips steeply before veering right and climbing through a series of S-bends to emerge in a large clearing adjacent to **Mweka Hut** (3100m).

Two large uniports are set amidst a series of clearings. There are a large number of tent pitches straggling alongside the path leading south-west from the huts. There are also long-drop toilets here. Mweka Hut is frequently dry, so water must be carried from the high campsite or retrieved from a stream 30 minutes further down the mountain. ◄

STAGE 2
Mweka Hut to Mweka Gate

This is a short, relatively swift final day that sees you descend the remaining distance through the forest to Mweka Gate. The forest section is lush and extremely picturesque. The track here used to be very narrow and after rainfall would degenerate rapidly into a slippery trench. A lot of work has been done recently to improve this section of track and much of it has been graded and levelled. Steps have been cut into the steeper sections and water channels line the path to prevent its future deterioration.

Track through the forest below the Mweka hut

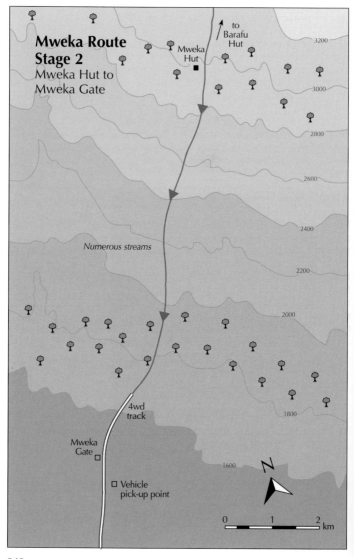

**Mweka Route
Stage 2**
Mweka Hut to
Mweka Gate

Mweka
Hut

to
Barafu
Hut

3200

3000

2800

2600

2400

Numerous streams

2200

2000

4wd
track

1800

Mweka
Gate

1600

Vehicle
pick-up point

N

0   1   2 km

The path **from Mweka Hut** passes south-west through a copse of skinny trees and giant heathers before dropping quite suddenly into much denser cloud forest. The path passes along the crest of a narrow ridge with steep-sided valleys to either side. After half an hour there is a **signpost** that indicates the indistinct track that winds down through the vegetation to the left of the path, to reach the stream at the bottom of the valley.

The path snakes through the forest and in places crosses the old route. The old path is set up to 2ft deep in the ground as a result of heavy erosion and is worn smooth to resemble a dry irrigation channel. In wet weather it resembles a muddy stream. ▶

After 1½–2hrs the path broadens into a dusty 4WD track, which used to be used as a logging road. The forest opens up as you near the Mweka Gate until 30-45 minutes later you emerge amidst a bustle of people and Landrovers at the **Mweka Gate**. Register at the hut here to complete your climb.

Unfortunately, most outfitters will not have a vehicle here to collect you, so you must gird yourself and walk a further 15 minutes downhill through banana plantations to arrive at the road end, where you will find a host of curio shops and the Tobit Kilimanjaro View Centre, which is ostensibly a bar full of exhausted, exhilarated climbers.

As you continue to descend steeply, be aware of teams of porters rushing past you. Step to one side and allow the faster moving people to pass. Conversely, you ought to walk slowly and admire the forest. Enjoy the tall forest trees, dense tangled patches and sunlit glades where mosses and lichens glow rich and green in the sunlight. Watch too for the reappearance of *Impatiens kilimanjari*.

N: ALTERNATIVE MWEKA ROUTE

Time on route:	2 days
Length:	29km
Start:	Barafu Hut (4640m)
End:	Kidia Gate (1500m)

During the time that the Mweka Route was closed for rehabilitation, from the end of 2001 to late 2002, the park authorities opened a new descent route along similar lines. Descending from Stella Point along the Barafu Route, the Alternative Mweka Route diverges from the traditional Mweka Route just beyond Barafu Hut. It then drops steeply just to the east of the original route and ends at the Kidia Gate. The route is sometimes referred to as the Kidia Route as a result. Some outfitters also know it as the Rau Route, since it follows the course of the Rau River.

Now that the original Mweka Route has been renovated and vastly improved, it has been reopened. This in turn signalled the closure of the Alternative Mweka Route, which remains shut. (Though a route description is included here, maps of this route are not). Although having a second descent on this section of the mountain was a good idea as it reduced the pressure and foot traffic on the Mweka Route, the temporary track took a severe pounding and is itself badly eroded now. Therefore, despite the fact that Kilimanjaro is in need of another descent route, this is not the solution.

Essentially the two routes are very similar, traversing near identical tracts of land. However, the original Mweka Route is shorter, more direct and slightly more scenic.

Horombo Hut sign

STAGE 1
Barafu Hut to Rau Campsite

At the time the track was open, this was a long, somewhat tedious descent from the summit of Kilimanjaro to the edge of the heath/moorland zone. The route is generally fairly monotonous and makes gentle progress down the mountain.

From the summit, follow the path around the crater rim until you reach **Stella Point**. From here commence the arduous descent on loose scree, dropping past the Rebmann Glacier on your right and on down towards Barafu Hut. After 10–15 minutes, a relentless series of switchbacks start, which will slowly lower you down Kibo's flank. Forty-five minutes to an hour after leaving the crater rim the gradient eases and the path veers across a broken plateau before dropping down two steep, stepped cliffs to the north of the **Barafu Hut**.

Having allowed you to rest, recuperate and rehydrate briefly, your guide will spur you on, rousing you from your stupor and driving you south. **From the Barafu Hut** the path climbs down a short section of the **South-East Valley** wall via a series of switchbacks. At the foot of the valley the path leads south-east across a barren, rocky surface. After 15 minutes it climbs steeply out of this valley before promptly dropping into a near identical one to the east.

▸ Half an hour after leaving Barafu Hut, the path forks at a **signpost**. The left-hand fork is a porters' path to Horombo Hut. Ignore this and take the right-hand fork as it descends through an increasingly interesting and diverse landscape.

Senecio and heathers appear along the trail as it undulates south, descending all the while.

After 15 minutes the South Circuit Path bisects the track. To the left lies the Horombo Hut, to the right the Barranco Hut. Ignore both of these options and continue to drop off the side of the mountain by plunging straight ahead. After a further 1½hrs the Rau campsite hoves into view. Unfortunately this mirage is a further 30-minute walk away.

The path trudges through a repetitive moorland landscape amidst *Senecios* and heather before crossing a small bridge, climbing a slight mound and arriving at the **Rau Campsite** (3250m). There are plenty of tent pitches, an actual sit-down toilet and a reliable water source here.

STAGE 2
Rau Campsite to Kidia Gate

The final descent from the mountain was initially very scenic and attractive, but having entered the forest the trail undulated endlessly before joining a 4WD track that looped across the lower slopes in a time consuming and unnecessary fashion.

Immediately **after the Rau Campsite** is a section of very pretty rolling hills. The trail leads south through meadows full of *Lobelia*. Beyond these, on the right-hand side, are a number of trees that thrive on the banks of one of the Rau River's tributaries.

An hour after leaving the campsite the trail passes a series of **signposts** that warn of the dangers posed by dropped cigarettes and the potential for forest fires. There is a picnic site set by a stream just next to these. Just down from here the path enters the forest and passes through an increasingly dense, mixed collection of trees eerily festooned with old man's beard and other lichens.

Impatiens Kilimanjari and other bright forest flowers are clearly evident admidst the buttressed tree roots.

◄ Once inside the forest, the path drops steeply before ascending a ridge that lies between two valleys. The path alternatively drops steeply and climbs roughly for an hour as it follows one side of a ridge before then switching to the eastern side of the ridge. It crosses a small stream on a wooden bridge and enters a section of lighter forest. Set here is another picnic table, confusingly called **Picnic Site No 1**.

Beyond the picnic site the path maintains its southerly direction, crossing a series of small streams and passing between a number of manmade water channels. It drops past a section full of tree ferns before climbing abruptly to the top of a small hill. At the summit of the hill is a large aerial tower. After this point the **4WD track** that leads to Kidia Gate begins. The path merges with the 4WD track and bends and winds downhill for an hour before eventually happening upon the **Kidia Gate** (1500m). Complete the requisite registration formalities here and relax now that the adventure is over.

APPENDIX A

Ascent Route Comparison Chart

ASCENT ROUTE:	MARANGU	UMBWE	MACHAME	LEMOSHO	SHIRA	RONGAI
LENGTH:	65km	44km	61km	72km	67km	54km
USUAL TIME:	5 days	5 days	6 days	7 days	6 days	6 days
GRADE:	Moderate/hard	Hard	Hard	Moderate/Hard	Moderate/Hard	Moderate/Hard
SUMMIT ASCENT ROUTE:	Normal/Marangu	Barafu Western Breach	Barafu Western Breach	Barafu Western Breach	Barafu Western Breach	Normal/Marangu
DESCENT ROUTE:	Marangu	Mweka	Mweka	Mweka	Mweka	Marangu
VEGETATION:	Good forest sections moorland sections.	Outstanding forest section. Short moorland section.	Superb ecological mix. Good forest and moorland sections.	Very good forest section. Interesting Shira Plateau section.	No route through forest section on ascent. Interesting moorland section.	Poor lower slopes, deforested and cultivated. Excellent moorland section.
INTEREST:	Lower slopes and forest very interesting. Tedious summit route. Must retrace footsteps on decent route.	Good lower slopes. Excellent views of Summit, Barranco Valley and Southern Icefields.	Stunning scenery and exceptional views.	Good forest approach, excellent moorland section and fine traverse of Southern Icefields.	Good Shira Plateau section and fine traverse below Southern Icefields. 4WD access to high trailhead reduces acclimatisation potential.	Good quality route that provides exceptional access to Mawenzi. Tedious summit bid and descent on Marangu Route, which can be crowded.
COST:	US$1300–1400	US$1500	US$1500–1600	US$1800	US$1800	US$1300–1400

245

APPENDIX B

Accommodation

There are a host of accommodation options at the foot of Kilimanjaro in Moshi. Those listed here represent a spectrum of the options available and ought to cater for most budgets.

GOLDEN SHOWER (Marangu Rd, Tel. 275 1990)
Camping US$3. Small shady site to pitch tents about 2km out of town.

YMCA (Taifa Rd, Tel. 275 1754, Fax. 275 1734, Email tzymca@africaonline.co.tz) Single/double rooms US$10/13, with bathroom US$18/25. Over priced, but safe and clean, if a bit run down. Very popular with backpackers. Good views of Kilimanjaro from some rooms. Pool and restaurant on site.

BUFFALO HOTEL (New St, Tel. 275 0270, Email twigacom2001@yahoo.com) Single/double rooms US$10/15. Very popular three-storey hotel that represents good value for money. All rooms have a fan and mosquito nets, whilst some are en suite. Also has a restaurant on site.

HOTEL DA COSTA (Mawenzi Rd, Tel. 275 4054, Email wilfredmberesero@yahoo.com, www.dacostahotel.com) Single/double rooms US$3/5. Very good value no-frills, budget hotel. Clean rooms with shared facilities. Rooftop bar and restaurant on site. The Kilimanjaro Porters Assistance Project have an office on the ground floor here.

HOTEL NEW CASTLE (Mawenzi Rd, Tel. 275 3203) Single/double rooms US$10/15. Reasonable venue. Rooms have fans but no mosquito nets. Also has a rooftop bar.

IMPALA (Lema Road, Tel. 027 275 3443) Welcoming and attractive place to stay, with its own pool and ensuite rooms. Single/double rooms US$80/100, with breakfast included.

KILIMANJARO BACKPACKERS (Nyeri Rd, Tel 027 275 5159, www.kilimanjarobackpackers.com) Dorm US$5, single/double rooms US$8/12. Despite being pretty basic, this is a popular place – in large part due to the reasonable rates.

NEW COFFEE TREE HOTEL, right next to clock tower, Tel. 027 275 1382. Rooms are basic, but essentially clean and secure. Rates start at Tsh8000 for a single and rise to Tsh 20,000 for an ensuite double.

KINDOROKO HOTEL (Mawenzi Rd, Tel. 275 4054, www.kindoroko.com) Single/double rooms US$15/30, with bathroom, TV and fridge US$20/25.

Small but functional place that has a good reputation Slightly pricey. Rooftop bar and restaurant on site.

BRISTOL COTTAGES (98A Rindi Lane, Tel. 027 275 5083, www.bristolcottages.com) Single/double rooms US$60/75. More expensive option that buys you a small, modern, immaculate cottage set in a tidy garden. Restaurant on site.

KEY'S HOTEL (Uru Rd, Tel. 275 2250, Email keys-hotel@africaonline.co.tz, www.keys-hotel-tours.com) Double rooms US$50. Air conditioning costs a further US$20. Quiet, comfortable and long-standing venue that has a superb reputation. Rooms in the main building are better than the cottages at the back. Pool, restaurant and bar on site.

KILIMANJARO CRANE HOTEL (Kaunda Rd, Tel. 275 1114, www.kilimanjarocranehotels.com) Single/double/triple rooms US$40/45/50. Double rooms with air conditioning cost a little more. Large, modern, plain hotel with reasonable amenities. Bar and restaurant on site.

MOSHI LEOPARD HOTEL (Market St, Tel. 275 0884, www.leopardhotel.com) Single/double rooms US$40/50. Large, modern hotel with good amenities, including fridge and TV, in busy part of town. Has a restaurant on site.

MOUNTAIN INN (Marangu Rd, Tel. 275 2370, wwwkilimanjaro-shah.com) Single/double/deluxe rooms US$35/45/65. Run by Shah Tours and located 6km east of town, this is an attractive, comfy place. Restaurant and pool on site. Discounts available for those taking Shah Tours' treks.

PARK VIEW INN (Aga Khan Road, Tel. 275 0711, www.pvim.com) Small but smart place to stay. Reasonably priced rooms (single/double US$45/50) with most mod cons and friendly service.

SPRINGLANDS HOTEL (Tel. 275 3105, www.springlands.co.tz) Single/double rooms US$50. Run by Zara. Located 1.5km south of town, this is a decent hotel with first-rate amenities. There is a pool, small shop, restaurant and bar on site. Unfortunately you are only likely to stay here if you book a climb with Zara, in which case you will receive a free nights accommodation before and after your trip.

APPENDIX C
Useful Addresses

KILIMANJARO SENIOR PARK WARDEN (PO Box 96, Marangu, Tanzania). The National Park Headquarters are situated at the Marangu Gate, 6km north of the Marangu village, and are accessible by tarmac road. They are 48km from Moshi and about 90km from Kilimanjaro International airport.

Outfitters

There are a large number of outfitters in Moshi who will volunteer to organise and equip a limb of Kilimanjaro for you. Many of these are professional, reliable outfits, but there are some charlatans about. The outfitters listed below represent the most recognised, established groups. Contact each outfitter direct to obtain an up-to-date list of the services they provide, the routes that they cover and the rates that they charge.

AKARO (Old Moshi Road, Tel. 275 2986, www.akarotours.com) Friendly, efficient and dependable budget outfitters.

AHSANTE TOURS (New St, Tel. 275 3498, www.ahsantetours.com) Small but reliable outfitter that specialises in budget trips. Reasonable value, but no frills.

DOTCOM SAFARIS (Kaunda Street, Tel. 275 4104, www.dotcomsafaris.com) Well-organised and professional outfitters that garners good feedback.

KEY'S (Uru Rd, Tel. 275 2250, Email keys-hotel@africaonline.co.tz www.keys-hotels.com/climbing.htm) Long-standing outfitter who provides solid, professional packages for most routes. Reasonably priced, without being cheap.

KINDOROKO (Kindoroko Hotel, www.kindoroko.com) Ambitious outfitters offering competitive, good value rates that include a stay in the New Kindoroko Hotel.

MAULY (Mawenzi Rd, Tel. 275 0730, Email enquiries@mauly-tours.com, www.mauly-tours.com) Reliable budget outfitter that provides a pretty decent service.

MEM TOURS (Kaunda Street, Tel. 275 4574, www.memafrica.com) Three standards of trek offered at varying rates and levels of luxury that include nights in one of Moshi's hotels, depending on which price picked.

SAMJOE (KNCU Building, Tel. 275 1484, Email samjoetours@yahoo.com). Very basic, cheap outfitter that has in the past proved a little unreliable.

SHAH TOURS (Mawenzi Rd, Tel. 275 2370, Email kilimanjaro@kilonline.com, www.kilimanjaro-shah.com). Very well established outfitter with a superb reputation for offering excellent climbs. Reasonable rates for most routes that also include a night's accommodation in the Mountain Inn.

SUMMIT EXPEDITIONS (Tel. 275 3233, www.nomadicexperience.com) Focuses on the Lemosho Route, but includes several nights' stay at the owner's farm. A member of the KPAP Partner's scheme, it has a very good reputation for taking care of its porters and staff.

TRANS-KIBO TRAVELS (YMCA Building, Tel 275 1754, Email transkibo2001@yahoo.com, www.transkibo.com).Reasonable travel agency organising tours and trips with reasonable prices.

ZARA (Rindi Lane, Tel. 275 0011, Email zara@zaratours.com or enquiries@kilimanjaro.co.tz, www.zaratours.com, www.zara.co.tz). Very well established, reliable, professional institution. Slightly more expensive, but provides an outstanding service on all routes.

Trekking Clubs
MOUNTAIN CLUB OF KENYA (Wilson airport, Nairobi, Tel. 020 501 747, www.mck.or.ke) Meets weekly. Members can participate in treks and climbs around the country.

KILIMANJARO MOUNTAIN CLUB
(PO Box 66, Moshi, www.geocities.com/thetropics/ island/8543/kilimanjaro.html) Less of a club and more of an information service, although the website is very old and prices are out of date.

Private bus services between Nairobi and Arusha and Moshi
BOBBY
Nairobi address: Muindi Mbingu St, Tel. 0722 763 818

IMPALA
Impala (www.impalahotel.com)
Nairobi address: Silver Springs Hotel, Hurlingham Roundabout, Tel. 271 7373
Moshi address: Impala Hotel, Tel. 275 1786

RIVERSIDE
Nairobi address: Pan African Insurance House, 3rd Floor, Room 1, Kenyatta Ave, Tel. 02 229 618, Fax. 02 241 032, www.riverside-shuttle.com
Arusha address: Sokoine Rd and desk at the Novotel Mt Meru Hotel, Tel. 027 250 2639, Fax. 027 250 3916, email riverside_shuttle@hotmail.com

Moshi address: Room 122, 1st Floor, THB Building, Tel. 275 0093

PALLSONS
Nairobi address: Pan African House, Kenyatta Ave, Tel. 02 708 999)

Foreign Embassies
UK
Tanzanian High Commission
43 Hertford St, London, W1Y 8DB, Tel. 020 7499 8951, Fax. 020 7491 9321, email visa@tanzania-online. gov.uk

Kenya High Commission
45 Portland Place, London, W1N 48S, Tel. 020 7636 2371

KENYA
Tanzanian High Commission
Taifa Rd, Nairobi or 4th Floor, Continental House, PO Box 47790, Nairobi, Tel. 02 331 056, Fax. 02 218 269

British High Commission
Upper Hill Road, Nairobi, Tel. 02 714 699, email bhcinfo@africaonline.co.ke

USA Embassy
United Nations Avenue, Nairobi, Tel. 02 363 6000

Australian Embassy
ICIPE House, Riverside Drive, Nairobi, Tel. 02 445 034/39

Canadian High Commission
6th Floor, Comcraft House, Haile Selassie Avenue, Nairobi, Tel. 02 214 804

Irish Embassy
Owashika Rd, Lavington, Nairobi, Tel. 02 578 043

France – Barclays Plaza, Loita St, Nairobi, Tel. 02 339 978

Germany – 4th Ngong Ave, Nairobi,
Tel. 02 712 527

TANZANIA
Kenya High Commission
4th Floor, NIC Investment House, Samora
Machel Ave, PO Box 5231, Dar es Salaam,
Tel. 051 112 955

British High Commission
Umoja House, Garden Avenue,
Dar es Salaam, Tel. 211 0101,
email bhc.dar@fco.gov.uk
(Used to be at Hifadhi House, Samora
Avenue, Azikewe St, Dar es Salaam,
Tel. 211 7659/2953, but recently moved to
new premises along with German and Dutch
consulates.)

USA Embassy
686 Old Bagamoyo, Msasani, Dar es Salaam,
Tel. 266 8001, email embassyd@state.gov

There is no Australian embassy or high
commission in Dar es Salaam. Australian
citizens are advised to contact the Canadian
High Commission, who will offer consular
assistance.

Canadian High Commission
38 Mirambo St, Garden Ave, Dar es Salaam,
Tel. 211 2831/2832,
email dslam@dfait-maeci.gc.ca

Irish Embassy
1131 Msasani Rd, Msasani Peninsula,
Dar es Salaam, Tel. 266 6211/6348

France – Ali Hassan Mwyini Rd, Kinodoni,
Dar es Salaam, Tel. 266 6021
Germany – Umoja House, Garden Avenue,
Dar es Salaam, Tel. 211 7409
Kenya – 14 Ursino, Old Bagamoyo Road,
Dar es Salaam, Tel. 270 1747)
Netherlands – Umoja House, Garden
Avenue, Dar es Salaam, Tel. 211 0000
South Africa – Mwaya Rd, Msasani,
Dar es Salaam, Tel. 260 1880

Information on health
Nomad Travellers store and Medical Centre
STA Travel, at 41 Bernard St,
London, WC1N 1LJ

British Airways Travel Clinic
Walk-in centre at 213 Picadily, London W1J
9HQ 156 Regent St, London W1
(www.britishairways.com/health) (Monday–
Friday 9.30–17.30,
Saturday 10.00–16.00)
Appointments at 101 Cheapside, London
EC2V 6DT (Tel. 0845 600 2236)
(Monday–Friday 9.00–16.30)

APPENDIX D
Bibliography and Further Reading

Interest Books

There has been a great deal written about Kilimanjaro over the years, from early explorer's accounts of their expeditions to contemporary glossy, coffee-table style accounts of trips up the mountain.

Perhaps the best-known title is Ernest Hemmingway's celebrated short story, *The Snows of Kilimanjaro* (first published by Jonathan Cape in 1939 and reproduced in 1994 by Arrow). Written in 1936, two years after Hemmingway returned from his first African safari, it tells the story of a wealthy writer on safari, who has contracted gangrene in his leg and is dying in the shadow of the great peak. The gangrene in his leg forces him to confront the fact that he has betrayed his vocation and frittered away his literary talent on a life of luxury. He realises that he will never produce anything as enduring or enchanting as the brilliance of the snow capped summit nearby. The story celebrates, and made famous, the leopard found frozen on the summit. The leopard's upward exploration, whilst not explained, stands for artistic endeavour and its frozen carcass remains as a testament.

The book was made into a film in 1952 starring Gregory Peck, Susan Hayward, Ava Gardner and a giant painting of Kilimanjaro as a backdrop. Rewritten in order to guarantee a happy ending, whereby the protagonist recovered from gangrene and resolved to not let his literary talent go to waste, the film outraged Hemmingway who railed at this version of his vision.

Interestingly, Hemmingway never actually climbed Kilimanjaro, and only came close to the mountain when flying to Arusha.

The following books provide a broad commentary on Kilimanjaro. Some of them, particularly the older expedition accounts, are out of print and can only be found in second hand bookshops or the British Library:

Peter Beard *The End of the Game* (Thames and Hudson, 1988) Pointed photographic and narrative account of the decimation of African wildlife and the African landscape.

Stephen Carmichael *Climbing Mount Kilimanjaro* (Medi-Ed Press, 2002) Plenty of pre- departure guidelines and advice as to what to take, but contains no details relating to the mountain or the routes on it.

Richard and **Nicholas Crane** *Bicycles up Kilimanjaro* (Oxford Illustrated Press, 1985) An account of mountain biking to the summit of Kilimanjaro in order to raise money for charity project looking to build windmills to pump water in East Africa.

Charles Dundas *Kilimanjaro and Its People* (H, F and G Witherby, 1924; Frank Cass and Co 1968) Very authoritative, fascinating description of the Chagga people, their daily lives and rituals.

Rolf Edberg *The Dream of Kilimanjaro* (Pantheon, 1976) Recounts his pilgrimage to the Rift Valley and contains a digression on the development and evolution of mankind in Africa.

H H Johnston *The Kilima-njaro Expedition* (Kegan Paul, 1886) A record of scientific exploration by the explorer and administrator who was to effect a series of treaties with local chiefs and preempt the founding of the British East Africa protectorate. Contains some fanciful details but also good descriptions of the natural history, ethnology and the commercial prospects of the region.

Peter MacQueen *In Wildest Africa* (LC Page, 1909) A record of his hunting and exploration expedition in East Africa at the time of the German occupation. Includes an account of his ill-fated ascent to the snowfields on Kilimanjaro.

Hans Meyer *Across East African Glaciers: the First Ascent of Kilimanjaro* (G Philip and son, 1891) A fantastically detailed, enlightening account of the first ascent of Kilimanajro. Beautifully illustrated.

Charles New *Life Wanderings and Labours in Eastern Africa* (Hodder and Stoughton, 1873) Interesting account of New's time on the slopes of Kilimanjaro and of his encounters with the Chagga.

David Pluth *Kilimanjaro – The Great White Mountain of Africa* (Camerapix, 2001) Photographic book detailing the history and appeal of Kilimanjaro. Lyrical text and good photographs describe the main routes on the mountain in brief.

Johannes Rebmann *Church Missionary Intelligencer* articles, Vol 1, May 1849 (Seeleys, 1850) First reports of Rebmann's three trips to the Kilimanjaro region and his assertion that there was indeed snow on the equator.

John Reader *Kilimanjaro* (Elm Tree Books, 1982) Outstanding photographic guide to the mountain, that also contains detailed historical and geological sections.

Rick Ridgeway *The Shadow of Kilimanjaro: On Foot Across East Africa* (Bloomsbury, 1998). An incredible journey that in the course of a month took him up and over Kilimanajro, across the plains of Tsavo to the coast. Well written, it provides a good ground-level view of East Africa both past and present.

Geoffrey Salisbury *The Road to Kilimanjaro* (Minerva, 1997) Contains an account of an expedition led by Salisbury that took a group of eight blind African children up Kilimanjaro along the Loitokitok Route.

Audrey Salkeld *Kilimanjaro: To the Roof of Africa* (National Geographic Books, 2001) Sumptuous coffee-table book full of contemporary photographs. Text describes the history and background to the mountain as well as details an ascent of Kilimanjaro via the Machame Route in the company of an IMAX film crew.

Neville Shulman *On Top of Africa: the Climbing of Kilimanjaro and Mount Kenya* (Element, 1993) Spiritual tinged trekker's tale of climbing Kilimanjaro.

Eva Stuart Watt *Africa's Dome of Mystery* (Marshall, Morgan and Scott Ltd, 1930) An early descriptive account of the Wachagga people and of an ascent to Kibo's crater rim by a young colonial.

Rob Taylor *The Breach: Kilimanjaro and the Conquest of Self* (Wildeyes, inc, 1981) An account of Taylor's 1978 attempt to climb the Breach Wall, which ended in disaster and resulted in Taylor making a daring escape from the mountain many days after his accident. Highly contentious at the time of publication, it provoked strong reactions and disagreements with his companion on the climb.

Wilfred Thesiger *My Kenya Days* (Harper Collins, 1994) Autobiography detailing Thesiger's 30 years in Kenya. Includes an account of his ascent of Kilimanjaro.

HW Tilman *Snow on the Equator* (Bell and Son Books, 1937) Reproduced in *Seven Mountain Travel Books* (Baton Wicks, 2003) Rumbustuous account of Tilman's failed ascent of Kilimanjaro with Eric Shipton in 1930 and his later solo success in 1933.

Guide books

Iain Allen *Guide to Mount Kenya and Kilimanjaro* (Mountain Club of Kenya, 1998) An excellent guide to both mountains that is primarily designed for climbers, although it does detail the trekking routes on each mountain.

Cameron Burns *Kilimanjaro and Mount Kenya, A Climbing and Trekking Guide* (Mountaineers/Cordee, 2006) Good guide to tackling the more extreme climbing routes on both mountains. Also contains practical information and descriptions of the trekking routes available.

Henry Stedman *Kilimanjaro* (Trailblazer, 2010) Comprehensive guide to the mountain and the surrounding towns. Contains descriptions of most of the routes on Kilimanjaro. Also has good sections relating to Dar es Salaam, Nairobi, Arusha and Moshi.

TANAPA *Kilimanjaro National Park* (Tanzania National Parks, 1987) Only available in Tanzania. Slightly dated but still very useful pamphlet that describes the history, flora and fauna and main routes in brief detail.

David Hosking *Wildlife of East Africa* (Harper Collins, 2002) Straightforward, illustrated checklist of the animals most frequently encountered on a trip to East Africa.

Ber Van Perlo *Birds of Eastern Africa* (Harper Collins, 1995) Useful introduction and checklist for bird spotting in the region.

Dale Zimmerman *Birds of Kenya and Northern Tanzania* (Christopher Helm, 2001) High quality, illustrated guide to the bird species found in this region.

Websites

A simple search on any Internet search engine for references to Kilimanjaro will turn up a myriad list of sites. A vast number of these are personal accounts of trips or advertisements by trekking outfitters.

Many of the trekking outfitters that offer climbs on Kilimanjaro have websites that outline the itineraries available on the various routes. These sites often also have a smattering of background information relating to the mountain.

For general information, try www.tanzania.gov.tz, the official site of the Tanzanian government, or www.africatravelresource.com, which has a printable factfile.

Otherwise, you may wish to look at the official Tanzanian Tourist Board website, www.tanzania-web.com, which has a section dedicated to Kilimanjaro. Alternatively, try www.kilimanjaro.com or www.kilimanjaroworld.com or www.kiliweb.com, all of which have trekking details and interesting links.

APPENDIX E
Language Glossary

Whilst it would be entirely possible to climb Kilimanjaro without ever speaking a word of Swahili, a little effort and the simplest of phrases can elicit a very positive response. Whilst trekking with a guide and porters plenty of opportunities to practise a few words and sentences will arise and any attempt to speak the language will be appreciated.

The following glossary lists a handful of words that may be useful on the trail. There are also a number of small, pocket-sized phrasebooks and dictionaries available that may be worth consulting.

Hello	Jambo
How are you?	Habari
	(response: Good – Nzuri, Fine – Salama)
How's things?	Mambo?
	(response: Cool – Poa)
Welcome	Karibu
Do you speak English?	Unasema Kiingereza?
I don't speak Swahili	Sijui Kiswahili
Goodbye	Kwa heri
Please	Tafadhali
Thank you	Asante
Thank you very much	Asante sana
You're welcome	Karibu sana
No problem	Hakuna matata
Yes	Ndiyo
No	Hapana
I want to go to …	Nataka kwenda …
I'm looking for …	Natafuta …
How many hours to …?	Masaa mangapi …?
Is it far?	Ni mbali?
How many kilometres from here?	Ni kilomita ngapi kutoka hapa?
Left	Kushoto
Right	Kulia
Straight ahead	Moja kwa moja
East	Mashariki
West	Magharibi
North	Kaskazini
South	Kusini

Mountain	Mlima
Guide	Mwongozi
Porter	Mchukuzi
Map	Ramani
Path	Njia
Stone	Jiwe
Summit	Kilele
Scree	Mawe kidogo
Cliff	Mlima mdogo
Valley	Bonde
Let's go!	Twendai!
Slowly, slowly	Pole, pole
Hotel	Gesti/Hoteli
	(hoteli also means restaurant)
Campsite	Kambi
Tent	Hema
Hot water	Maji ya moto
Toilet	Choo
Bath	Bafu
Telephone	Simu
Fan	Feni
Key	Ufunguo
Hungry	Njaa
Thirsty	Kiu
Meat	Nyama
Chicken	Nyama kuku
Beef	Nyama ng'ombe
Fish	Samaki
Milk	Maziwa
Vegetable	Mboga
Potato	Kiazi ulaya
Bread	Mkate
Coffee	Kahawa
Tea	Chai
Drinking water	Magi ya kunywa
Ice	Barafu
Beer	Bia (order by brand name)
Wine	Mvinyo
What's the weather like?	Hali ya hewa ikoje?
It's cold	Ni baridi
It's hot	Ni joto
It's raining	Mvua inanyesha

It's sunny	Kuna jua
It's windy	Kuna upepo
Snow	Theluj
Cloud	Mawingu
Danger!	Hatari!
Help!	Nisaidie!/Saidia!
I need help	Naomba msaada
I'm lost	Nimepotea
I'm ill	Ninaumwa
I feel dizzy	Nasikia kizunguzungu
I feel nauseous	Nataka kutapika
I feel weak	Najisikia mnyofu
I've been vomiting	Nina tapika
Is the water good to drink?	Maji haya ni safi ya kunywa?
0	sifuri
1	moja
2	mbili
3	tatu
4	nne
5	tano
6	sita
7	saba
8	nane
9	tisa
10	kumi
11	kumi na moja
12	kumi na mbili
20	ishirini
30	thelathini
40	arobaini
50	hamsini
60	sitini
70	sabini
80	themanini
90	tisini
100	mia/mia moja
200	mia mbili
1000	elfu
2000	elfu mbili

Cicerone's mission is to inform and inspire by providing the best guides to exploring the world

Since its foundation 40 years ago, Cicerone has specialised in publishing guidebooks and has built a reputation for quality and reliability. It now publishes nearly 300 guides to the major destinations for outdoor enthusiasts, including Europe, UK and the rest of the world.

Written by leading and committed specialists, Cicerone guides are recognised as the most authoritative. They are full of information, maps and illustrations so that the user can plan and complete a successful and safe trip or expedition – be it a long face climb, a walk over Lakeland fells, an alpine cycling tour, a Himalayan trek or a ramble in the countryside.

With a thorough introduction to assist planning, clear diagrams, maps and colour photographs to illustrate the terrain and route, and accurate and detailed text, Cicerone guides are designed for ease of use and access to the information.

If the facts on the ground change, or there is any aspect of a guide that you think we can improve, we are always delighted to hear from you.

Cicerone Press
2 Police Square Milnthorpe Cumbria LA7 7PY
Tel: 015395 62069 Fax: 015395 63417
info@cicerone.co.uk www.cicerone.co.uk

CICERONE